Edible Plants of the Pacific Northwest

Edible Plants of the Pacific Northwest

A Visual Guide to Harvesting and Cooking with 40 Common Species

Natalie Hammerquist

SKIPSTONE

For my mom, who always helps me even when I don't know I need it.

Copyright © 2025 by Natalie Hammerquist

All rights reserved. No part of this book may be reproduced or utilized in any form, or by any electronic, mechanical, or other means, without the prior written permission of the publisher.

Published by Skipstone, an imprint of Mountaineers Books—an independent, nonprofit publisher. Skipstone and its colophon are registered trademarks of The Mountaineers organization.
Printed in China
28 27 26 25   1 2 3 4 5

Design: Melissa McFeeters
Layout: Jen Grable
Cover photographs clockwise from top left: *Chicory flower; Bee pollinating a fireweed flower; Rugosa rose hip; Making fermented fireweed tea; Evergreen violet; Oneseed hawthorn berries; Making chokecherry jam; Ladyfern fiddlehead; Feral apples; Spring nettle shoot*

All photographs by the author unless otherwise noted.

Disclaimer: Please use common sense. This book is not intended as a substitute for professional instruction. Harvesting, using, and/or eating any wild plant is inherently risky, and it is incumbent upon any user of this guide to assess their own skills and experience and to be aware of any plant-based allergies or similar personal risks. Readers should assume responsibility for their own actions, including awareness of changing or unfavorable foraging conditions. The author has made every effort to ensure the accuracy of the information in this book; however, wild plant research and knowledge is always evolving. The publisher and author are expressly not responsible for any adverse consequences resulting directly or indirectly from information contained in this book.

Library of Congress Cataloging-in-Publication Data is available at
https://lccn.loc.gov/2025932413

Printed on FSC®-certified materials

ISBN (paperback): 978-1-68051-732-3
ISBN (ebook): 978-1-68051-733-0

Skipstone books may be purchased for corporate, educational, or other promotional sales, and our authors are available for a wide range of events. For information on special discounts or booking an author, contact our customer service at 800.553.4453 or mbooks @mountaineersbooks.org.

Skipstone
1001 SW Klickitat Way
Suite 201
Seattle, Washington 98134
206.223.6303
www.skipstonebooks.org
www.mountaineersbooks.org

LIVE LIFE. MAKE RIPPLES.

Contents

7 Introduction

Part One: Learn to Forage for and Prepare Wild Edible Plants
(starts on page 10)

12 Harvesting Wild Foods
34 *Seasonal Harvest Calendar*
40 Traditional Ways to Make Wild Food Safe for Consumption

Part Two: The Plants and Recipes
(starts on page 44)

49	Apple	127	Hawthorn	204	Pineapple Weed
55	Bigleaf maple	134	Hazelnut	208	Purslane
61	Bittercress	140	Huckleberry	212	Rose
65	Blackberry	147	Huckleberry, Evergreen	220	Salal
71	Blackcaps			225	Salmonberry
75	Burdock	152	Indian Plum	229	Serviceberry
81	Chickweed	157	Japanese Knotweed	234	Sheep Sorrel
86	Chicory	164	Lady Fern	239	Sow Thistle
92	Chokecherry	169	Lambsquarters	245	Strawberry
98	Dandelion	174	Mallow	250	Thimbleberry
104	Dock	179	Miner's Lettuce	255	Violet
110	Fennel	185	Mountain Ash	263	Watercress
116	Fireweed	191	Nettle	268	Wood Sorrel
123	Hairy Cat's Ear	198	Oregon Grape		

Part Three: Poisonous and Toxic Plants
(starts on page 274)

278	Columbian Monkshood	286	Bittersweet Nightshade
279	Death Camas	287	Cascara Sagrada
280	False Hellebore	288	English Ivy
281	Foxglove	289	Manroot
282	Larkspur	290	Snowberry
283	Poison Hemlock	291	Twinberry
284	Water Hemlock	292	Pacific Yew
285	Baneberry		

293 Acknowledgments
294 Resources
297 Recipe Index
298 Index

Introduction

In 2021, I took a solo trip to rural Italy, where I learned about the local wild food plants there. Everyone I met was surprised that a person like me wanted to learn such things. All that the Italian young people wanted, they said, was to live in the city, have a desk job, and go out to the club. I have heard similar things from elders in most of my travels abroad. People's connections to the wild food traditions of their ancestors are quickly disappearing.

But you have picked up this book, and I assume you've done so because you want to eat wild things. Perhaps you are drawn to foraging because you yearn for a deeper relationship with nature, and with your ancestors. And why not? We are all wired to be in relationship with nature. And that, to me, means we're wired to forage, and to do it in a healthy way that links us to the past.

Some people still are raised to forge a strong bond with the land, just as their ancestors were; they've been carefully educated in the art of gathering wild plants: learning where to look, how much to take, how to store a harvest, and how to prepare it for human consumption. I think about women in rural China collecting fern root to make flour that can be deep-fried into dumplings. I think of Italians roaming olive groves for wild asparagus and thistle crowns for their Easter meal, farmers in Japan who harvest fiddlehead ferns and Japanese knotweed shoots on their tea plantations, and Native Alaskans who travel miles from home to harvest huckleberries.

In my own family line, we lost our land-based traditions several generations back. Most of my ancestors left their failing farms in Europe to homestead in an entirely new place, making their traditional knowledge nearly obsolete. On top of that, my Scandinavian ancestors chose not to teach their native

TOP: Harvesting salmonberry in western Washington. (Photo: Sydney Hammerquist) **BOTTOM:** Harvesting black hawthorn berries on the eastern slope of the Cascades (Photo: Lukas Speckhardt)

languages to their children, perhaps out of shame and fear of ostracism. There was so much pressure (and still is) to fit in and assimilate into the culture. I feel sad for what was lost and for the things that I wasn't able to learn from my elders. I wish I could have cooked alongside my Danish great-grandmother, Inge, and learned to make the traditional foods she made as a girl in Denmark.

But not having grandmothers to learn from does not mean we *can't* learn. Many people today, including me, are reimmersing themselves in crafts, foraging, gardening, traditional foods, and traditional medicines. Something is calling them back. As I weave baskets with foraged material, eat wild berries, or use wildcrafted medicines, I feel a deeply fulfilling sense of connection and purpose. I can only imagine that others are searching for the same thing. This is part of what motivates me to teach people about plants and what motivated me to write this book. I want us all to have a shot at having a heart-nourishing relationship with the wild.

As modern foragers, we have to constantly remember that just as foraging is becoming more and more popular, wild spaces are becoming smaller and more fragile. Part of the practice of foraging requires protecting these spaces, to ensure that our wild plants and animals continue to thrive. Sometimes this means scaling back our harvests, tending a favored patch to ensure its longevity, or just taking the time to observe and educate ourselves about the plants we work with.

The Pacific Northwest landscape I call home was carefully managed by Native groups until colonization, when they were removed from their own land. Their tending of wild plants was stopped and replaced with imported agriculture, natural resource extraction, development, and industry. Now we are witnessing the legacy of those halted practices in the form of intense wildfires, species decline, and the increase of tree diseases.

Native people today are successfully reclaiming some of their traditions and practices, traditional foods, and even land-management practices, such as cultural burning (see the Huckleberry entry in Part Two). Getting involved in local, Native-led restoration projects can be a great way to support these efforts and learn more.

In our quest to reconnect and relearn, we must observe closely, tread carefully, ask and listen to our elders, and help each other. Above all, we must be driven, not by lust but by generosity. I pray that we learn to love ourselves, so that we may have the full hearts we need to serve the communities of nature that surround us: people, plants, animals, fungi, insects, and the unseen organisms. May the cycles of life continue to thrive and find balance.

How to Use This Guide

Wild plants, unlike their domesticated counterparts, were not bred for human consumption. Some of them have toxins, some of them taste bitter or astringent, and some are extremely fibrous and hard to digest if harvested too late. This book is your guide to learning how to harvest and prepare wild edible plants in the Pacific Northwest, to eat the plants on their terms, and to enjoy their unique flavors and textures.

For the purposes of this book, the Pacific Northwest includes the southern part of British Columbia, Washington, Oregon, Northern California, and the Idaho panhandle. Some of the plants in this book are found throughout the region, while others are found only in specific areas. Harvest windows are based on the central part of our region, where I live, so you may find that if you live in the northern or southern reaches, your harvest times may be a bit earlier or later.

Turn to Part One to gather the basics of identifying, harvesting, and preparing wild plants. In Part Two, dive deeper into individual edible plant profiles and recipes. And finally, in Part Three, learn some of the poisonous and toxic plants to avoid while out harvesting.

As you develop your foraging skills, you will quickly discover that there are edible plants all around. You will notice them growing in the grocery-store parking lot, in your lawn, and in the woods near your house. Learning about wild plants will change the way you experience the "green wall" around you. Soon you will be walking through your neighborhood and greeting all of your new green friends, commenting that they are blooming a bit early this year, or that they are looking particularly tender in that damp patch of grass. And in this way, you will feel more connected to the place you call home.

Part One

Learn to Forage for and Prepare Wild Edible Plants

Carefully plucking the scented petals of Nootka rose (*Rosa nutkana*)

These chapters cover the basic skills needed to identify, harvest, and prepare wild plants. I recommend that beginner foragers peruse this section before heading out for the first time. Intermediate foragers will find valuable reference material here and perhaps some new ideas about stewardship.

Harvesting Wild Foods

A successful harvest outing depends on identifying the plant you want to harvest and what part to harvest, determining where and when to go, and knowing what equipment you will need and how to process your harvest when you get home. Use the information in this book as your starting point, then add to your knowledge by learning more from experienced harvesters and through your own observations and direct experiences.

Before you forage, it's important to consider how your actions will affect the local plants, ecosystem, and wildlife. The impact of harvesting edible plants in wild spaces can be ecologically devastating or ecologically beneficial. For example, harvest what's rare, and you may contribute to that plant's extinction; harvest too much of a food source that wildlife on, and the local fauna may go hungry. On the other hand, local native plants and wildlife may benefit when we harvest non-native species that are crowding out the local flora.

The best place to start is to harvest what's abundant, which is why I chose the most common plants to feature in this book. Some of these plants are considered native, which means they occur naturally and were not introduced by humans. Some of the native plants have sustainability concerns and should be harvested in small amounts; I point these out in the Sustainability sections of the plant entries in Part Two. Other plants featured in the book are non-native, also known as exotic species or introduced species. These plants were introduced by humans to the Pacific Northwest ecosystem and became naturalized, meaning they now grow spontaneously without human intervention. Plants in this category are often considered weeds and can be harvested in abundance.

As you start down the path of foraging for wild foods, I invite you to strive toward maximum ecological benefit in your harvests, and I have provided further recommendations on this topic in the Harvesting for the Health of Our Ecosystems section.

Developing Your Plant ID Skills

Plant identification is one of the most difficult skills to learn, yet perhaps the most critical. Make sure your ID is 100 percent correct before you put anything in your mouth. The same species of a plant can differ in color, size, and shape depending on where it's growing and the time of year. Learning to note small details like hairs on the stem, serrations on the leaf edge, the shape of the flowers, the inflorescence (the arrangement of flowers along the axis of the stem), and where the plant is growing will help you immensely on your identification journey. Plant identification apps and plant identification forums can be helpful too, though keep in mind that there is a margin for error in both.

There are several strategies you can use to get better acquainted with local plants:

- Go outside and spend time looking at plants. Get curious about them.
- Take an in-person class out in the field.
- Use plant identification apps on your phone (but don't trust them 100 percent).
- Use social media plant identification forums (but don't trust them 100 percent).
- Buy local field guides.
- Use the internet (science or research-based YouTube, podcasts, blogs, etc.).
- Learn about plant families and taxonomy.

Using Plant ID Apps

Plant ID apps are designed to identify a plant you find in nature by analyzing a photo you submit. These apps are getting better and better, especially if your picture is a good one. That said, apps can get things wrong, so it's good to have other sources to cross-reference. Think of the app as a good place to start, as it's a lot easier to verify an app's suggested ID than to come up with an ID yourself. Once you get an ID from the app, I suggest googling the scientific name of the plant or looking it up on iNaturalist (see Resources) to see some images, descriptions, and range that can help you confirm the ID.

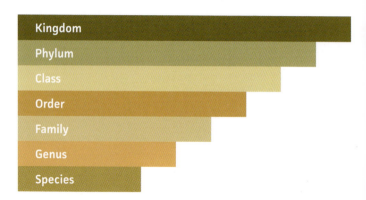

Understanding Scientific Names and Taxonomy

Plant taxonomy is the study of how plants are related and categorized. All living organisms can be categorized using the Linnaean system (named after the Swedish botanist Carolus Linnaeus). It helps immensely to know a bit about the classifications of plants and their Latin names as you learn to identify them. The levels of classification are summed up in the hierarchical chart above, starting with the largest categories and ending with the most specific.

Foragers are most concerned with the last three lines of the chart: family, genus, and species. The plant **family** is a group of many plants that share similarities in flower type and DNA because they have the same ancestors. Without a trained eye, you might not know that plants are related. For example, several plants in this book are in the rose family, such as blackberry and rose. They share certain characteristics, but that doesn't mean they look alike. Families are composed of genera (the plural form of *genus*). A **genus** is a smaller grouping of related species within a family that can often look quite similar. Some entries in this book will contain two or more plants in the same genus, such as one-seed hawthorn (*Crataegus monogyna*) and black hawthorn (*Crataegus douglasii*), which are both in the *Crataegus* genus. A **species** is a single, genetically distinct organism that typically cannot mate with other species (though there are exceptions to this).

The classic two-part botanical name that you will see throughout this book, such as *Rubus ursinus*, is called a Latin binomial. The name contains the genus (first word) and species (second word). Let's take a look at an example of the botanical names found in this book.

You might be asking why you should bother with all of this technical information. Though you can go out and forage without knowing about plant families and plant taxonomy, having a basic understanding is helpful for a few key reasons:

- If you know by sight what family a plant is in, identifying the genus and species will be much easier. Many field guides are organized by family.
- Other species in the same genus may also be edible. This is certainly true of the *Viola* genus, most of which have edible leaves and flowers. Several species grow in the Pacific Northwest.
- The more we understand the distinctions between certain species, the less likely we are to harvest the wrong plant. Some species in the same genus may be rare or toxic and should not be harvested.
- Plants in the same families may share the same toxicity concerns or human health cautions. Roots of plants in the sunflower family, for example, commonly cause gas when consumed. Plants in the buckwheat family tend to contain oxalates, which can interfere with calcium absorption and irritate the kidneys (see sidebar "What Are Oxalates?").
- You will better understand more advanced sources, such as floras (technical books that list all the plant species of a given location or region), scientific articles, and essays.

To get started, simply take note of the scientific names in this book. Say them out loud and look for Latin roots you may recognize. There's a game I play on hikes and road trips, which is naming the plants I recognize by common name and Latin name. Not only is this a fun way to pass the time, but it helps reinforce the names in your head. Before you know it, you'll be rattling them off like a pro!

Preparing to Harvest

When you first begin harvesting wild plants, spend more time observing than harvesting. Study this book in your free time to get familiar with the plants: how to identify them, where to search for them, and how and when to harvest them when the time comes. It's okay to wait until you feel more confident to harvest something. It can also be helpful to go out with an experienced friend or teacher.

On every walk you take, identify as many plants as you can. Sometimes, I even say the names in my head to reinforce them. Do they seem to be abundant or rare? Are there obvious signs of pollution around? What are the legalities of harvesting there?

Take special care to go out in April, May, and June, which are the best months for foraging in our region. You may even find yourself pulled off-trail by something you see through the trees. Always step lightly when going off-trail, and avoid it all together in sensitive ecosystems, such as montane, subalpine, and alpine habitats. Remember that the most interesting plants are often on the edge of things: forests, streams, meadows, and even roads. Edges are a great place to start.

Finding Good Foraging Spots

It can take time and effort to find good, clean, legal harvesting patches. In fact, this is perhaps the thing that new foragers struggle with the most. Generally speaking, experienced foragers keep their patches secret, which means you'll need to find your own.

The best way is simply to get out where the plants are, and do it often. Plan outings with the intention to find new foraging spots. Drive forest service roads for a day or wander through a park where foraging is allowed and note good spots. Don't take the same walking route every time; change it up and get your eyes on as many different spots as possible. Since plants often are present and identifiable even when it's not time to harvest from them, you can mark them for later in the season when the fruits are ripe. Use a map app on your phone to drop pins and label foraging spots you find. Just recently I returned to a St. John's wort patch that I had marked on an excursion the previous fall and had a great harvest!

One absolutely wonderful characteristic of plants is that they tend not to move much year to year, so once you find a patch, you can return to it. Building this type of close relationship with a place is one of the beautiful things about foraging, and it also helps you to not unintentionally overharvest: when you see the same patch year after year, you'll notice when it has a less productive year or if the population starts to decline and you can adjust your harvests accordingly.

Harvesting on Public Land

Laws governing the harvesting of wild plants from shared lands, like parks, have existed for a long time across cultures. Most settled cultures learned quickly that harvesting as much as they liked led to the decline of that resource. In Britain, for example, harvesting timber and allowing livestock to graze in the forest led to massive deforestation, and land-use regulations were implemented as a result. Among Native groups in the Pacific Northwest, there were complex hierarchies of who was allowed to harvest what and where, all to conserve food resources for everyone.

Picking chokecherries to make chokecherry jam (Photo: Lukas Speckhardt)

Today, regulations around harvesting plants and mushrooms on public lands in the Pacific Northwest vary widely depending on what jurisdiction owns and manages the land. Information provided here is specific to the United States, where I live. If you live in Canada, please do your own research on Canadian laws.

American public land can be managed by a city, county, state, or national jurisdiction. Each has its own unique regulations around harvesting, some of which vary site to site. In most cases, the harvest of berries, nuts, fruits, and mushrooms is allowed without a permit, while the harvest of other plant parts, such as leaves, barks, and roots, is either not mentioned at all or requires a special permit. Commercial harvesting is also usually categorized differently and is more heavily regulated and permitted than harvesting for personal use, which tend to be limited to 1, 2, or 5 gallons per person per day.

Foraging in city parks is usually not allowed, especially in urban centers such as Seattle. County park regulations vary. Notices are sometimes, but not always, posted at trailheads or entrances. You can usually get the information you need by visiting the park's website or reaching out to park employees.

State lands tend to have the most liberal foraging policies, varying depending on the type of land. Some state parks allow foraging; just check their website before you go. The Department of Natural Resources (DNR) lands do not require a permit for personal harvest of plant parts, berries, nuts, and mushrooms. There are, however, specific limits as to how much a person can gather in one day and over the course of one year for things like berries, pine cones, and other forest products. These regulations aim to conserve plant resources, some of which are particularly threatened by commercial and private harvesters. For example, huckleberries and fiddlehead ferns are both heavily harvested in the Pacific Northwest, which negatively impacts their populations.

Harvesting in national parks also varies from park to park. In some areas it is not allowed at all, and in others, only personal harvest of fruits, nuts, and berries is allowed. Commercial harvesting of mushrooms is strictly prohibited, though this does not deter many commercial pickers from taking mushrooms illegally, especially in places like Mount Rainier National Park, where commercial harvesters sneak large amounts of valuable mushrooms out of the park to sell.

The United States Forest Service (USFS) also manages a lot of land in the Pacific Northwest, and these are usually great places to harvest. Each ranger district has its own regulations on harvesting forest products, some of which require free or paid permits. Some items have an upper limit on how much can be harvested by one person in a year. Contact your local ranger station or look up regulations online. But be aware that USFS regulations focus on the harvest of mushrooms, fiddlehead ferns, firewood, tree and shrub transplants, Christmas trees, and green cuttings for floral arrangements. Many edible and medicinal plants are not mentioned, and many ranger districts don't have clear answers on those things. Most regulations are designed to help control the impacts of certain industries—such as salal harvesters—that have been problematic and damaging in the past. The US government isn't currently focused on making regulations that take small-scale harvesters into account or that protect edible and medicinal plants in a meaningful and specific way.

That said, if you are planning to forage on public lands, I invite you to extrapolate beyond these regulations and learn to be a respectful and positive presence in natural spaces. If we show up as the responsible and educated foragers that agencies hope for, it is more likely that new regulations will be in our favor. The more people who march into natural areas and destroy, on the other hand, the more conservative the regulations will become. It is a least-common-denominator phenomenon, so get on your soapbox and educate others. Our ancestors held each other accountable because their livelihoods relied on responsible collective harvesting practices, and we must do the same.

Harvesting on Private Land

From a legal standpoint, private land is the best place to harvest wild plants. All you need is permission from the landowner. I do not currently and have never owned land, as I'm sure is the case for many of you, so I've had to rely on the generosity of landowners who let me harvest on their property. In this section, I provide a few tips for reaching out to local landowners. (If you do own land, you'll find information about growing and sharing many of the plants in Part Two of this book as well as in the section titled The Power of Growing Native Wild Edibles. Plant native plants and help local ecosystems thrive!)

Contact local organic farms, especially U-pick ones, about whether you can harvest some weeds or other wild plants on their farm. Be specific about the species you are after, who's coming, and when you are able to visit. I have reached out to and visited several local farms in Washington and Oregon that have a lot of edible weeds and are happy to have me harvest from there. Lambsquarters and dandelion grow prolifically in tilled farmland, as do so many other delicious edible weeds.

Ask your neighbors for permission to harvest specific things, or post on local Facebook groups or bulletin boards. I am a bit shy to knock on doors, but I have asked a lot of neighbors who are out in their yards if I can harvest hawthorn berries or apples from their trees. Many people are happy to oblige because it means they don't have to clean up as much fruit from the ground. Just be respectful and don't break branches or leave a mess when harvesting.

Reach out to friends and family who own land to see if anyone is willing to have you over to harvest things. In these cases, I typically focus on harvesting weeds and lesser-known berries like hawthorn. Some might also be willing to let you plant native plants in their yard. Be creative!

What to Bring

A variety of tools and equipment can be useful for your foraging outing. Most importantly, use sharp, clean tools for harvesting to help prevent the spread of disease. Always carry a few bags or containers in your car or backpack in case you find a good patch when out on a hike or walk. Note that I don't bring everything on this list for every outing, but I pack the specific tools I'll need to harvest what I'm out to get.

- Bags (paper and plastic)
- Rigid plastic containers with lids
- Bucket
- Basket
- Clippers
- Hori hori (a Japanese digging knife)
- Scissors
- Digging fork
- Gloves
- ID book or app

For more extended outings, be sure to take along other gear as well, just as you would for a hike. However, keep in mind

Harvesting in a giant patch of Bohemian knotweed at a local farm. I received permission from the owners to forage here. (Photo: Anne Norton)

that you create quite a bit of heat when hiking, whereas foraging can involve staying still, so wearing warmer clothing is a must. Always take a look at the weather report before you go. I've been surprised by a lightning storm before! Foragers also leave the trail more often than hikers and are more likely to get lost, so having some kind of navigational tool is also a good idea. Suggested equipment for longer outings:

- Backpack
- Water bottle
- Snacks
- Closed-toe shoes, preferably waterproof
- Long pants (insulated pants are great on cold days)
- Long-sleeve shirt
- Rain jacket
- Additional warm layer
- Sunglasses and/or hat in summer
- Warm hat for cooler weather in winter, spring, and fall
- Brightly colored clothing (if harvesting in an area where people hunt)
- Cell phone or other communication device, such as an inReach
- Map and compass

Staying Safe in Wild Places

Always exercise caution when traveling to remote areas. There are many potential hazards, including wildlife, hunters, unexpected weather, cliffs, rivers, and more. Here are a few tips to keep you safe.

- Travel in the wilderness with another person when possible. If you travel alone, always carry a form of communication and bear spray, and tell a family member or close friend where you will be going and when you expect to return.
- Avoid traveling at dusk or dawn, which is a common time for cougars and other predators to prowl and hunt.
- Make noise in areas known to have a lot of bears. Bears don't like to be surprised and will most often retreat when they hear humans coming. The same is true of many other animals.

- Wear sturdy shoes and watch your footing on rugged and uneven terrain to avoid rolling an ankle, or worse. Sometimes leaves can cover large holes, or there can be unexpected cliffs or drops. Use extra caution in remote areas where other people may not happen upon you to help. Keep your wits about you and have an exit strategy.
- If traveling in deep wilderness, consider bringing the Ten Essentials, and take a class or two in wilderness survival or navigation. Always carry a topographical map of the area, and know how to use it. Most people who hunt mushrooms have at least one story about getting lost in the woods. Most tales thankfully end happily, but sometimes people do get lost and die in the woods, especially in colder seasons.
- If you don't know how to navigate well, stick to established trails and don't take chances. I have a terrible sense of direction, so I limit myself to a certain distance from the car or trail, at which point I turn around. I also pay a lot of attention to landmarks like large rocks or mountains in the distance.

Avoiding Contaminants

It is important to avoid harvesting edible plants from contaminated sites. Plants can uptake toxic compounds in the soil they grow in, and chemical sprays can remain on their leaves. In order to stay safe, read the following section carefully so you know what to look out for.

A petroleum slick on the edge of a puddle—a definite sign of contamination

SOIL POLLUTANTS

Sadly, a lot of soils contain pollutants that can make plants harvested there harmful to human health. Potential pollutants include heavy metals, agricultural chemicals, fire retardants, mining chemicals, petroleum products, and car exhaust.

Paved roads are a common source of soil contamination, both from car exhaust and the asphalt itself. It's generally recommended to harvest at least 20 feet from roadsides, though I give a wider berth to highways and other high-traffic roads.

Creosote is another common soil pollutant. Wooden pedestrian bridges, railroad ties, and utility poles are typically treated with creosote to preserve them and prevent them from burning. Avoid harvesting around telephone poles and other treated wood. Short-term exposure can cause nausea, skin irritation, dizziness, and other symptoms. Long-term exposure can cause cancer and neurological disorders, among other things. Unfortunately creosote also impacts local ecosystems, building up in smaller organisms and accumulating in the food chain. Some former creosote treatment facilities are now designated Superfund sites, like the one very near where I grew up on the shores of Lake Washington in Renton, Washington. A Superfund site is a location with heavy industrial contamination that has been officially recognized by the Environmental Protection Agency (EPA).

Mines are also a large source of soil contamination, as many mining processes involve using chemicals of some kind in the refining process. Gold mining, for example, leaves behind mercury and other heavy metals. Abandoned coal mines (of which there are many in the Pacific Northwest) can also leave behind a host of harmful chemicals in the soil, including heavy metals, sulfur compounds, and polycyclic aromatic hydrocarbons (PAHs).

Recent burn sites may also be contaminated. A flame retardant called Phos-Chek, used to fight high-severity or fast-moving fires, is dyed red before it's dropped from airplanes, so firefighters can avoid treated sites. The chemical can be harmful to humans and can contaminate the

Some old mines are marked, but others are not. Look into the history of the area where you want to forage.

water, plants, and animals where it is applied. There are several documented cases of Phos-Chek used in wildland firefighting causing large fish die-offs. If you'd like to check if Phos-Chek was used on a specific wildfire site, you can look up the incident report on the fire agency's website, or the Incident Information System (https://inciweb.wildfire.gov/).

If you live in Washington State, check out the Department of Ecology's tool called "What's in My Neighborhood" (https://apps.ecology.wa.gov/neighborhood/), which allows you to view documented sources of contamination near you using an interactive map. Other states and jurisdictions have similar resources, so check your state's Department of Ecology and the EPA website, which lists Superfund sites along with information about their history, the type of contamination, and their cleanup status.

FECAL CONTAMINATION

Contamination from human and animal excrement can be a concern for foragers in the same way that it's a concern for backcountry hikers, who have to treat their drinking water to avoid contracting giardia and other parasites.

In Seattle, several parks, including the popular Discovery Park and Carkeek Park, share space with sewage-processing facilities. In some areas of these parks, raw sewage can seep out of the facilities and contaminate local streams, ponds, and even the ocean. Lands with septic tanks may also have effluent fields that could cause bacterial contamination.

In general, avoid harvesting in wetland areas and places where water emerges from the ground. If you have any doubt, wash and cook your harvest thoroughly.

HERBICIDES AND PESTICIDES

Herbicides and pesticides are unfortunately incredibly common these days, both in urban and rural areas. They are used on public and private lands in a lot of different contexts.

The Department of Transportation sprays roadsides quite frequently. Look for browning and dead vegetation. In general, it is a good practice to harvest at least 20 feet away from roadsides to avoid contamination from not only herbicides and pesticides but also creosote, car exhaust, and runoff, mentioned earlier.

LEFT: The curled head of a bull thistle that has been sprayed with herbicides. **CENTER:** Herbicides are often colored blue, to make it obvious where they have been applied. **RIGHT:** Signs are sometimes posted after spraying, with the date and herbicide type.

Railroad tracks are also heavily sprayed with various chemicals to prevent plants from growing on the tracks. Give railroad tracks a wide berth of 30 feet or more.

Parks and other public lands often use herbicides to remove invasive species such as Himalayan blackberry, Japanese knotweed, and poison hemlock. Look for deformed and wilting stems and leaves, bullet-shaped herbicide plugs in tree trunks (see Hawthorn entry in Part Two), and blue dye on leaves. Herbicides are often dyed blue so that the person applying them can see what they have sprayed and to provide a warning for the public. Signs are sometimes displayed to inform the public that the area will be sprayed that day or has recently been sprayed, but not always.

Some timber companies use pesticides to prevent certain insects and other diseases from infecting their trees. These chemicals are typically broadcast from the air using crop dusters. They're most commonly used in private timber units but are occasionally used by the DNR and USFS.

Also keep in mind that less stringent regulations around pesticide and herbicide use may apply to non-farm areas, where it's not assumed anyone would harvest plant material for consumption. And though many agricultural chemicals claim to have a short half-life (meaning that they break down quickly in the soil and become harmless), there is a lot of controversy around this. You will have to decide for yourself how concerned to be.

GIVEN ALL THESE risks, it can be quite difficult to find good places to harvest, and sometimes you may need to concede on some of these points. We each have to decide for ourselves which of these things really matter and do our own research. We are all exposed to pollutants and chemicals on a daily basis, so it may be unproductive to demand perfect purity from our wild plants. As always, I encourage you to make educated decisions based on your research and direct observations. I also encourage you to advocate to your local authorities for less chemical use on public lands and in public parks!

Harvesting for the Health of Our Ecosystems

The harvesting of wild food in this country has long been an extractive venture, meaning that too much has been taken

Dock is a very common non-native plant that grows in a lot of scrubby, weedy areas. It is abundant and low-impact. (Photo: Sydney Hammerquist)

without a thought to how that may affect the ecosystem and others who may need access to that food. Now that you are a forager, you are a functioning part of the ecosystem, like a deer browsing for food, and your impact can be positive or negative. Unlike a deer, you have the capacity to use information and logic to make decisions to sway the outcome. We foragers can support healthy, functioning ecosystems by following some general guidelines:

- Harvest what you need and nothing more. When you first begin, start by harvesting small amounts.
- Don't harvest the first plant you see. Instead, take time to observe how much there is of a plant and where it is growing most abundantly.
- Focus on harvesting what's abundant which sometimes means non-native plants or even invasive plants. Himalayan blackberry is a great example of this.
- Avoid harvesting what's not abundant. This changes from area to area, but usually plants growing in sensitive habitats fall into this category.
- Tend to your patches, especially of native plants. This could mean weeding out invasives, propagating, spreading seed, pruning, and more.
- Step lightly when traveling off-trail. So much life happens in the soil that you can't see, and it all needs air!
- Use clean tools. You can pass diseases from tree to tree by not washing your tools between uses.

- Leave some for other animals and insects. Plants are important sources of food and habitat for many other species.
- Find a way to give back. This looks different for everyone. For me, it's educating other humans on how to harvest respectfully and connect with nature. For you, maybe it's replanting and propagating, removing English ivy, picking up trash, or offering tobacco to the plant. One of the most important things people can do for plants is to advocate to protect their habitats.

Scaling Harvests and Respecting Other Stakeholders

Something I rarely see discussed in foraging guides is the difference between harvesting in rural areas and harvesting in or near population centers. In large cities, where parks and wild areas are limited, a patch of nettles may have many more

Sensitive Wild Edibles to Avoid Harvesting

Though these species may be edible, they are not abundant enough to handle heavy harvesting from humans. Consider growing these if you are able.

- Mariposa lily (*Calochortus* spp.)
- Chocolate lily (*Fritillaria affinis*)
- Shooting star (*Dodecatheon* spp.)
- Tall bluebells (*Mertensia paniculata*) and other species of bluebells
- Camas (*Camassia* spp.)
- Wapato (*Sagittaria* spp.)

TOP ROW (L TO R): Mariposa lily, chocolate lily, shooting star
BOTTOM ROW: Tall bluebells, camas, wapato

harvesters than a similar patch in a rural location. It is therefore extremely important to look for signs of previous harvest when we forage in densely populated areas and avoid harvesting if there has already been a large impact.

It is also important to consider the aesthetic value of certain plants. For example, Portland has a lot of public rose gardens. Harvesting roses there would be frowned upon because it would impact the enjoyment that others get from the roses. This also applies to trailside wildflowers on popular hikes.

In addition, some plants have important cultural significance to local Native people and thus, non-Native foragers must give special consideration to the plants before harvesting them to ensure that Native Americans have first access to their culturally significant foods. In some cases, this means that non-Native folks should not harvest certain species in the wild at all, such as camas root. Not only is camas an important food to many Native people, but its habitat has almost disappeared compared to its historic range. If you live where camas grows, consider volunteering at a local prairie restoration project to connect more with that plant (see sidebar "Get to Know Your Ecosystem").

A bee pollinating a camas flower at Mima Mounds Natural Area Preserve, Washington

Review the websites and social pages of local tribes to learn more about the specific issues around native plants and harvesting concerning them and what their recommendations are. The Snoqualmie Tribe Ancestral Lands Movement is just one example of many helpful resources.

If you are not Native, I recommend discovering what your own cultural foods are so you can develop relationships with them. There are many plants in this book that my ancestors used, including apple, nettle, rose, hawthorn, wild strawberry, dock, dandelion, and burdock.

Many plants offer important food for wildlife as well. I once witnessed a chipmunk in a field of osha (*Ligusticum porteri*) that had its cheeks entirely stuffed with osha seeds. Had someone harvested those plants or removed the seeds, the chipmunk's winter food store would have been reduced significantly. Even non-native plants can offer food sources, such as the berries of

A robin eats one-seed hawthorn berries on a winter morning at Discovery Park in Seattle.

one-seed hawthorn (*Crataegus monogyna*), which feed many birds in the wintertime when other food sources are scarce. Also, let's not forget insects, who pollinate, feed on, and live in plants.

Patch Tending

Patch tending is an ancient concept that involves caring for a group of plants that you harvest from. This may include pruning, reseeding, selective harvesting, removal of invasive plants, and even advocacy. The concept of "untouched wilderness," which you sometimes see mentioned in environmentalist narratives, is entirely untrue. Native groups have been tending patches in the Pacific Northwest for time immemorial, which has included prescribed burns, transplanting plants, creating beds, weeding, pruning, reseeding, and even fertilizing. This is also true of most other countries. It is important that when we do this, it also benefits the ecosystem the patch is in. It would be inappropriate, for example, to encourage a patch of Japanese knotweed. However, pruning dead canes off your favorite blue elderberry bush could be really helpful.

Cultivating a Relationship with the Land Around You

Having a deep relationship with the land is a radical invitation in a world that fetishizes exotic destinations and where few people remain in their hometowns. Nature is everywhere, so find the natural spaces near you and visit them regularly. Harvest wild foods in the same patches year after year. When you have this kind of intimate relationship with a place, you are a far better tender and advocate. You may notice that some years a

> ### Get to Know Your Ecosystem
>
> Volunteering at a local restoration project is one way to gain an understanding of the plants and ecosystem in your area. I have learned so much from participating in ivy pulls at my local parks, pulling Scotch broom out of prairies, and hearing restorationists tell the stories of the pieces of land they tend. I have since realized just how much work goes into preventing plants like Himalayan blackberry from taking over every inch of our region and crowding out native plants.
>
> I am also a lover of quiet observation. During peak berry season, I go to my favorite berry patch and sit quietly nearby for at least ten minutes. Once your presence fades, birds and other wildlife will return to eat. This is a great opportunity to learn about the other animals that access the patches where you harvest and how important it is to leave enough for them. We have access to grocery stores, and they don't!

plant did not produce as much or that the local parks department mowed something down. Though sometimes heartbreak happens, your relationship with a place puts you in a unique position to better protect and serve that place.

The Power of Growing Native Wild Edibles

If you own land or have access to a yard or other growing space, planting native wild edible plants not only gives you immediate access to them but benefits the local ecosystem in a lot of ways. Native plants, especially those with berries and fruits, tend to attract and feed wildlife. Serviceberry in particular is super popular among birds—just before writing this, I witnessed seven bird species eating from one serviceberry tree in a twenty-minute period!

Ecosystems and the creatures that live in them benefit greatly from habitats. Developed areas disrupt these habitats, leaving isolated pocket populations of native plants that become less genetically resilient over time. We can help connect these pocket populations by planting native plants, allowing access to more genetic diversity. Native plantings can also help take foraging pressure off public lands.

Perhaps the largest benefit of planting native plants in your own yard is that it is the best way to form a close relationship with a plant and learn about it deeply. You get to observe it in all the seasons, and you'll see whichwildlife interact with it, and you'll figure out how best to tend it.

These native species are easy to find at local nurseries:

- Beaked hazelnut
- Black hawthorn
- Indian plum
- Lady fern
- Oregon grape
- Pacific crabapple
- Salal
- Salmonberry
- Serviceberry
- Wood sorrel

Wood sorrel plants for sale at a local nursery

When tending native plants, especially food plants, try to avoid using chemicals in your yard for the benefit of anyone who consumes that plant as well as for the ecosystem as a whole. Make a commitment to go chemical free and explore alternatives to pest and weed control and disease prevention. Climate change and habitat fragmentation have introduced many new tree diseases that may impact your native plants, but there are often things you can do to prevent these diseases. For example, avoid planting serviceberry near juniper or cedars to help prevent cedar-apple rust (read more in the Serviceberry entry). Before planting, do a quick internet search of potential diseases of a given species to see if there is anything you can do to ensure the health of your plants. Let's give the plants we steward the same loving care we give our four-legged friends.

If you are feeling charged up about planting natives, I recommend a visit to a local native plant nursery (see Resources at the back of the book for a list of suggestions). And remember that the more people in a given area are planting natives, the more effective it is, so spread the word to your neighbors!

Getting Your Timing Right

Part of learning to harvest wild foods is learning how to show up at the right time. Many wild foods can be harvested only once a year in a particular window of time, which in some cases can be just a few days or a few weeks. Others are available year-round.

Thick, crunchy Japanese knotweed shoots at the perfect stage for harvesting (Photo: Ann Norton)

Several different factors affect when plant parts are ready to harvest, including elevation, latitude, heat from cities, microclimates, and annual fluctuations in weather. For example, where I live in Roslyn, Washington, the harvest windows are an entire month behind Seattle's because of the higher elevation. This section outlines some general guidelines for plant parts; the plant entries in Part Two provide specific guidelines for individual species.

Shoots

If you want to harvest shoots, you will need to keep a keen eye out and check your patches frequently. It can be hard to catch plants in this stage as it is so fleeting and sometimes happens before you expect it. Fireweed shoots, for example, are tender and nice for only a short time in the early spring when they are six-inch shoots. They quickly develop fibers and astringent compounds that make them inedible. For this reason, I usually end up harvesting fireweed up high in the mountains because there it sends up shoots much later in the season.

Leaves

Most edible leaves are best before the plant flowers; after that, most plants become bitter and fibrous. For instance, dandelion leaves are best harvested in February and March before they bloom. Chickweed and nettle leaves also should be harvested in early spring when they are still tender. Nettles develop cystoliths as they flower and mature. Cystoliths are calcium-based crystal structures that can irritate the skin and kidneys.

Flowers

Most plants listed here flower sometime between March and July, with an especially large number blooming in the month of May. Some species flower for a short period of time, like hawthorn. Others, such as roses, flower continuously for a month or more. Bloom times vary from year to year and by elevation and location. Plants at sea level and near warm cities or roads tend to bloom first, whereas those at high elevations and in more northerly areas bloom later. It is best to harvest flowers just after opening and on a dry day, especially if they are aromatic.

Fruits and Seeds

Once pollinated, flowers develop into fleshy fruits or seeds. The first fruits usually begin to ripen in June, with the last ripening as late as October. It can often be tempting to harvest these things before they are ripe, so be patient and wait until the full flavor has developed. A few fruits or seeds are harvested before they are completely ripe, such as wild fennel seed.

Roots and Rhizomes

Roots can be dug either in the spring or fall, though most edible roots are harvested in the spring. Roots such as chicory and burdock become much more fibrous when they are in full flower in the dry summertime.

Processing and Storing Your Harvest

After a day of foraging in the wild, there is often much to do to ensure your harvest is clean and ready to use or store. Remember to factor this processing time into your day and avoid harvesting more than you have time to process; many plants go to waste when people don't account for the processing time.

SEASONAL HARVEST CALENDAR

PLANT	JAN	FEB	MAR
apple (fruit)			
bigleaf maple (flower)			■
bigleaf maple (seeds)			
bigleaf maple (sprouts)			
bittercress (leaf)	■	■	■
blackcaps (fruit)			
blackberry, Himalayan (fruit)			
blackberry, laceleaf (fruit)			
blackberry, trailing (fruit)			
burdock (root)			■
cattail (shoot)			
cattail (pollen)			
chickweed leaf and stem	■	■	■
chicory (leaf)			
chicory (root)	■	■	■
chokecherry (fruit)			
dandelion (leaf)		■	
dandelion (buds)		■	
dandelion (flower)			
dandelion (root)	■	■	■
dock (leaf)			
dock (seed)			
fennel (leaf)			
fennel (flower)			
fennel (pollen)			
fennel (seed)			
fireweed young (shoot)		■	■
fireweed (leaf)			
hairy cat's ear (leaf)		■	■
hairy cat's ear (flower shoot)			
hairy cat's ear (root)	■	■	■
hawthorn, one-seed (fruit)			
hawthorn, black (fruit)			

■ Ideal time to harvest.

APR	MAY	JUN	JUL	AUG	SEP	OCT	NOV	DEC
					■	■	■	
■	■							
						■	■	
■	■							
							■	■
		■	■					
				■	■			
				■	■			
			■	■				
■						■	■	
	■	■						
	■	■	■					
■							■	■
■	■							
■	■					■	■	
					■	■		
■								
■	■							
					■	■	■	■
■	■							
				■	■			
■	■							
	■	■	■					
			■	■	■			
				■	■			
■								
		■	■					
■								
	■	■						
					■	■	■	■
						■	■	
			■	■				

PLANT	JAN	FEB	MAR
hawthorn (flowers and leaves)			
hazelnut, beaked (nut)			
huckleberry (fruit)			
huckleberry, evergreen (fruit)	■		
Indian plum (fruit)			
Indian plum (leaf buds)		■	
Japanese knotweed (shoot)			
lady fern (fiddlehead)			■
lambsquarters (leaf)			
mallow, common (leaf)			■
mallow, dwarf (leaf)			
miner's lettuce, Siberian (leaf)			■
miner's-lettuce (leaf)			■
mountain ash (fruit)			
nettle (spring shoots)		■	■
nettle (seed)			
Oregon grape, low (fruit)			
Oregon grape, tall (fruit)			
pineapple weed (whole plant)			
purslane (leaf)			
rose (flower)			
rose (hip)			
salal berry (fruit)			
salmonberry (fruit)			
serviceberry (fruit)			
sheep sorrel (leaf)			■
sow thistle (leaf)			■
strawberry (fruit)			
thimbleberry (fruit)			
violet (flower)			■
violet (leaf)		■	■
watercress (leaf)			■
wood sorrel (leaf)			■

Ideal time to harvest.

APR	MAY	JUN	JUL	AUG	SEP	OCT	NOV	DEC

HARVESTING WILD FOODS

Tiny insect eggs on the surface of an Oregon grape berry. There are all kinds of creatures that make their homes on and in plants, so don't be surprised when you sort through your harvest!

Cleaning and Sorting

My foraging students are frequently alarmed at the amount of insects that crawl out of their foraging bags. It is truly a testament of how much insects love and live in plants. If you notice a mass exodus of bugs crawling up the sides of your bag, it's best to set the bag outside for an hour or two and let them crawl out. They don't want to be eaten by you just as much as you don't want to eat them!

To sort through a large harvest for twigs and bugs, spread it out on a baking tray and pick detritus out into a mixing bowl. Even nettle harvests may carry some leaf duff and unexpected aphids that you will need to pick out; be sure to wear gloves while sorting nettle.

Washing

It is generally a good idea to wash things that you are going to eat. The only exception is if you are planning on drying your harvest. If plant material is wet when laid out on a drying rack, it is likely to mold. For this reason, I avoid washing plants that are destined to be dried.

Rinsing a freshly picked batch of chickweed

Leaves can be washed the sink or in a large bowl of water and then dried in a salad spinner or mesh strainer. Most fruits, too, can be put into a large bowl of water and sloshed around to scrub them off a bit.

Softer, perishable fruits like blackberries will spoil more quickly once washed, so if you plan on storing them in the fridge for a period before using them, wash them directly before using.

Before taking roots into the kitchen, wash them off with a hose outside. I use the jet-spray nozzle setting to pressure wash them. Use a mesh bin to prevent them from being blasted off while spraying.

Refrigerating and Freezing

Store-bought mixed greens tend to be sold in plastic bags and clamshell containers to keep them from wilting too quickly; do the same with your wild-harvested greens by storing them in an airtight container. I use resealable freezer bags both for harvesting and for storing greens in the fridge.

Most berries freeze well. After washing and picking through them, line a baking tray with parchment paper and fill it with a single layer of berries. Freeze the whole tray, and then pour the frozen berries into a clearly labeled gallon freezer bag. This method keeps berries from freezing together into a giant mass. If freezing leaves or roots, it is best to blanch or cook them before freezing.

Roots keep better with the dirt still on them, as was traditionally done in root cellars. Note that different roots will have different levels of tolerance to being stored for long periods. I usually store roots in sealed plastic bags in the fridge.

Traditional Ways to Make Wild Food Safe for Consumption

Wild food culture is experiencing a period of revival, but it is still developing and maturing. Many people today seem to believe that if a plant is edible, you can eat it any way you want, and if it is toxic, you cannot eat it at all. But the edibility of wild food is nuanced; some so-called edible plants need to be prepared in specific ways to make them more digestible, and some "toxic" plants may be edible in tiny portions or after being cooked. I once watched a man on a hiking trail snap off a bracken fern fiddlehead and pop it right into his mouth. My jaw dropped, because I had learned that bracken fern contains carcinogenic compounds and should not be eaten raw. And when I was in Italy, I was shocked when my host told me we were eating wild poppy greens in the dish he made. I considered poppies to be medicinal and too toxic to be eaten in any quantity. But he stressed that he had only put a small amount in, along with a mix of other wild greens, and that the leaves should be young when harvested.

Humans can handle eating a little bit of many toxic plants, as it turns out. Some great examples from this book are sheep sorrel, wood sorrel, and Siberian miner's lettuce, which contain oxalates and thus should be eaten raw only in small quantities (see "What Are Oxalates?" sidebar). Traditional cultures that consume bracken always soak it, cook it, or ferment it. Learning proper preparation techniques opens up a whole world of new wild food options, flavors, textures, and even nutritional values.

In many of the countries where I've studied, traditional knowledge around consuming wild foods has been prioritized and consistently passed down for many generations. Japan, especially, because of their limited food supply, has had to develop ways to eat many toxic things, relying on precise preparation techniques. A great example of this is konjac root, which is the corm—a bulblike type of root—of a very strange plant also known as devil's tongue (*Amorphophallus konjac*). Because of toxic and bitter alkaloids in the corm, it must be shredded, soaked in an alkaline solution, boiled, solidified, and rinsed. The final product is a fairly tasteless gray gelatin-like cake called *konnyaku*. It is much loved in Japan in hot pot and *oden*, though I have still not developed a taste for it.

Traditional wild food preparation techniques can enhance the flavor, texture, and digestibility of many wild foods. These techniques can be broken down into four main categories: cooking, soaking, fermenting, and peeling. Sometimes just one of these is used, but often, multiple methods are used in succession. You'll find specific cooking recommendations within each plant entry in Part Two. This section serves as an overview of some of the techniques employed.

Cooking

Heat can soften fibrous leaves, reduce astringency, break down complex starches, and destroy toxic compounds. Many of us already use heat in this way when we cook potatoes, which contain a toxic compound that is destroyed in the cooking process. Slow cooking can also reduce prebiotic starches like inulin, which can cause gastrointestinal distress if your gut isn't used to it; burdock roots, for example, contain large amounts of inulin, and cooking them slowly for a long period of time makes them more digestible and less likely to cause severe gas.

You can soften later-season hairy cat's ear leaves by parboiling them for 20 minutes.

Soaking

Soaking plants in water is also a common preparation technique to remove toxins or bad flavors from certain plants. This can be done with hot water, boiling water, cold water, alkaline water (made by adding lye), or acidic water (made by adding vinegar), depending on the plant.

What Are Oxalates?

Many wild plants, and even some store-bought vegetables, contain mildly toxic compounds called oxalates that wild food enthusiasts should be aware of. Plants such as wood sorrel, sheep sorrel, Siberian miner's lettuce, dock, Japanese knotweed, and even violet leaf contain varying levels and types of oxalates. The leaves and stems of the plant typically contain more oxalates than the roots, fruits, or flowers.

Oxalates come in soluble and insoluble forms. The soluble ones can be removed with water, but not the insoluble ones. Insoluble oxalates are found more often in nuts and seeds than in greens, but greens still do contain them. One way to detect the presence of insoluble oxalates is that they will feel gritty between your teeth, because they form calcium oxalate crystals. Spinach is a great example of this. Soluble oxalates make a plant taste sour.

Oxalates can negatively impact human health in a few ways: The first is that overconsumption of oxalates can lead to the formation of kidney stones, especially in susceptible individuals. If you already have kidney stones, then it's best to avoid high-oxalate plants where possible. Second, they tend to bind to minerals like iron and calcium, making it difficult for your body to absorb the minerals. Over time, this could lead to deficiencies of key nutrients. Third, oxalates can be irritating to the gastrointestinal tract in some people. If you experience bowel distress after consuming high-oxalate plants, it may be best for you to avoid them altogether or parboil them before consuming. Unfortunately, I am one of those people and can handle eating only small amounts at a time.

The negative effects of oxalates become an issue only when large amounts are consumed, so it's best to eat them in moderation. This could even mean just eating them in combination with other greens that don't contain oxalates. Another method is to parboil the greens and discard the water, which can significantly reduce the amount of soluble oxalates. However, parboiling removes on average only 50 percent of the oxalates, so moderation is still important. Parboiling is especially appropriate for some of the less sour oxalate-containing plants like dock. Simply bring a pot of water to boil, reduce to a simmer, and add the leaves. Simmer for 10 to 15 minutes—more time for more fibrous plants and less time for less fibrous plants. Strain the greens, press out the excess water (discarding the oxalate-rich water), and rinse under cold water for 10 seconds.

Fermentation is also commonly used to reduce oxalate levels, as the microbial activity can break them down. I don't use this method often, but it's something to look into.

Acorns are one of the best examples: They are soaked in several batches of water to remove their tannins. Depending on the species of acorn, they are soaked two to ten times or more. White oaks apparently have less tannins and are much more palatable than red oaks. We use this same method on bigleaf maple seeds, which can also be quite astringent.

Dock leaves, sheep sorrel, and other leaves that contain oxalates are boiled in water, drained, and then added to soups or sautéed. The water soaks up the oxalates and must be discarded (see sidebar "What Are Oxalates?").

Many other wild greens are soaked in cold water to remove the bitterness, which is a practice I have seen in both Japan and Italy during my travels. This is often but not always done after cooking them.

Fermentation

Fermentation can break down compounds like inulin, which is found in dandelion, burdock, Jerusalem artichoke, and other roots high in complex and indigestible starches. This is usually done by soaking pieces of the root in brine for several days or several months. Oxalates can also be reduced through fermentation (see sidebar "What Are Oxalates?").

Peeling

Peeling fruits, stems, and roots often removes fibrousness or astringency in some way. Many stems can be eaten if the outer skin is peeled off, much like rhubarb. I always peel Japanese knotweed shoots, as the skin can be annoying and fibrous even after cooking. Some people also peel mature fireweed shoots that have become a bit bitter and eat only the inner part.

Although many wild plants require cooking, soaking, fermenting, or peeling to make them more palatable or digestible, others can be eaten raw or treated like cultivated crops. Chickweed or blackberries make delicious raw snacks, for example, and lambsquarters can be treated like spinach in most cooked recipes. In Part Two, you'll find specific cooking tips for each plant featured in the book.

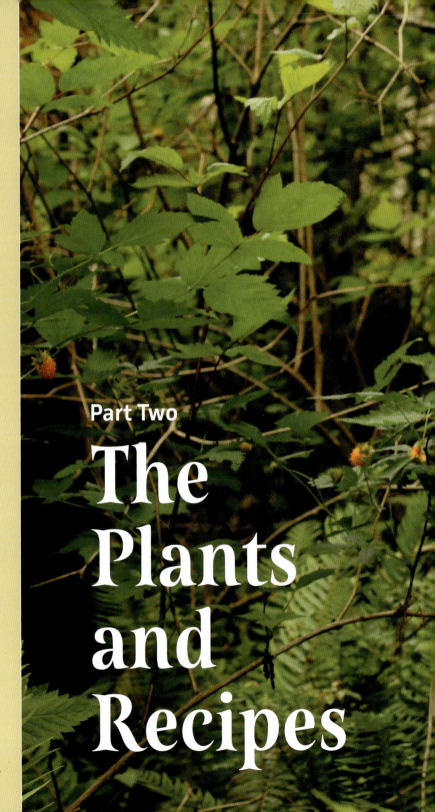

Part Two

The Plants and Recipes

Grazing on salmonberries on a hike near Issaquah, WA (Photo: Sydney Hammerquist)

This practical, accessible guide is designed to lead you to wild foods you will want to eat and that won't harm the plants and ecosystems. In selecting plants to include, I chose those that are commonly known, palatable to most people, fairly abundant in places where people can actually harvest them, and available throughout the Pacific Northwest.

Many of the plants I expected to include were cut because they did not fit these guidelines. For example, I made a seemingly lovely blended soup of dead-nettle, which I thought would overpower the leaf fuzz nicely. Wrong! It was inedibly fuzzy. I omitted other plants, such as camas and wapato, because of their sensitive habitats and relative scarcity. I encourage people to avoid harvesting such plants and to instead enjoy them on hikes and plant them in your garden.

The Plant Listings

Each plant entry provides key information to guide your foraging efforts, along with cooking tips and a recipe. Entries open with the plant's common name, Latin name, family name, and then a brief description. The rest of the entry is divided into the following sections.

Where to Find It

This section lists each plant's range and habitat in the Pacific Northwest, including tips on where to look for the best of the best. I also include the geographic range for some plants that grow beyond the Pacific Northwest.

How to Harvest

Learn what time of year to harvest, what parts to harvest, how to tell if it's ready, and how to harvest.

Look-Alikes

Correct ID is important, so be sure to review this section before harvest. Some look-alikes grow in the same habitat, and

I met these two jovial fellows harvesting huckleberries near Snoqualmie Pass.

some are also toxic! I break down any obvious look-alikes and describe how to tell them apart from the plant being discussed. There may be look-alikes not covered here, so if you have even a hint of doubt, get help from a nerdy friend, a professional, or an app.

Sustainability

This section includes information about how to harvest respectfully and sustainably. In some cases, that may mean harvesting one in ten and only from abundant patches. In other cases, it might mean leaving some for wildlife. And sometimes, it may mean harvesting as much as possible because the plant is invasive. Each plant has different needs and requires different treatment from us foragers.

Grow Your Own

For some plants, I provide information for anyone wanting to introduce that plant into a home garden. Planting wild edibles in your garden typically requires far less maintenance than growing domesticated vegetables and can benefit wildlife too!

Cautions

Some wild food plants can be toxic if not processed or harvested correctly. If a plant entry includes this section, be sure to check it out before eating your plant.

Cooking With

This section includes preparation instructions and suggestions on what to make with the plant. Pay careful attention to information about how to cook the plant so it doesn't upset your stomach!

Recipe

For each plant, I have provided one basic recipe. For the most part, I selected and tested what I would be most likely to make with the plant. Some of the recipes are from other foragers and cooks who have generously given me permission to include them here.

Apple

Malus domestica, M. fusca
Rosaceae (rose family)

Cultivated apple trees often naturalize and bear fruit in forgotten places, and it is common to run into ancient apple trees from old homesteads from the pioneer days. I call these "feral" apple trees. Without the constant pruning and care that commercial apple trees receive, their apples tend to be smaller, and the trees a little more dense and mossy. If you really start looking, you'll start seeing feral apple trees hiding around every corner. I can't think of a more abundantly available wild food.

Back in college, my friends and I would bike out to an overgrown feral apple orchard and fill our backpacks and bike baskets to the brim with small hard apples. Then we'd go home and make apple juice, apple cider, applesauce, apple cider vinegar, and anything we could think of.

Pear trees (*Pyrus communis*) also sometimes go feral, though not quite as often. I suggest looking for those in Central Washington, where the climate is prime for them.

TOP: A feral apple tree in bloom **LEFT:** Apple flowers have delicate, white-pink blooms.
RIGHT: Small, feral apples grow in a scrubby corner of my local park.

Fruit

Blossom spray

Leaf

Some leaves have irregular lobes, but others do not

Flower

Where to Find It

Feral apple trees are common on old homesteads. Many city parks were once homesteads, and thus some parks have a ton of apple trees hiding around. You can also sometimes find them growing alongside a country road or an irrigation canal. Just be sure that if it's on private property, you ask for permission first.

How to Harvest

Because there are many varieties of apple, some trees bear excellent fruit and others tasteless and mealy fruit. Find yourself a tree with fruit you like, and come back year after year. Some people even prune wild trees to improve the tree's health, lifespan, and fruit production.

Different species of apples ripen at different times—some will ripen starting in early September, and others may not ripen until as late as November. Sample them to see if they are ready and make a note in your calendar for following years. Take a sturdy bucket to harvest into and place the apples carefully to avoid bruising them. I prefer to harvest apples off the tree, not the ground, as the ground apples tend to have more maggots

Pacific Crab Apple

Pacific crab apple (*Malus fusca*) is the only native apple species in the Pacific Northwest. It grows in the lowland areas around Puget Sound and on the Pacific coast down into Oregon. The trees like moist areas, growing especially in wetlands, near streams, and in riparian areas in general. You'll find them growing alongside willow, red osier dogwood, cramp bark, red alder, and hardhack. They are easy to spot when they bloom in the spring as their flowers are large and pinkish white.

Pacific crab apple fruits are very small and the trees don't produce very many, so I advise against trying to harvest them in the wild. However, Pacific crab apple would be a great tree choice for a native garden on the west side of the Cascades. They can be pruned in the same manner apple trees are pruned, or they can be allowed to grow in their wild shape. Pacific crab apple trees can be purchased at some, but not all, native plant nurseries, so just be sure to check the inventory before you go. Planting native plants like these in our yards benefits wildlife and helps us deepen our relationship with them.

Several non-native species of crab apple also grow in our region, like Siberian crab apple (*Malus baccata*), plumleaf crab apple (*Malus prunifolia*), and tea crab apple (*Malus hupehensis*). These are easy to tell apart from Pacific crab apples once you have the fruit, as Pacific crab apples are the smallest of them all (about the size of a kidney bean) and are oblong rather than round. Feel free to harvest the non-native species. The fruits tend to be small, seedy, and astringent but can make a fun jelly or liqueur.

(fly or moth larvae) in them. To reach apples higher in the tree, you could use an apple harvesting pole—a contraption with a pole, a hook, and a receptacle, like a yogurt container, to catch the fruit.

The fruits of domesticated apples can withstand hard frosts on the tree, but they don't tolerate wet weather well. Where I currently live, on the eastern slope of the Cascade Range, the apples stay fresh on the tree well into December. I harvested a whole basket full of great apples that had ice around the stems for a Thanksgiving apple pie one year. However, on the west side of the Cascades, they fall off the tree and spoil quickly in the wet weather that brings insects and rot.

All apple species are prone to insect larvae, so inspect the outside of the apples for brown spots with holes in the middle before putting them in your bucket. Some trees will be more "wormy" than others. You can still harvest these apples; you will just need to do more cutting at home to remove the affected parts.

Look-Alikes

Before the fruits set, Pacific crab apple very closely resembles black hawthorn due to their similar leaves and tree habits. Look for the long thorns of black hawthorn to tell them apart.

A deer munches on apple greenery and feral apples. Bears sometimes visit apple trees, as well!

Domesticated apple trees can be difficult to distinguish from the closely related cherry and plum trees before they bear fruit. However, a botany trick will help you identify cherries and apples by looking at the flower: Apple flowers have a five-pronged pistil in the middle of the flower (corresponding to the five seed chambers), and cherries have just one single pistil in the middle (corresponding to the single pit).

Sustainability

I think it's nice to leave some apples for the deer and other wildlife, though most trees produce so many that it's a bit of a moot point.

Also note that I do not recommend harvesting Pacific crabapple in the wild (see sidebar "Pacific Crab Apple").

Grow Your Own

Planting an apple tree is playing the long game, as it could take many years for it to bear fruit. Still, apple trees are a great addition to any garden, and if you take tender care of your trees, you can harvest a great crop of apples every year.

I recommend going to a nursery and getting a strong variety that's been bred for resistance to common diseases. The older the tree, the quicker you will get fruit.

When you have an apple tree, there are several things you can do to keep it healthy. First, keep trees well pruned for airflow and sunlight. There are classes and books on tree pruning, so get into it and learn this ancient art! It's also important to clean up dropped fruit and leaves from the ground regularly, as some diseases can reinfect a tree through leaves and fruit

EASY SLOW-COOKER APPLESAUCE

Fills 2 to 3 quart-sized jars

Always test the apples you are going to use first. The best applesauce comes from crispy, sweet, and tart apples. Some feral apples can be a bit bland for applesauce, in which case you can add a Granny Smith apple to the recipe to liven things up a bit. I think the plain applesauce is delicious by itself, but you can add ½ teaspoon cinnamon and sugar to taste, if you like.

3 pounds apples
½ cup water

Wash the apples by submerging them in a large bowl of water. Cut into quarters and remove brown spots or larvae. Some trees have a lot of larvae, so be ready to spend time on this step. As you work, add the quartered apples to the bowl of a slow cooker.

If you don't have equipment to easily strain the applesauce after cooking, it is best to peel the apples and remove the cores first so there is nothing to strain out at the end. The only downside is that the peels offer some great flavor when they are kept on during the cooking process.

A food mill is a great way to remove apple skins from the sauce and saves a lot of peeling time.

Add the water, set the slow cooker to high, and cook for 4 hours. Or leave the sauce in longer if you like a more concentrated, caramelized flavor. Eventually it will turn into apple butter as the moisture evaporates off and more caramelization occurs.

Once cooked, stir the apples and mash with a potato masher if necessary. If the apples were peeled, then the sauce will be ready immediately after a good stir to mash it up. If you left the peels on, then run it through a food mill (or other straining method) into a glass bowl.

Store in an airtight container in the freezer for up to a year or in the fridge for up to a week.

Browsing the tangles of a forgotten apple tree

that overwinter under the tree. If you're having issues, you could even net your tree, or net individual apples, to prevent animals or insects from getting into the fruit.

Cooking with Apple

Apples are such a well-known kitchen ingredient that you probably already have ideas for how to use them, but feral apples can differ from store-bought apples in a few ways. Feral apples are much smaller, less sweet, and sometimes less flavorful than domestic apples, depending on the tree you harvest from. They also sometimes have in them that need to be cut out before eating.

Applesauce is an excellent venue for these apples (see recipe in this entry). You can also peel them, dry the peel, and use it to flavor teas. With the tastier apples, you can make pies, crumbles, and cakes, or cut them into thin apple rings and dry them. If you have a cider press, you can make apple cider, which you can drink as is or ferment to make hard apple cider and apple cider vinegar.

The tiny fruits of Pacific crab apple are tart, a little astringent, and fairly sweet when ripe. They do have seeds, so you wouldn't necessarily want to pop the whole thing in your mouth. As with other crab apples, they are best soaked in liquor or made into a syrup. They combine well with flavors such as pomegranate, rose, lemon, hawthorn, and strawberry.

Bigleaf maple
Acer macrophyllum
Sapindaceae (horse chestnut family)

Bigleaf maples are perhaps the most iconic deciduous tree in the Pacific Northwest. You can find these majestic trees in city parks and young forests, on mountain slopes, and more. They are fairly easy to identify, as the leaves are so large it could hardly be anything else.

The spring flowers and the fall seeds of bigleaf maple are both edible, and some more ambitious folks make maple syrup from the sap. You can also eat the very young sprouts, of which there are many on the forest floor in the spring.

Maple trees host a lot of life in their branches. Tiny licorice ferns (*Polypodium glycyrrhiza*) prefer to grow in mossy patches far up in the branches of bigleaf maples. Lungwort lichen (*Lobaria pulmonaria*) also often grows on the branches of bigleaf maple trees, along with a host of other lichen, including old man's beard lichen (*Usnea* spp.). Woodpeckers, sapsuckers, and creepers love picking out insects hidden in the moss and lichen covering the trunks. Oyster mushrooms often grow on the dead logs. In other words, bigleaf maple trees are teeming with life!

LEFT: The fissured bark of a big leaf maple tree with a few tufts of moss **RIGHT:** The lime-green flowers emerge in early spring.

Bigleaf maple seeds, found in the "helicopters" that come down in the fall, are eaten or secreted away by squirrels. Their buried caches often go forgotten and germinate into trees.

Where to Find It

Bigleaf maples grow all up and down the West Coast in a variety of forest types. I have spotted them in the Yosemite Valley growing alongside the Yosemite River, they grow among the ponderosa pines near my house on the eastern slope of the Cascades, and they are especially prolific in the forests of Western Washington and Oregon. In those moist forests, they grow alongside red alder, Douglas-fir, and western hemlock.

How to Harvest

Harvest bigleaf maple flowers just as they emerge in late March to early May, depending on where you live. They are quite easy to spot, as they are a sudden lime-green flush among stark brown. The flowers of some trees will emerge before others, especially if they are in a warm microclimate, such as those that highways and cities create. Pluck the clusters within reach with your thumbnail. If they are too fibrous to be easily severed with your fingernail, then they won't be good for eating. Place them in a small bag or basket, preferably where they won't get squished. Store them in the fridge for up to 3 days.

Maple sprouts emerge soon after the flowers, germinating by the hundreds on the forest floor in April or May. Take only 10 percent of what you find, and pick the ones with only one set of round seed leaves, as they are less astringent and bitter. Either pick the dirty root off or give it a quick wash and eat the whole thing. Once the regular-shaped leaves start sprouting, they are too old.

TOP: These young bigleaf maple flowers are tender and perfect for harvest. **BOTTOM:** A maple flower harvest after a windstorm.

These maple samaras form quickly, but the nuts inside take a long time to ripen. Be patient!

Maple seeds ripen in their pods in October or November, when the samaras (winged pods) turn entirely brown. They become more bitter as they age, so it's best to harvest right when they finish ripening. You can harvest whole clumps at once. You'll have to stick to the ones you can reach from the ground or use a long pole or ladder. The seeds are in the bulb end of the samara. Pry it open with your fingers to get the seeds out.

Tapping bigleaf maples for sap to make syrup is out of the scope of this book, but there is a lot of information online and even some folks who teach in-person classes on it.

Look-Alikes

There are some non-native ornamental maples that grow in parks and gardens that could be mistaken for bigleaf maple. These other maples are edible as well, but their flower clusters tend to be a bit fibrous and their seeds small and more astringent. American sweetgum (*Liquidambar styraciflua*) and western sycamore (*Platanus racemosa*) can also sometimes be mistaken for bigleaf maple due to their similar leaf shape, but their flowers and seedpods are entirely different, so it would be unlikely you would harvest them. Neither of those trees is naturalized here but may be found growing in parks and gardens.

Sustainability

Bigleaf maple flowers are a very sustainable harvest, as long as you ensure the leaves remain on the branch and you stick to picking the blossoms and seeds in your natural reach. Leave the higher bounty for the birds and squirrels. If a tree is young or very small, refrain from stripping it, but if you find a downed branch after a spring windstorm, then by all means, take all the blossoms.

Cooking with Bigleaf Maple

Maple flowers are tender and delicate and can be eaten raw, cooked, or pickled (see recipe). The most common way to prepare

PICKLED MAPLE BLOSSOMS
Makes about 2 cups

This recipe is from my friend Amy Pennington, a Northwest writer, gardener, and food expert and the author of six books, including Apples: From Harvest to Table *and* Fresh Pantry. *Amy has been featured in* Bon Appétit, *the* Wall Street Journal, *the* Huffington Post, goop.com, *and* Apartment Therapy. *These quick-pickled maple blossoms are a breeze to prepare and make an interesting spring condiment. They're particularly tasty on crackers with goat cheese.*

2 cups maple blossoms
1½ cups white vinegar
3 tablespoons sugar
2 whole star anise (optional)
1 teaspoon whole black peppercorns
1 teaspoon coriander seeds
Pinch of salt

Place the maple blossoms in a glass pint jar and pack them down. Set aside.

In a medium saucepan, heat the vinegar, sugar, star anise, black peppercorns, coriander seeds, and salt over medium heat until simmering. When the liquid is near boiling, pour it over the blossoms and let the mixture sit on the counter until cool, stirring gently on occasion.

Once cool, seal the jar and store the pickled maple blossoms in the refrigerator until ready to serve, up to several weeks.

Making a spring nettle, miner's lettuce, and maple sprout stir fry. Delicious!

them is by dipping them in batter and frying them in oil, like a fritter, or even tempura.

Maple sprouts can be eaten raw in salads or cooked into soups. They also make a fun garnish.

Maple seeds are less often eaten by the casual food enthusiast, as they are harder to harvest and sometimes taste bitter. Roasting them with salt improves their flavor, and bitterness can be removed by boiling them in water and discarding the water.

You can also make maple syrup from bigleaf maple sap, but bear in mind that because the sap of bigleaf maple contains far less sugar than East Coast sugar maples, it takes a larger volume of sap to make the same amount of syrup. It can take 30 gallons of sap to make just 1 gallon of syrup, which equates to hours, and even days, of boiling and reducing. A large endeavor indeed. If you are interested in doing this, I recommend getting some training so you don't damage the tree and so you harvest the sap in the correct season. This precious syrup can be purchased online from small purveyors, and I've occasionally seen it being sold at farmers' markets and fairs.

Bittercress

Cardamine spp.
Brassicaceae (mustard family)

Bittercress is one of the only edible greens that grows throughout the winter in the Pacific Northwest and is best harvested then. It is in the mustard family and has the same spicy flavor as mustard greens and arugula.

The seeds of bittercress are formed inside a pealike structure called a silique. Many of these are spring-loaded and when brushed can cause seeds to fly out far enough to get in your eyes! That is where the common name *shotweed* comes from. It is a highly effective seed-dispersal mechanism that keeps this weed in the seed bank.

Where to Find It

Several species of bittercress, some native and some introduced, grow in the Pacific Northwest. Either hairy bittercress (*Cardamine hirsuta*) or few-seeded bittercress (*Cardamine oligosperma*) is likely the kind that is growing in your garden. They enjoy the bare soil in fallow garden beds suburban landscapes. Bittercress are quite easy to remove, having only a thin taproot. Many of the native species prefer to grow near ponds, streams, and other water sources.

Hairy bittercress (*Cardamine hirsuta*) sprouting up in early spring at a local park

The different *Cardamine* species can be hard to distinguish from each other, but they share the fairly universal leaf shape, flower structure, and seed structure that make easy to identify.

How to Harvest

Bittercress is best harvested from November to March. In March the flower stems start emerging, which get quite fibrous and thus are not as nice to eat. You can still pick the leaves off anytime of the year, but they become much more difficult to harvest in quantity.

The best plants have abundant large leaves. When bittercress is happy, it can really get large! For easy harvest, lift up the leaves and snip the taproot underneath the plant with scissors or a knife, harvesting the entire plant minus the roots. When you get it home, cut off the fibrous base that attaches everything together and wash the leaves. Be sure to pick out any slugs and dead leaves that may be caught in the multitude of leaf stems.

Sustainability

Bittercress is a common and non-native weed, so it can be harvested freely. Most people weed it out of their gardens anyway,

---

BITTERCRESS AND CHICKWEED ITALIAN SALSA VERDE *Makes about 1.5 cups*

This unique and flavorful green sauce can be served on meat, crackers, or pasta. Feel free to experiment with other greens here, such as miner's lettuce, dandelion, sheep sorrel, bigleaf maple flowers, or even store-bought parsley and arugula. The red pepper flakes will add just a bit of heat, but you can omit them if you like.

2 cups bittercress leaves
2 cups chickweed
⅓ cup extra-virgin olive oil
4 mini gherkins
3 anchovies
1 clove garlic, peeled
1 tablespoon capers
¼ teaspoon red pepper flakes (optional)
Zest and juice of ½ a lemon

Wash the greens, removing any brown parts, bugs, or poor-quality leaves. Chop them roughly.

Put the greens and all the other ingredients into a food processor. Process until it becomes a thick paste, scraping down the sides with a spatula as needed.

Store in a sealed container in the fridge for 3 to 5 days.

Wash your bittercress, pick out any small bugs or debris, and cut out the fibrous centers to prepare it for eating.

so you could even ask neighbors if you can harvest them. The many native species of bittercress, on the other hand, should be harvested only in small amounts as a trail snack unless they are found in great abundance.

Cooking with Bittercress

The leaves are the best part of bittercress. They taste like mustard greens and arugula, so definitely a bit spicy, and can be eaten raw or cooked. Because the leaves are quite small, it can be difficult to get enough to make a dish with, so I often mix them with other greens. In the Italian Salsa Verde recipe, I mix bittercress with chickweed.

Blackberry

Rubus bifrons, R. ursinus
Rosaceae (rose family)

I've picked blackberries every year since I can remember. My mom used to suit us up in long sleeves and thick jeans to battle the insane thorny brambles in a park near our house. We'd go home with gallons of berries to make pie, sorbet, and sauce.

Three species of blackberry grow in our region: trailing blackberry (*Rubus ursinus*), Himalayan blackberry (*Rubus bifrons*), and laceleaf blackberry (*Rubus laciniatus*).

Trailing blackberry is native to the Pacific Northwest and has delicious small berries. It is a common forest-understory plant, but it also grows in open thickets, which is where the best berries are to be found.

Himalayan blackberry berry cluster

You will encounter laceleaf blackberry alongside Himalayan blackberry, but it is nowhere near as aggressive in its habit. The berries are less tasty, so I often leave those in favor of the Himalayan blackberries. Laceleaf blackberry was introduced from Europe.

Himalayan blackberry is incredibly invasive, sometimes covering huge swaths of land. You can occasionally see it doing battle with fellow invasives Japanese knotweed, English ivy,

LEFT: Trailing blackberry blossoms **RIGHT:** Trailing blackberry vine tangle

and reed canary grass, and it is a clash of titans to be sure. However, the berries of Himalayan blackberry are delicious and extremely abundant, so we foragers can enjoy them for at least a month out of the year. You can also thank Himalayan blackberry for feeding the honeybees an ample harvest of nectar during its bloom.

Himalayan blackberry is actually an engineered species, created by botanist and horticulturist Luther Burbank. His goal was to create a delicious, resilient, thornless cultivar of blackberry that would be profitable for farmers all over the West Coast. He supposedly used stock that was sent to him from India (thus the name), though some people say it was from Europe. It escaped into the wild quickly after being sent out to farms and subsequently reverted to its thorny genetics. That was the beginning of the Himalayan blackberry nightmare that we live in today. I have recently begun to wonder if Himalayan blackberry would cover the entire state of Washington if it didn't have humans working constantly to eradicate it!

Where to Find It

Himalayan blackberry grows all up and down the West Coast, avoiding only the particularly dry areas. Look in a corner of your local park, at the edges of forests, or in neglected patches of land. It seems to prefer growing in lowland areas and will even grow on beaches.

Trailing blackberry is a bit more limited in its range, growing mostly on the lowland coastal areas of the Pacific Northwest and all the way down into California. You will find it in forest understories, especially in younger forests with red alder and bigleaf maple. It also can dominate open fields, so check local parks.

Laceleaf blackberry has a similar range to trailing blackberry but grows more commonly is disturbed areas, like Himalayan blackberry does.

How to Harvest

Harvest Himalayan blackberries when they ripen at the peak of summer in August. Wear thorn-resistant long sleeves and pants and closed-toe shoes. Pick into large sealable containers.

TOP: Himalayan blackberry vines dripping with fruit in August
BOTTOM: Trailing blackberry vines producing fruit in a sunny meadow

A trick I learned from my mom is to lay a small piece of cardboard or thin plywood over the lower blackberry vines and use that as a platform to get even higher and farther in without getting stuck with thorns. This is a good technique for those moments when you see those nice juicy berries just out of reach.

As they age on the vine, and especially after a rain, blackberries can become infested with small white worms (spotted wing drosophila fly larvae). Check for these by pulling apart a berry or two. I have had my whole harvest ruined by these. Harvest on the earlier side of the season to avoid them.

BLACKBERRY SYRUP *Makes about 1 pint*

As a kid, I remember watching my mom painstakingly strain our blackberry syrup I put it on vanilla ice cream and would eat it in tiny bites to savor it. We would also have it on pancakes on Sundays. As an adult, I make mocktails and fancy sodas with syrup, which my husband loves. You can use a lot of different berries in this recipe, such as huckleberries, Indian plums, strawberries, or blueberries, but juicy Himalayan blackberries are the best. If you'd like your syrup to last longer in the fridge, use twice the amount of sugar. For a more intense sauce, use less water.

2 cups (10 ounces) blackberries, fresh or frozen
½ cup water
Cane sugar, as needed

Put the blackberries and water in a small saucepan and bring to a boil on medium heat. Turn down the heat to low and simmer for 5 minutes, mashing each berry well with the back of a wooden spoon. Once it is well mashed, remove from the heat.

In batches, pour the pulp through a fine-mesh metal strainer into a heatproof bowl to separate the seeds from the dark-purple liquid. Discard the seeds.

Measure the resulting liquid and add an equal volume of sugar. Stir thoroughly. If the sugar does not dissolve easily, put the mixture back on the stove in a saucepan and heat gently over low heat until it dissolves completely.

Transfer the syrup to an airtight jar or bottle and store in the fridge for 1 to 2 months or in the freezer for up to 6 months. As with any perishable item, always check for mold or strange smells before using.

Laceleaf blackberries ripen at the same time as Himalayan blackberries and often grow among them. Their berries are a bit firmer and sour, not a favorite of mine.

Trailing blackberries are much more scarce than Himalayan blackberries and shouldn't be harvested heavily for the sake of wildlife that relies on them. Harvest a handful and gorge yourself on the trail, but there's no need to collect large quantities of them when we have Himalayan blackberries around. They ripen slightly earlier than Himalayan blackberries, in July and August. They don't often fruit a lot when they grow with tree cover above them, so seek them out in open spaces. Where they have access to the sun, they form thick tangled mats that can be up to 3 feet deep, and they fruit prolifically. The tangles are often so thick that you can step on top of them to get farther into the patch; just don't let them pull you into the fairy realm.

Look-Alikes

Blackcaps (*Rubus leucodermis*) and salmonberry (*Rubus spectabilis*) are both in the same genus and could be mistaken for blackberry when not in fruit. However, the fruits are a dead giveaway. Blackberry fruits (both *R. bifrons* and *R. ursinus*) have a white center that does not separate from the black drupelets when the fruit is picked. Blackcaps and salmonberries both separate from their white center, resembling a thimble.

Cautions

Himalayan blackberry is the target of a lot of herbicide applications. The city of Seattle definitely sprays blackberries in their city parks, and they post signs when they spray, so keep an eye out. Sprayed blackberries will look a bit warped and start to brown shortly after spraying. Steer clear. As far as I know, no research has been done on whether herbicides persist in the berries in future years after application, so you will have to make your own call on that one. Personally, I avoid patches for at least a few years after I know have been sprayed.

Sustainability

Pick all the Himalayan blackberries. Seriously. The fewer seeds there are out there, the less we have to worry about them spreading to new areas. Birds and other animals eat the berries and spread them far and wide through their poop, further cursing us with Himalayan blackberry. Because they block new trees from the light they need to survive in their early years, Himalayan blackberries actually make it quite difficult for forests to grow.

Cooking with Blackberry

Blackberries are a classic kitchen ingredient, so you can likely find many creative recipes. My family's favorite is blackberry pie. You can also make jam, jelly, sorbet, syrup, infused vinegar, and more. They can sometimes be quite sour, so adding sugar to them can improve their flavor a lot.

Dark, juicy himalayan blackberry are the best for cooking.

Before you use blackberries in a recipe, wash them well in a large colander and pick out any bugs or leaves that may have made it home with you. Sometimes I soak them in a big basin of water for a minute and then drain.

To freeze the berries for later use, cover a baking sheet with waxed paper or parchment paper. Lay the berries out on the baking sheet so they are mostly not touching and put them in the freezer for a few hours. You can do this in batches if your freezer has limited room. Once frozen, transfer them to a labeled container, such as a gallon plastic freezer bag. This technique ensures they do not freeze into a single mass. Store in the freezer for no longer than 6 months, as they will eventually get freezer burn.

Blackcaps

Rubus leucodermis
Rosaceae (rose family)

I have fond memories of picking blackcaps (also known as blackcap raspberries) up the hill from my house as a kid. We were usually out for blackberries and were especially excited when we came across our coveted blackcaps. None of them ever made it home.

The flavor of blackcaps is different from closely related blackberries, and the berries come off like a thimble, like raspberries do. The plants are easy to spot in all seasons as they have a frosted neon stalk with thorns in it that sets it apart from other brambles. The stalk can be neon pink, purple, or green.

Where to Find It

Blackcaps grow on both sides of the Cascades from British Columbia all the way to Southern California. They grow in the temperate rainforests of the Olympic Peninsula, in scrubby waste lots, at montane elevations in the Cascades, in ponderosa pine forests, and even on coastal bluffs. This plant is fairly versatile,

LEFT: When black caps turn red, they aren't ripe yet! Wait until they are dark purple. **RIGHT:** The upright canes of blackcap bushes jut upward and then curve back toward the ground.

though they don't prefer the driest parts of our region, like the Columbia Basin.

How to Harvest

Blackcaps ripen from late June to July. At higher elevations, they may be ripe into August. Pick them when they are darker. The berries with hints of red are good, but they are more sour and less sweet.

Whereas Himalayan blackberries grow in huge clusters, blackcaps grow in very small clusters that ripen one at a time, making it hard to find a lot at once. For this reason, it's best to eat blackcaps directly off the bush rather than try to take them home.

Look-Alikes

Himalayan blackberry, trailing blackberry, and salmonberry all look fairly similar to blackcaps. In fact, they are all in the *Rubus* genus. The leaf shapes are similar, and they all have thorns. But the berries are a foolproof way to tell blackcaps apart: they are black like a blackberry and cap-shaped like a salmonberry.

Sustainability

Blackcaps are not common enough nor do they fruit enough to be harvested heavily. For that reason, it is best to treat these like a special trail snack, eating only a few at a time. As with other berry plants, it's important to leave some for the birds so that they can eat them and disperse the seeds to new locations. Birds play an important role in helping berry plants spread and propagate. Blackcaps are also one of the many native berry species important to the Native Americans of the Pacific Northwest.

A Handful of Trail Berries

Many trail berries are often either too scarce to collect in large quantities, too goopy to take home, or too sour to eat many of, so they're best enjoyed in moderation when we are out on the trail. Following is my personal list of favorite trail berries, along with the reason they aren't suitable for me to take home; your list may look different depending on how common certain berries are in your area. A few of these berries aren't even in this book!

- Blackcaps (too scarce)
- Chokecherry (too astringent)
- Cloudberry (too scarce)
- Grouseberry (too scarce)
- Red huckleberry (too scarce)
- Thimbleberry (too goopy)
- Trailing blackberry (too scarce)
- Western teaberry (too scarce)

The benefits of trail berries are many—not only are you consuming them at the moment when they are most nutritious and delicious, but you are also leaving a lot of berries for wildlife by not picking bushels of berries to take home. If you sit quietly for ten or more minutes near the patch of ripe berries, you may see the critters that come to eat the berries!

Picking a few blackcaps to eat while on a mountain bike ride

Grow Your Own

Blackcaps are one of the first native berries that I would plant in my yard. They are hardy, versatile, not too wandering, and very tasty. You can buy seeds online, buy plants from native plant nurseries, or dig up a plant from the wild. If you choose to go for wild stock, dig it up from a place where there are many other plants, and make sure you have permits or permission. Caring for them is very similar to caring for raspberry, so you can follow instruction for pruning raspberries. When cared for properly in a yard, blackcaps can actually produce quite a bit more fruit than they do in the wild.

You could also potentially propagate this plant from a cane cutting, though because the stem is only semi-woody, it will be a bit more finicky than something like elderberry.

Cooking with Blackcaps

Blackcaps make a fantastic trail snack, one that I will stop my mountain bike for in a heartbeat. They are fantastic raw, though they are quite seedy, so be ready to floss your teeth after eating them.

Burdock

Arctium lappa, A. minus
Asteraceae (sunflower family)

Burdock root is a delicious wild root vegetable, similar in shape and texture to carrot, but more fibrous. It is commonly eaten in Asia, where it is pickled, stir-fried, roasted, or boiled.

Burdock is a biennial, which means that it lives for two years. In its first year, it grows a set of large basal leaves and puts much of its energy into developing its long taproot. In the second year, it sends up a flower stalk, blooms, produces seed, and then dies in the fall.

Two species of burdock grow in the Pacific Northwest. The most prevalent one is common burdock (*Arctium minus*). Less common is great burdock (*Arctium lappa*), which is the species of burdock commonly eaten in Asia. The two plants are very similar, but you can tell them apart by the fact that great burdock is much larger, and common burdock is smaller with longer leaf stems. Both are non-native to our area and are equally edible.

TOP: The purple flowers of burdock have burrs that will grab your clothes and hair if you're not careful. **BOTTOM:** Late in the season, burdock sprawls out and creates burr-covered seedpods at a farm in Carnation, WA.

Flower

Leaf back (top) and front (bottom)

Seed

This ring can be found on all burdock roots

Root and cross sections of root

Root with basal leaves

Harvest at this young stage for the most tender roots

Where to Find It

Like many other introduced, weedy species, burdock likes disturbed areas and wastelands. I find it growing on forgotten corners of farmland, on the sides of paths and roads, in open grassy fields, and near and on train tracks. It seems to grow in most parts of the Pacific Northwest, except for the very driest areas, such as the Columbia Basin in Washington and the John Day area in Oregon.

How to Harvest

Burdock root is best when harvested in the first year, before the root becomes too fibrous to eat. Harvest the root before the plant sends up a flower stalk, which is usually in the spring of the second year or late fall of the first year of growth. Plants in this stage of growth will have just a set of basal leaves, with no flower stalks or flowers.

Harvesting burdock root takes some persistence, as it tends to grow in hard soils and the taproot grows deep. I recommend starting with a digging fork to loosen the surrounding soil and then moving to a shovel or trowel. The key is to not hit the root with the digging tools, because they will scar and bring soil into the inner white flesh of the root, which is hard to clean out.

After excavating as much root as possible, wash it thoroughly. I start with a good spray from the garden hose and then fill a basin with water and use a stiff scrub brush to scrub off the remaining dirt.

Digging up the deep taproots of burdock from compacted, rocky soil without scarring them is a unique test of patience.

Another option is to grow it in your garden, where it will thrive happily. In Japan, burdock roots are grown in 3- to 4-foot-long tubes to make the harvest easy. The roots that result from this are tender, long, and unbranched. To grow your own, you can collect wild seed (expect a more fibrous root) or get special burdock seeds from an Asian grocery store that have been bred for eating.

Look-Alikes

The closest look-alike for burdock is broadleaf dock (*Rumex obtusifolius*), which can be easily distinguished by its lack of

KINPIRA GOBO

Makes 4 servings

This is one of my favorite Japanese dishes, one I learned how to make during college, when I spent three months in Japan staying at organic farms. The Japanese consider burdock to be a healing food, and it was very popular among the families I stayed with. In the Japanese name for this dish, kinpira means "julienned," and gobo means "burdock." An easy way to julienne the burdock and carrots is to slice them diagonally, producing long oval-shaped slices, and then stack those pieces and slice them into matchsticks. You can find mirin—sweet rice wine—in Asian markets or in the international section of some grocery stores. When selecting roots to harvest for this recipe, it is important to choose first-year roots with no flowering stalks to ensure they are tender enough to chew.

1 cup julienned burdock root (cut into 2-inch matchsticks)
1 cup julienned carrot (cut into 2-inch matchsticks)
1 to 2 tablespoons light oil, such as sunflower, avocado, or canola oil
1 tablespoon toasted sesame oil
1½ tablespoons soy sauce
1 tablespoon mirin
1 tablespoon sake (Japanese rice wine; optional)
1 tablespoon sugar
1 tablespoon toasted sesame seeds

Put the burdock into a bowl and cover with cold water. Soak for 5 minutes, drain, replace with more cold water and soak for another 5 minutes. Drain well.

In a sauté pan, wok, or cast-iron skillet, heat the two oils over medium heat. Once hot, toss in the burdock and stir-fry for 2 to 3 minutes, until it begins to soften. Add the carrot and continue to stir-fry for another 2 to 3 minutes.

Add soy sauce, mirin, sake, and sugar and cook, stirring, until all the liquid has evaporated and a browning reaction has begun. Be careful not to burn it at this stage.

Turn off the heat, add the sesame seeds, and serve hot with steamed rice.

hair on the undersides of the leaves. The undersides of burdock leaves have a distinct whitish velvet fuzz. Contrary to what the names may lead you to believe, burdock and broadleaf dock are not related. Broadleaf dock is in the buckwheat family (Polygonaceae) and thus related to Japanese knotweed and sheep sorrel. Burdock is in the sunflower family, and is related to dandelion and artichoke.

Sustainability

Burdock is a non-native weed and can be harvested at your leisure. The only hesitation I would have about harvesting it is that digging up burdock roots can cause a lot of disturbance that may not be appropriate in a park or other maintained area.

Grow Your Own

Burdock is very easy to grow in your garden from seed. You can harvest seeds from wild plants if you'd like, which are ready to be gathered when they are hard and gray in August and September. However, if you buy seeds at the store, those cultivars have been bred to have long, less-fibrous roots to maximize edibility. Choose a sunny spot with well-drained soil. Sow the seeds directly in spring, right after the last frost. You can harvest the roots in the fall of the first year or the following spring. You don't need to baby it like you would a tomato plant, as burdock is a weed and will do well in dry, rocky soil. However, a little

Cautions

Burdock root contains inulin, a prebiotic starch that can cause gastrointestinal (GI) distress and gas if consumed in large amounts. Though not technically toxic, it can cause a lot of discomfort. Inulin is actually beneficial for large-intestine bacteria because it feeds the good bacteria, but it is something that your gut must get used to. This affects some people more severely than others. Traditional cultures likely ate a lot more prebiotic foods like burdock and thus would not have had a problem with gas when consuming them. Theoretically, if you were to consume burdock regularly, your bacteria would become more accustomed to it and the GI distress would lessen over time. You can reduce the inulin by slow cooking the root (see "Cooking with Burdock").

water and good soil will yield more tender roots, and planting it in softer soil will make them easier to dig up. In Japan, farmers sometimes grow commercial burdock in long pipes that ensure an easy harvest and allow the roots to grow 2 feet long or more! There are tutorials online showing how to build burdock planters; something to check out if you are a burdock fanatic.

Cooking with Burdock

Because the outside skin of burdock tends to retain dirt and is more fibrous, people tend to peel it. If the skin is thin, this can be done by scraping the back of a butter knife back and forth to remove the outermost brown layer. Some roots may have a thicker bark-like skin that may require a vegetable peeler to remove.

It is traditional in Japan to soak freshly sliced or cut burdock root in cold water for 5 to 10 minutes. This keeps it from oxidizing (turning brown), keeps it fresh and crunchy for stir-frying, and removes bitterness and excess starch. After the soak time is complete, mix it around a bit, drain the water, and then rinse once more with cold water.

Burdock is delicious cut into thin matchsticks and stir-fried. See the recipe for *kinpira gobo* in this section for a traditional Japanese stir-fried dish.

One of my favorite ways to prepare burdock is to make burdock chips, which involves thinly slicing the root (1 to 3 millimeters thick), coating them in oil and salt, and roasting them in the oven at 400 degrees F until they start to turn brown. When crispy, burdock produces delicious and addictive flavor compounds that will tempt you to eat enough to give you gas, so be warned.

When adding burdock to soups, it can be prudent to precook the burdock in a slow cooker for a few hours before adding it to the pot, to reduce inulin (see Cautions).

Wild burdock roots are more fibrous, thicker, and more oddly shaped than the ones available at Asian markets and some specialty grocery stores. It is often necessary to cut out rotten bits, discard overly fibrous sections, and wash them very well. Some methods of preparing—like burdock chips—are a better way to use the more fibrous roots. You can also chop, dry, and roast the roots, which make a delicious and healthful tea.

Chickweed

Stellaria media
Caryophyllaceae (pink family)

Common chickweed (*Stellaria media*) is a delicious early season edible green that thrives in soft, disturbed soil in moist gardens, parks, and at the edges of some forests. It is one of my favorite and most-eaten wild edible greens.

Many other members of the *Stellaria* genus are native to the Pacific Northwest, but a lot of them are rather rare and thus should be avoided. Crisped starwort (*Stellaria crispa*), can be found in the forest and shaded areas on the west side of the Cascades tangled with nettle, trailing blackberry, and fragrant bedstraw. Though edible, it is much more fibrous than chickweed. I stick with the tasty and abundant common chickweed and leave the others alone.

Chickweed is also used for medicinal purposes. It is a gentle medicine, used to discourage cysts, that grows in the body over time. It is not a fast-moving or miraculous remedy; chickweed is in the category of medicines that are best used as part of a daily routine to maintain health.

TOP: Chickweed's V-shaped flower petals **BOTTOM:** A bright green, early spring patch of chickweed coming up on a lawn

82

Where to Find It

Chickweed loves soft, rich soil. I often see it overtaking an empty garden bed or a forgotten planter. The biggest patch of chickweed I've ever seen was in an old horse-manure pile on someone's property. The spot was not particularly sunny, as it was surrounded by trees, but there were gallons of thick bright-green chickweed there. It also often grows in moist grassy areas, and even on the forest floor.

It is found mostly on the west side of the Cascades at lower elevations, though it can be found occasionally in farms and gardens in the drier parts of the region.

How to Harvest

Chickweed is an early spring green, one of the first besides bittercress to emerge. If there are warm stints in the winter, especially in warm microclimates, chickweed will emerge in bursts. It is best harvested before it flowers, when the leaves are green, succulent, and tender. Once it flowers and seeds begin to form, the stem becomes fibrous.

To harvest, use scissors to trim the top halves of shoots. The plant often grows in patches, so you can trim it much like you would hair. Just be sure to pick out grass and any other plants that might be hiding among the chickweed.

Chickweed often grows in places that you should not harvest from, like abandoned patches of land near commercial buildings or at the local dog park. Take care to harvest chickweed from an uncontaminated spot and wash it before eating it.

Store it in a sealed plastic bag in the fridge for no more than 2 days. This is a delicate green and should be used as soon as possible.

An abundant November harvest of chickweed

CHICKWEED SPRING SALAD

Makes 4 servings

This is a bright spring salad with a fresh, homemade vinaigrette you can use on other wild salads, if you like. Wild-harvested chickweed usually needs to be sorted through before use. Wash it in a colander and then lay it out on a cutting board and remove brown parts, slugs, bugs, leaves, and sticks. Chop into 1-inch sections for the salad. If the chickweed you've harvested has fibrous stems, you may need to remove the lower part of the stem, keeping only the tops. You can also add in other early spring greens, such as sheep sorrel, miner's lettuce, or bittercress.

FOR THE SALAD
1 bunch asparagus
3 to 4 cups chopped chickweed shoots
1 bunch red radishes, finely sliced
1 large carrot, grated or julienned
½ cup chopped, toasted almonds

FOR THE DRESSING
⅓ cup extra-virgin olive oil
3 tablespoons champagne vinegar or other light vinegar
Juice of ½ a lemon
1 clove garlic, finely minced
1 teaspoon Dijon mustard
1 teaspoon honey
¼ teaspoon salt
Dash of pepper

Bring a pot of water to boil and prepare a bath of ice water in a Pyrex dish large enough to fit the asparagus. Blanch the asparagus by plunging it into the boiling water to cook for 3 minutes. Remove from the water and transfer it to the ice bath for at least 5 minutes.

Chop the asparagus into ½-inch sections and put into the salad bowl along with the chickweed and other salad ingredients.

In an 8-ounce jar, add the dressing ingredients and shake well. Dress the salad right before eating.

Look-Alikes

Chickweed has a few look-alikes, some of which are edible (but not as tasty), like mouse-ear chickweed (*Cerastium glomeratum*). Watch out for toxic look-alikes such as milk spurge (*Euphorbia maculata*) and related species, as well as scarlet pimpernel (*Lysimachia arvensis*). Scarlet pimpernel is not very common in Washington and Oregon but is more prevalent in California.

Sustainability

Chickweed is an abundant non-native weed that produces thousands of seeds, so harvest to your heart's content.

Grow Your Own

You can introduce chickweed into your garden by broadcasting seeds in the fall. They will come up in the early spring and form a low mat. Plant them in rich, moist soil for the best results. It can be a nice groundcover or early season crop for your vegetable garden beds.

Cooking with Chickweed

Chickweed is among my favorite wild foods. Its flavor is subtle relative to other wild greens—it has a refreshing, watery, nutty flavor that is a real joy. It has very little toxicity, so you can eat quite a bit of it. Chickweed is high in vitamin C, calcium, iron, and many other nutrients.

The aerial parts of chickweed, especially the leaves and stems, are edible raw or cooked. I prefer them raw as they can get a little slimy when cooked. I usually put a little chopped chickweed in a green salad, and I also love to make chickweed pesto and Italian salsa verde (see recipe in the Bittercress entry).

You can also make a hot infused tea from fresh chickweed that is gently detoxifying and nutritive.

Chickweed pesto is my favorite wild pesto, especially spread on warm sourdough bread.

Chicory

Cichorium intybus
Asteraceae (sunflower family)

Wild chicory, introduced to this continent by European settlers, is eaten all over Eurasia in places as disparate in their cuisines as South India and Russia. The Italians have a special love for chicory, where it is known as *cicoria*. The leaves, roots, young flower stems, flower buds, and flowers are all edible.

Radicchio, one of my very favorite vegetables, is actually a cultivated variety of chicory that was bred from the wild species about two hundred years ago. It is more tender and less bitter than the wild stuff.

Where to Find It

Like some of the other Mediterranean escapees in this book, this plant likes sunny spots with well-drained soil and a little gravel. Think roadsides, ditches, farmland, and vacant land. Chicory has a wide distribution, occurring in most parts of the Pacific Northwest, including Idaho and most parts of California.

To my delight, chicory is incredibly common where I live on the eastern slope of the Cascades. My guess is that it loves the gravelly, clay-like soil here. At houses that have less fastidious lawn care, it readily replaces the grass, creating an epic purple bloom in July. It also loves my neighbor's gravel pile—it's the only plant growing there.

It's easy to miss chicory until it blooms, and these beautiful purple flowers emerge.

How to Harvest

The young basal leaves are the least bitter and most tender in March through May, before the plant sends up a flower stalk. The inner leaves, the most recent growth, are the ones you want to harvest. Once the flower stalk emerges in the middle, the leaves start to get more bitter. You can either harvest the whole basal rosette by cutting it off at the root crown, or you can be highly selective and pinch individual leaves off.

In Italy, they also harvest the tips of the tender developing flower stalk. Just pinch off 1 to 2 inches of each branch. June is the best time to search for these, before they flower in July.

The thick taproot is best dug in the spring when the leaves are just emerging, usually in March through May. However, you can harvest later in the season or even in the fall, but note that roots may be more fibrous and harder to chop at those times. The roots can be a foot long or more and thicker than your thumb, if you're lucky. They can be difficult to dig up because the soil they like to grow in is usually gravelly and hardpan. Bring a digging fork or even a small pickax to loosen up the soil around the plant as much as possible. You want to get as much of the root as possible without nicking it or breaking it, so take your time. Once you've got the upper part loose, you may need to cut off what you've managed to excavate from the rest of the root that delves to unimaginable depths. There is only so much digging one can do in one session, after all.

A bee with visible pollen sacs collects the bright yellow-or-ange pollen of chicory

Harvest the flowers when they have freshly opened, plucking them off and gathering them carefully in a plastic container to prevent crushing them.

Look-Alikes

Chicory is among the many dandelion look-alikes and can be quite hard to distinguish before it shoots up its distinctive branched flower stalk. The leaves look very similar to dandelion and, further complicating things, they both have a fairly wide range of leaf shapes. One sneaky way to tell the two apart is this:

A Close Look at Chicory's Central Leaf Vein

One sneaky way to distinguish chicory leaves from two of its close look-alikes, dandelion and prickly lettuce, is by taking a close look at the central leaf veins. The central leaf vein of chicory has fine white hairs, and the central veins of dandelion leaves are smooth and mostly hairless. Prickly lettuce has a distinctive row of soft spines along the underside of the leaf rib. These distinctions are especially helpful since you'll probably be identifying and harvesting leaves of these plants early in the season, before the flower stalks emerges.

Central vein comparison of dandelion (left), prickly lettuce (middle), and chicory (right)

when you cut dandelion leaves or stems, the exposed inner parts leak a white sap, chicory leaves do not.

Prickly lettuce (*Lactuca serriola*) can also be easily mistaken for chicory before they are in bloom. Prickly lettuce has a row of soft spines along the underside of the leaf rib, distinguishing it from chicory.

Sustainability

Chicory is a non-native weed, so you can harvest to your heart's content.

Grow Your Own

You can easily plant wild chicory in your yard by collecting seeds from wild plants (select ones from plants with big, healthy leaves) and broadcasting them in some rich, tilled soil in the early spring. However, keep in mind that it is a non-native

ROASTED CHICORY COFFEE

Makes about ¾ cup

Roasted chicory coffee is one of the best coffee substitutes out there. Not only is making it yourself rewarding, but you can control the roast level and the flavor. You can play with blends by adding other ingredients, like roasted carob or roasted dandelion root, or grind it and combine it with real coffee.

6 ounces fresh chicory roots

Wash the roots thoroughly using a jet-spray nozzle on an outside hose, and finish them off inside if needed.

Preheat the oven to 300 degrees F.

Put all the roots in a food processor and roughly chop until they are of equal size. You can also finely chop them with a knife, if you like. The larger the pieces, the longer it will take them to dry and then roast.

Line a baking tray with parchment paper or a silicone baking mat and spread out the chopped roots with as much space between them as possible.

Put them in the oven and roast for 60 to 90 minutes, checking regularly to make sure they aren't burning. About 30 minutes in, take them out of the oven and stir the roots, then put them back in.

Smell and use your eyes to determine doneness. The roots should be dark brown, not black, and completely bone-dry. They should smell chocolatey and toasty.

If you like more of a roasted flavor, increase the oven temperature to 400 degrees F and roast for another few minutes. It is easy to burn them this way, so monitor closely and use your nose to tell when they're done. Remove the pan from the oven and let it cool for at least 20 minutes.

In an herb grinder, food processor, or other grinding method of your choice, grind them into a rough powder.

Prepare as you would coffee, using about 1 tablespoon of powder per 8-ounce cup water, depending on your preference. Add milk and/or sugar if you'd like.

weed and will spread. That said, if you plant it in softer soil, the roots are much easier to dig up and can save you a lot of trouble.

Cooking with Chicory

Chicory leaves can be eaten raw in salads or cooked. Be sure to wash the leaves, especially if you are taking home the whole basal rosette, as roly-poly bugs and other insects like to live between the leaves.

The most traditional way to eat chicory leaves is to plunge them into boiling water for 2 to 3 minutes, strain, squeeze, and sauté with good olive oil, garlic, lemon juice, and salt. The soaking process reduces the bitterness and makes them tender. This is a simple dish and a classic way to prepare many wild greens. You can mix other greens with it, if you like.

Roasted chicory root has been added to and used in place of coffee for hundreds of years, either because wars made coffee unavailable or too expensive. The famous "coffee and chicory" from Café du Monde in New Orleans is an example of a tradition that came from poverty and became a local specialty. Chicory coffee was also consumed in East Germany during the partition. Dandelion root is another common coffee substitute, but in my opinion, chicory is much better. It is richer, darker, and more complex. To be clear, neither contains caffeine.

Starting to dry chicory in the sun helps prevent mold. If it's cloudy and cold outside, you can mimick this in a gently warm oven.

The flowers can be added to salads to add color or used to garnish cakes or other dishes. Be creative!

Chokecherry

Prunus virginiana
Rosaceae (rose family)

Chokecherries are native to North America and grow all over the northern part of the US, especially in the Mountain West and the Northeast. Though the Pacific Northwest is not its primary range, it is still quite abundant in some areas.

Chokecherries are an important food plant for many First Nations, especially those living where it grows more abundantly, such as the northern plains, Rocky Mountains, and Midwest.

Chokecherries are in the *Prunus* genus, which is the same genus as the sweet cherries (*Prunus avium*) you get at the supermarket. The fruits are similar to regular cherries in that they contain a very hard pit that you don't want to chew on or swallow. Also, the bark is red and striped like other members of the *Prunus* genus. The stripes on the bark are lenticels, which facilitate tree respiration. Its leaves are finely serrated, like those of other cherry trees, and its five-petaled white flowers are also characteristic of the *Prunus* genus.

Where to Find It

To find chokecherries in the Pacific Northwest, you will have the best luck east of the Cascades, where there are more distinct seasons, less shrubby competition, and drier soils. Chokecherry

Chokecherry has distinctive, spike-shaped berry clusters

CHOKECHERRY

Cherry cluster

Flower spike

Flower

Cherry

Look-Alike ⚠
Bitter cherry flowering branch

Leaf front and back

Look-Alike ⚠
Bitter cherry leaf front and back

Look-Alike ⚠
Bitter cherry berry cluster

Look-Alike ⚠
Bitter cherry berry cluster

prefers well-drained yet moist soils, such as gravelly areas near streams where they get consistent moisture. They also like disturbed soils, which tells us to look in flood zones around rivers and near human development (which unfortunately includes roadsides). You will not find chokecherry in shrub steppe regions, such as the Columbia Basin in Washington, as there is not enough water there.

West of the Cascades, you can find pockets of chokecherry on the south side of Vancouver Island, around the Puget Sound, in dry spots in western Oregon, and a lot in Northern California. Look to prairie lands rather than the moist, dense forests.

How to Harvest

The berries turn dark red or black (depending on the tree), ripen in late August, and can be found through September and sometimes October. Berries are astringent (which is where the *choke* in the name comes from) but will become less so as they ripen. Black-colored berries are supposedly more astringent than the more common red ones, and they all have a small, hard pit in the center that must be removed.

I pick whole cluster together with the stems into a basket or bucket and then take them home to wash and pick out insects and bad berries. To store the berries for later use, freeze them in resealable freezer bags, clearly labeled, with or without the stems. Sometimes berries can be easier to remove from stems when frozen, so that's a plus, but you will have to remove the stems and pits either way. I prefer to do the work upfront and have a ready-to-go item when I take it out of the freezer.

Like other fruits, the fruit production of this tree varies depending on the year. One year you'll have a huge fruiting (a mast crop), and another year you may return to the same tree and find only a few clusters. In meager years, it's best to leave what's there to the birds and other animals, who enjoy chokecherry immensely. Bears enjoy chokecherries, and I often see bear scat with chokecherry pits in it during September and October.

Birds love to eat chokecherries in the late summer and fall.

LEFT: Chokecherries have distinctive white flowers spikes. RIGHT: The white flowers make for a lovely spring bloom.

Look-Alikes

The berries grow in spikes, which sets them apart from bitter cherry (*Prunus emarginata*) and other ornamental cherries that are naturalized. However, their spike form resembles cherry laurel (*Prunus laurocerasus*), an introduced shrub that grows around the Puget Sound, western Oregon, and coastal Northern California. Thankfully, those habitats don't overlap much with chokecherry's range. Cherry laurel fruits are much darker in color, and their leaves are dark, shiny, and waxy, with smooth edges. The edibility of cherry laurel fruits is debated, with the consensus being that some fruits are edible while some have higher concentrations of cyanogenic glycosides, which can be harmful in large doses. In any case, you would not want to mistake the two!

One could also mistake chokecherry for buckthorn (*Frangula purshiana*), as the berries are dark and of a similar size. To differentiate, look for chokecherry's signature spike-shaped fruit clusters, and note that buckthorn leaves are not finely serrated like those of chokecherry. Buckthorn berries are mildly toxic when ingested and can upset the stomach and cause diarrhea. Incidentally, aged buckthorn bark is used medicinally as a laxative, but is so strong that it must be aged for a whole year before

Cautions

Chokecherry pits, leaves, and bark contain cyanogenic glycosides, which can be toxic if consumed in large enough amounts. This will not affect you if you are just eating the fruits.

> **How to Sterilize Jars**
>
> Canning is a useful technique for many of the plants in this book. Sterilize jars by putting them in the canning bath full of water. Bring it to a boil, and boil for 10 minutes a lid on the pot. Once sterilized, line them up on a clean towel, ready to have jam poured into them.

it can be safely used. Definitely not a mistake you would want to make! But buckthorn prefers a wetter climate and is more common on the west side of the Cascades.

Sustainability

The primary sustainability concern for chokecherry is leaving enough of it for wildlife. As mentioned in How to Harvest, avoid harvesting during meager years. If the berries seem really abundant where you are, harvest to your heart's content.

CHOKECHERRY JAM *Makes 6 pints*

For this recipe, you will need a food mill (see picture in the Hawthorn entry recipe) or similar equipment to remove the pits while retaining the flesh. If you don't have a food mill, you can make this a jelly instead of a jam and strain the cooked and mashed pulp through a metal sieve, muslin, or even a nut-milk bag, though this method is painstaking. The resulting juice can be substituted for the 3½ cups of pulp mixture used to make the jam.

4 cups water
4 cups chokecherries
3 tablespoons powdered pectin
2 tablespoons fresh lemon juice
4 cups sugar

Add the water and chokecherries to a large pot, put the lid on, and bring to a boil. Once boiling, reduce the heat and simmer for 30 minutes. Let cool for 10 minutes.

Remove the seeds from the pulp in batches using a food mill. Most food mills have several plates with holes of different sizes, so select one with small enough holes that the seeds can't make it through.

Measure 3½ cups of the pulp mixture and put it into a large saucepan. (If you have leftover pulp, add an equal amount of sugar and make it into a syrup, or discard.) Over medium heat, whisk in the powdered pectin and add the lemon juice.

Grow Your Own

Chokecherry trees are easy to grow in the drier areas of our region. The best time to plant is in the early spring or fall. Find a dry, sunny, well-drained spot to plant it and water it heavily once a month during the summer for the best fruit and tree health. You can find chokecherry trees at some nurseries, but you can also order them online or even grow them from wild-harvested seed, if you are ambitious.

Cooking with Chokecherry

Chokecherries are not great to eat raw because of their astringency, so people tend to cook them into syrups, jams, jellies, and fruit leather (usually combined with other fruits like apple or pear). They are not as sour as other cherries are, which means the jam has a surprisingly mild flavor that is tasty on scones or even between layers of a yellow cake.

Turn the heat up to high and bring the mixture to a rolling boil while whisking vigorously. Add the sugar and bring to a rolling boil again, whisking constantly to prevent burning. Boil hard for one more minute. Remove it from the heat.

Using a jar-filling funnel, ladle the hot jam into six sterilized pint-size canning jars (see sidebar "How to Sterilize Jars"), leaving about a ½ inch of room in each one. If you are planning on canning the jam, having consistent headspace in each jar is important. Jam-making kits include a tool that measures the headspace. Wipe the jar rims clean with a damp towel.

Screw fresh canning lids onto each jar. Put the jars in a canning bath full of water, making sure that each jar is covered by an inch or more of water. Bring the water to a boil, and then process the filled jars in vigorously boiling water for at least 10 minutes, adding 5 additional minutes for each additional 1000 feet above sea level. Remove the jars from the water using jar tongs and let them sit on the counter overnight to seal. In the morning, remove only the rings to see if the lids have sealed. For any jars that have not sealed properly, put them in the fridge and use within a month or freeze and use within a year.

Dandelion

Taraxacum officinale
Asteraceae (sunflower family)

The common dandelion (*Taraxacum officinale*) should need little introduction, for who has not encountered this humble and ubiquitous plant? With its yellow flowers that morph into puffs that children wish upon, and its leaves eaten in many corners of the globe, this is a forager's staple. All parts of this plant are edible: leaves, flowers, roots, stems, and seeds.

The dandelion is native to Europe and central Asia but has spread to every continent except Antarctica, thriving in a wide range of habitats.

Other members of the *Taraxacum* genus grow in our region. The native ones seem to be mostly rare alpine plants, such as horned dandelion (*Taraxacum ceratophorum*). Red-seeded dandelion (*Taraxacum erythrospermum*), also introduced from Europe, is common enough that you might run into it. It looks almost identical to the common dandelion except it has terracotta-colored seeds rather than the grayish-white ones of common dandelion.

Where to Find It

Where do you *not* find dandelion? It grows from the coast all the way up into the alpine and on both sides of the Cascades.

I love to find a good dandelion specimen like this and harvest the whole thing--roots, leaves and flowers.

It grows in sidewalk cracks, under black tarps, in frequently mowed lawns, and in gravel roads, where it gets run over. This is one versatile and adaptive plant. But where do you find the best dandelion plants for eating? I tend to look in community gardens with a lot of bark chips; in sandy, wet areas; in gardens; and in gravel lots. When given rich, loose soil with a fair amount of moisture and organic material, it grows abundant tender leaves and large roots. Organic farms often have a lot of dandelions, and I can't think of a better place to get a lot of high-quality flowers, roots, or leaves at one time.

How to Harvest

Dandelion leaves are least bitter when they are new and before the plant flowers, so harvest them from February to April for the best taste. To harvest, gather the leaves of one plant together, like a ponytail, and cut the whole thing off at the base. You can also harvest individual leaves, which may be better when there are some older leaves or insect predation. Sort them when you get home because small insects and snails love living between the leaves. I typically store the leaves in a plastic bag in the fridge to prevent wilting and use them as soon as possible. Wash them directly before using.

Buds begin to emerge in February and sometimes hide at the center of the plant until conditions warm up a bit. Push aside the upper leaves and see if you can find small dark-green buds hiding in there! You can pop them off with your fingers and gather several handfuls in a good patch.

The flowers emerge March through May and flower sporadically throughout the summer. You can snap the flowers off easily and harvest them into a small bag or basket. For recipes that require a lot of flowers at once (like dandelion-flower soda or dandelion-flower wine), harvest the flowers in batches as they bloom and throw them into a single bag in the freezer as they accumulate.

TOP: A fresh harvest of dandelion flowers, ready to make a lacto-fermented soda or wine
BOTTOM: Reisha Beck washes dandelion roots harvested from her farm in Ferndale, WA.

Dandelion roots are best harvested in the spring and fall and are probably better when the plant is not in flower. However, I harvest them any time of year, except when the soil is too frozen. Look for plants with the widest crowns and in soft soil, where they will be easy to dig up and wash. I use a four-pronged digging fork to loosen the soil around the plant and then pry it out of the ground. Knock it on the ground to get most of the dirt out. When you get them home, spray them with the garden hose in the grass to get off the largest dirt chunks, then scrub them in a basin with a stiff vegetable brush. Be advised that cleaning roots is hard work! When harvesting roots in the early spring, you can also use the leaves that come with the root.

Look-Alikes

Dandelion has many look-alikes, all of which are closely related. Thankfully, all are edible. However, it is always good to do your homework and make sure you know exactly what species you are eating. This is a great way to sharpen your plant-observation skills!

Hairy cat's ear (*Hypochaeris radicata*) shares nearly the same habitat as dandelion and has a very similar leaf shape and flower. However, as its name suggests, the leaves of hairy cat's ear are very hairy. See Hairy Cat's Ear entry on page 123 for more identifying characteristics.

Smooth hawksbeard (*Crepis capillaris*), which is also edible but bitter, can be a bit harder to distinguish from dandelion before flowering. Like dandelion, its leaves do not have hair, but they are narrower and more finely toothed than dandelion's leaves. I find it helpful to compare the leaves side by side.

Chicory (*Cichorium intybus*) can look identical to dandelion before blooming. Fortunately, it is equally edible, so a mistake would not be harmful. Once the flower stem emerges, the differences become obvious. While dandelion has a single bare stem with no branches, chicory has a complex, branched flower stem that has leaves at each branch. Also, chicory does not leak white sap when cut like dandelion does.

Salsify (*Agoseris* spp.) is a less common look-alike. Many species in the *Agoseris* genus resemble dandelion to varying degrees. Its leaves tend to be the shape of a sawfish, with narrow lobes jutting out in pairs. *Agoseris* tends to grow in prairies and dry, open areas rather than the disturbed weedy spots that dandelion prefers.

Cautions

Do not eat too many raw dandelion leaves, especially when the leaves get a bit old and more bitter. When I was first getting into foraging, I ate five to seven leaves while out on a walk, and all the joints in my body suddenly felt like crystals. Dandelion is, after all, a medicinal herb that cleanses the liver and kidneys, an action that should be respected. Dandelion root can be *too* cleansing for some people, so if you have a reaction to it, it is best to avoid it. Dandelion leaves can also be fairly diuretic and can dehydrate some people.

The whole dandelion plant contains natural plant latex, posing a theoretical concern for people with latex allergies.

Dandelion roots contain a large amount of inulin and can cause gas and cramping in some individuals.

Sustainability

Dandelions are not only extremely common, but they are a non-native weed, so you can harvest them to your heart's content. Not only that, but it is hard to kill a dandelion even by digging it up. They tend to come back from root fragments left in the ground. The only thing you might consider is that dandelion flowers tend to be a good early spring forage for bees, so leave a few when harvesting flowers.

Cooking with Dandelion

Dandelion leaves are a bitter spring green that can be eaten cooked or raw. Cooking can remove some of the bitterness, especially if you boil them and discard the water. Spring dandelion leaves are commonly cooked by parboiling for a minute or so and serving with butter or olive oil and salt or a sauce (see recipe). Many people enjoy the raw greens chopped in salads as well, just make sure to balance the dandelion with less bitter greens.

BOILED DANDELION LEAF WITH CREAMY SESAME-GINGER SAUCE

Makes 2 to 4 servings

Boiling dandelion leaves is a great way to reduce their bitterness a bit and make them more palatable. When boiled, they become tender like spinach. A good sauce is also a great way to hide some of the bitterness and make them more appealing to the whole family. Serve these greens as a side dish or over rice.

½ cup tahini
1 tablespoon soy sauce
1 tablespoon rice vinegar
1 tablespoon maple syrup
1 tablespoon toasted sesame oil
1 tablespoon grated fresh ginger
1 clove garlic, finely minced
½ teaspoon chili crisp or sriracha (optional)
¼ cup water
8 cups fresh dandelion leaves

To make the sauce, combine the tahini, soy sauce, rice vinegar, maple syrup, sesame oil, ginger, garlic, and optional chili crisp in a jar and mix with a fork. Once combined, add water bit by bit and stir well until it is smooth. Set aside while you prepare the greens.

Bring 6 quarts of water to boil in a large pot. Once boiling, lower the heat to medium and plunge the dandelion greens into the pot, either all at once or in two batches. Boil for about 1 minute, then pull the greens out with tongs into a colander and rinse with water. Once the greens have been cooled a bit by the water, squeeze the excess water out and roughly chop them.

Top with the sauce and serve.

Dandelion flowers are most commonly used to make fermented beverages like dandelion-flower soda or wine. However, you can also pull out the petals and sprinkle them into a salad or even use them to decorate a cake.

The buds can be pickled to make an interesting version of capers. You can also lacto-ferment them or make fritters. The texture is very unique, loved by some and hated by others.

The most common way to prepare dandelion roots is to roast them in the oven to make a coffee substitute. I have a more adventurous wild-foodie friend who cooks them in soups and even ferments them. Like burdock, dandelion roots contain a lot of inulin and can cause gas if eaten in large amounts. Cooking and fermentation helps break down that inulin.

Dock

Rumex crispus, R. obtusifolius
Polygonaceae (buckwheat family)

Chances are some kind of dock is growing near you, possibly even in your garden. Broadleaf dock (*Rumex obtusifolius*) and yellow dock (*Rumex crispus*) are the two most common species in the Pacific Northwest, both are rather weedy and were introduced from Europe.

Telling the two apart can be challenging, but the easiest way is by looking at the leaves: the leaf edges of yellow dock are curly and more narrow (other common names for yellow dock are curly dock and narrow-leaf dock).

The edible leaves of dock aren't often sought out by foragers. In fact, in Italy I learned that dock leaves, once eaten extensively by peasants, are now largely ignored in favor of more flashy wild edibles. A leaf of necessity, then.

The special attraction of the dock plant is its edible seeds. It is one of the few edible-seed crops that grow in our area and the easiest to harvest and use. Wild seeds can be very nutritious, containing novel fatty acids and other nutrients that domesticated crops often lack. That's a definite win.

Many native species of dock grow in the Pacific Northwest, including sour dock (*Rumex arcticus*), which grows in Alaska

LEFT: A yellow dock seed head
RIGHT: The immature seeds of broadleaf dock (Photo: iNaturalist)

TOP: A field full of dock seeds in a local park. This kind of bounty occurs when parks forego mowing.
BOTTOM: Gently tug the seeds off each spike and check for spiders and other bugs before putting dock in a container.

and is commonly eaten there. Do some research about native *Rumex* species in your area, but remember to look up their edibility before eating them, as some species of dock have much higher levels of oxalates than others (see Cautions).

The root of yellow dock, so called because the root is yellow, is commonly used in herbal medicine to clean up the large intestine.

Where to Find It

Broadleaf dock is found mostly at lower elevations on the west side of the Cascades. Its range extends from British Columbia all the way to Southern California. It likes fields, garden beds, vacant lots, and other places where humans are. Chances are it's growing in your yard if you live in that area.

Yellow dock is much less picky, thriving on both sides of the Cascades. It grows in similar habitats to broadleaf dock but can tolerate much drier climates. It also thrives in muddy, marshy areas, which is where I usually find the largest patches.

How to Harvest

Young dock leaves are best harvested in the spring. The younger leaves have fewer oxalates in them and are less fibrous, making for better eating. The tender, young leaves are lighter green and found in the middle of the plant. You can browse a dock patch and remove just the young leaves from each plant, pinching them off with your fingers. Harvest into a plastic bag to keep them fresh while traveling home. Store in the fridge for no more than 3 days.

The edible seeds can be harvested in the late summer and fall, when the seed heads have turned brown and begun to dry. Don't wait too long to harvest them, as once the fall comes, they can mold and start dropping to the ground. Snip off whole seed heads and carry them home in a large grocery bag.

Look-Alikes

Because of its large leaves, burdock may be confused for broadleaf dock or yellow dock. However, the undersides of burdock leaves are silvery white with small hairs, while dock leaves have no hair and are the same color as the leaf surfaces. Despite the name, burdock is not related to these dock species.

Sustainability

The non-native docks grow abundantly, and harvesting leaves is very low impact, so you can harvest those freely. For roots or seeds, I recommend removing no more than half of what you find. Birds like the seeds too.

Grow Your Own

You may want to avoid introducing the weedy yellow dock and broadleaf dock into your yard, but it would be fun to collect seeds from a native species like willow dock (*Rumex salicifolius*) and plant it in your yard. If you live in the Columbia Basin area, you could seek out the sand-loving and strange-looking winged dock (*Rumex venosus*) and introduce it to a sandy area of your garden.

Cooking with Dock

Dock leaves are considered a "pot herb," which is a category of wild greens that are meant to be cooked and combined together. Many of them have undesirable textures or flavors, are toxic in large quantities, or simply must be cooked to be edible. In other words, it is best to combine high-oxalate plants with other plants to dilute them. Dock could be combined with nettle or a cultivated vegetable like kale. Note that spinach and chard both have oxalates as well; kale does not.

To further reduce oxalates, parboil dock before use: Bring a large pot of water to boil over high heat. Reduce the heat to medium and plunge the dock greens into the boiling water and boil gently for 10 to 15 minutes. Strain in a colander in the sink and give the greens a good rinse. After they cool, squeeze out excess water. Boiled dock greens have a neutral taste and can be

DOCK-SEED CRACKERS

Makes about 40 crackers

These crispy, dark crackers have a unique, nutty tasty and grainy texture. They will impress dinner guests on a charcuterie platter, yet are surprisingly easy to make. In testing, I discovered that the key to the recipe is to roll out the dough as thinly as possible, which yields nice crispy crackers. The amount of dock-seed flour may seem relatively low, but it is the maximum that can be added for the cracker to turn out well. Note that you can experiment with adding different herb blends to the crackers. You could even add powdered nettle seed or nettle leaf!

1 cup dock seeds (¼ cup ground)
¾ cup plus one tablespoon whole wheat flour
⅓ cup water
1 tablespoon extra-virgin olive oil, plus more for brushing
½ teaspoon salt
1 teaspoon finely minced fresh rosemary or ground dried rosemary

Preheat the oven to 300 degrees F.

Spread the dock seeds out on a baking pan lined with parchment paper and toast in the oven for 5 to 10 minutes. Monitor them closely to avoid burning They should smell nutty when ready. Remove the seeds and leave the oven on to bake the crackers. Let the seeds cool for at least 5 minutes before grinding them.

Grind the toasted seeds well in a Vitamix or an herb grinder. Note that a mortar and pestle will not get the seeds fine enough for the crackers to be enjoyable.

Measure out ¼ cup of the dock-seed flour, combine that with the rest of the ingredients in a medium bowl, and stir well. It should form a stiff dough, like you are making pasta. Add more whole wheat flour if it's too wet or more water if it's too crumbly.

Roll out the dough very thinly on a floured surface, ideally to the thickness of a quarter. Cut into desired shapes (such as diamonds) with a sharp knife and lay out on a baking sheet lined with parchment paper or on a silicone baking sheet. Brush with olive oil and sprinkle with salt. Bake for 25 to 30 minutes, or until the crackers are crisp and do not bend. Let cool for about 20 minutes before serving, during which time they will harden more.

Let the crackers cool and store them in an airtight container for up to 2 weeks. The crackers may get stale or soft with time, especially if you live in a moist climate, so seal the container well and eat quickly.

Serve the crackers with goat cheese, salami, hummus, or even a chimichurri sauce.

> **Cautions**
>
> Dock leaves contain oxalates, which can irritate the kidneys and gastrointestinal tract (see sidebar "What Are Oxalates?" in Part One), and should not be eaten raw. This is because dock leaves actually contain more oxalates than other oxalate-containing plants, such as wood sorrel, and the dominant type of oxalates in dock are more irritating than others. Oxalates can be reduced by parboiling the leaves before use (see Cooking with Dock).

used much how you would use spinach. You could finely chop them and throw them in a quiche, soup, ravioli filling, or curry, for example.

As for the seeds, once you get the seed heads home, use your fingers to pull the seeds off the stalk into a bowl. The seeds are actually inside a papery husk, though because the seeds are difficult to separate, most people just use the husk along with the seed. Pick out all stems, leaves, and insects. I dry these kinds of seeds by spreading them out on a baking sheet lined with parchment paper, setting the oven to the lowest setting (between 175 degrees and 200 degrees F), and letting them sit in the oven for about an hour. Remove and let cool, store in a jar, and grind them thoroughly in an herb grinder or Vitamix directly before using them as a flour in crackers, breads, cookies, and other baked goods. Store in a cool, dry place and use within a year.

Separating the dock seeds from stalks over a large baking dish

Buckwheat is a close relative of dock, and dock seeds share similar flavors. As such, the flavor can be a bit strong, and the flour is also coarse and non-glutenous, so substitute only about one-quarter of the total flour in a recipe with dock. You can make dock-seed crackers (see recipe), pasta, and more.

Fennel

Foeniculum vulgare
Apiaceae (carrot family)

Most people are already familiar with the sweet, aromatic flavor of fennel. Some love it; some hate it. Wild fennel tends to be more aromatic than the stuff you get at the grocery store, so buckle your seat belt. For those of us who love this licorice-like group of flavors, wild fennel is an exciting find.

Fennel is easy to identify because of its threadlike leaves, which are called filiform in botany. Dill also has filiform leaves, as do a few other members of the carrot family. Fennel's yellow flowers also set it apart from the mainly white flowers of other carrot-family members. Fennel is native to the Mediterranean and was likely introduced here as an herb by settlers from Europe.

Fennel has some medicinal properties as well, especially the seeds. The most common use is as a post-meal digestive aid. The fresh or dried seeds can be soaked in vodka with sugar to make a simple after-dinner liqueur. Check out the fennel entry in my book *Medicinal Plants of the Pacific Northwest* for a recipe.

Bright green fennel leaves emerge among the previous year's dead flower stalks. (Photo: iNaturalist)

Where to Find It

Wild fennel grows occasionally in Western Washington and Oregon, and it grows voraciously all up and down the coast of California. Being from the Mediterranean, it prefers growing in sunny gravelly spots, and it loves the coastline. It also loves roadsides, probably because of the extra heat the road provides. Seattle is full of fennel growing in waste areas, sidewalk cracks, and next

FENNEL

Leaf

Inflorescence

Immature flower

Individual floret

Seed cluster

Seeds

to highways. I've heard that it smells like fennel when they mow the side of the highway in California. Just remember not to harvest it within 10 feet of a road or 100 feet of a highway.

How to Harvest

Fennel leaves are best harvested in the spring, when they are tender and young. Use scissors to cut them off and harvest into a plastic bag to prevent wilting during transport.

Harvest the very young flower heads as they form in the late spring and early summer by pinching them off with your hands or using scissors. Some people eat whole inflorescence when they bloom, but I don't like the fibrous stems. They are much tastier when just emerging.

Harvest fennel pollen when flowers are freshly open. The flowers are out from May to July, with the most flowers coming out earlier in the summer. You can test whether the pollen is ready by simply shaking a flower into your hand to see if the yellow powder falls out. There may be a lot of beetles, wasps, flies, and other pollinators hanging out on the flower, so gently knock them off. Don't shake them off, because you will lose the pollen. Snip one flower head at a time and hold it upside down over a paper bag and shake the pollen out. Each flower head will have only a bit of pollen—$1/8$ to $1/4$ teaspoon or so—so you will need to snip several flower heads to gather any kind of quantity. An alternate method of collection is to collect a bouquet of flowers and put the whole thing upside down in a paper grocery bag, letting the pollen fall out slowly. Strain out the bugs and debris using a fine-mesh, metal strainer and dry it for later use by leaving it on a piece of parchment paper on a baking sheet, undisturbed, for a few days. Occasionally, small insect eggs can make it through the straining process and ruin the batch. Yuck. To kill these, you can either freeze it for a week or microwave for 10 seconds or so.

Fennel seeds can be collected from late summer to early fall. I prefer to harvest them before the seeds are mature, when they

A ladybug eats aphids on a fennel seed cluster.

ITALIAN SAUSAGE WITH WILD-HARVESTED FENNEL SEEDS

Makes 4 servings

To me, fennel seeds are what makes Italian sausage worthwhile. I love the burst of sweet, aromatic flavor that the fennel adds to the savory taste of the meat. This sausage is formed into patties and fried, but you can also use the sausage to make meatballs and bake them in the oven, use it as the base for a soup like minestrone, or combine it with cheese and peppers to stuff acorn squash. You can use dried versions of any of the fresh herbs called for in this recipe, just use about one-third of the amount called for.

FOR THE SAUSAGE
- 1 pound ground pork or chicken
- 1 tablespoon minced garlic (4 to 5 cloves)
- 1 tablespoon red wine or red wine vinegar
- 1 tablespoon smoked paprika
- 1 tablespoon minced fresh parsley
- 2 tablespoons fresh fennel seed
- 1 tablespoon finely minced fresh thyme
- 1 teaspoon salt
- 1½ teaspoons black pepper
- 1 teaspoon onion powder
- 1 teaspoon finely minced fresh rosemary
- 1 teaspoon finely minced fresh oregano
- 1 teaspoon finely minced fresh sage

FOR FRYING
- 1 tablespoon extra-virgin olive oil

Mix all the ingredients together in a medium bowl with your hands or a spatula until the herbs and spices are thoroughly distributed into the meat. Form 2-inch-wide, flat medallions.

Heat the olive oil in a large skillet over medium heat for a minute or two and add the sausage patties in batches so they don't touch. They should sizzle on contact with the pan. Fry them for 3 to 5 minutes on each side, until browned and the pink has gone from the center.

are still green and a bit juicy. They are much sweeter and aromatic at this stage and can actually be chewed like candy right off the stem. To dry them for later use, I snip off the entire seed head and spread them out on a basket or towel for a week or so and then remove the seeds from the dried stems. I then go back through the seeds to remove any remaining stems, insects, or stones. I use a flat pan or plate for this step.

> ### Cautions
>
> Do not harvest fennel growing next to the highway. Not only is that a contaminated area from car exhaust and asphalt runoff, but transportation departments spray herbicides heavily next to highways to keep the vegetation down.

Look-Alikes

Fennel is in the carrot family, so it's critical to be extra careful with your ID as there are some poisonous members of that family. Thankfully, fennel has unique hairlike leaves that are not flat like the poisonous members of the carrot family. It also has yellow flowers, which further set it apart from the white flowers of water hemlock and poison hemlock (see Part Three: Poisonous and Toxic Plants).

Sustainability

Fennel can be harvested freely as it is a non-native that can be hard to remove and spreads in patches. Wild fennel is a problem in areas including California, where it grows voraciously and crowds out native plant communities, especially in sensitive coastal habitats. It makes sense that fennel does well in California as the climate is so similar to its native Mediterranean climate. If harvesting in an area where fennel is a problem, take extra care to prevent its spread to new areas by not dropping any seeds. Harvesting all the seeds in this kind of scenario is actually helpful, as it helps prevent the plant from spreading more.

Grow Your Own

You can grow fennel in your garden quite easily, though I would avoid planting it if I lived in California, where it is more of a problem. Like most plants that have naturalized as weeds, they grow like weeds in our gardens too. Give fennel a dry, sunny spot. You can collect seeds from the wild or buy them from a seed distributor. Seed distributors will have different varieties available for different purposes, one of which will grow a nice bulb like you can buy at the grocery store.

Cooking with Fennel

Fennel leaves have a sweet licorice-like flavor that is very unique. They can be eaten raw or cooked. Their aromatic flavor can be overpowering, but when paired well with other flavors, like citrus, fennel can steal the show. Try adding orange slices, avocado, and fennel leaves to a salad with a homemade orange vinaigrette. Pair fennel with lemon juice and zest in chicken recipes and risotto for an Italian-inspired taste.

Fennel leaves can replace basil in a traditional pesto recipe with pine nuts, Parmesan, garlic, olive oil, lemon juice, and salt.

The flowers are delicious and make an eye-catching garnish because of their unique umbel shape.

Harvesting fennel seeds

Fennel seeds can be used fresh or dried. The fresh seeds are especially aromatic and delicious. I use wild-harvested fennel seeds in handmade Italian sausage, which is much tastier than the store-bought kind, especially if you use fresh oregano, rosemary, thyme, and parsley too (see recipe).

The dried seeds also make a nice tea: Combine 1 tablespoon of fresh or dried fennel seeds and 8 ounces of water in a small saucepan and cover. Bring to a boil on the stove, then reduce and simmer for 5 minutes, keeping the lid on throughout. Strain it into your cup through a fine-mesh, metal strainer and enjoy with honey, if desired.

Fennel pollen is an Italian spice with a delicate flavor that is used in both sweet and savory dishes. You might see it in fancy cured salami or infused syrup.

Fireweed

Chamaenerion angustifolium
Onagraceae (evening primrose family)

Fireweed, so named because it grows in abundance right after wildfires, is an abundant and delicious wild edible that grows all over the Pacific Northwest. I have hiked through many recent wildfire sites where the fuchsia-colored flowers of fireweed stretch as far as the eye can see, contrasting beautifully with the intense black of the charred trunks.

This plant is a survivor. In a world with increasing wildfires, many of which are high-intensity burns that eliminate all the vegetation, fireweed is abundant. Therefore, it is a great plant to befriend in these trying times. It has much to teach us about being a phoenix that emerges from the ashes of a literally burning world. Let us learn from this plant's incredible resilience.

Where to Find It

Fireweed grows in every province in Canada and all US states except those in the Southwest. It grows incredibly well even in alpine environments and boreal environments with deep freezes and short growing seasons. Because the flowers are not

A thicket of fireweed in full bloom along a forest service road in the Cascades

on display in early spring, the best way to find a good place to harvest shoots is to find established patches the summer before and return to the same spot in the spring for harvest. It can be difficult to differentiate from other shoots at this stage, so be sure to look closely (see Look-Alikes).

Fireweed thrives best in bare, disturbed soils with plenty of sun, making it an extremely successful plant after wildfires. It also germinates and grows quickly, even within a month of devastating wildfires or volcanic events, and establishes long root systems that persist in high heat. Unlike many other herbaceous plants, fireweed does not require endosymbiotic fungi to germinate and grow. Because of this, it can sprout and grow even after fires that have reached temperatures so high that the soil is sterilized. High-intensity fires like this can incinerate shrubs and trees all the way down into their roots, leaving branched holes in the ground. Roots are important for soil stability, and their absence creates very fragile soil conditions, susceptible to erosion and landslide events. Because of all its aforementioned traits, fireweed can provide early soil stabilization due to its rapid growth and extensive underground root network, a key part of post-burn remediation. That is all to say that fireweed is an incredibly heroic plant.

Once other vegetation starts to grow up around it, especially tree cover, the fireweed population will start to decline.

Avoid harvesting alpine fireweed (*Chamaenerion latifolium*), which looks like this. It is closely related but far less abundant.

This decline usually happens after seven years, which is congruent with other post-burn specialist plants, like red root and mullein. When looking for your fireweed harvest site, look for a site that has burned within the last seven years.

Fireweed can also be very successful in floodplains and recently logged sites, where similar soil disturbance helps fireweed thrive.

The seeds are attached to plumes that allow the seed to be dispersed by the wind, often traveling more than a hundred miles. The seeds do not remain viable for very long, unlike other plants, such as red root, whose seeds can last one hundred years or more in soil. However, fireweed seeds are numerous and travel far, so the seed bank is constantly getting a new batch of seeds, which have an extremely high germination rate in their first year.

How to Harvest

Fireweed shoots emerge in early spring and are the easiest and tastiest way to eat fireweed. Harvest them by snapping or cutting off the tender top of the shoot when they are 6 to 12 inches tall. It can be hard to catch them before they get too big, and their fibrous stems taste very astringent, so harvest fireweed around the time when nettles are coming up, just after the snow melts. This could be as early as February in warmer and lower-elevation parts of the region. At high elevations (above 3,000 feet), the shoots could emerge as late as June.

The leaves of fireweed should be harvested when they are still tender, which is best before the plant has flowered. It begins flowering in June at lower elevations and July at higher ones. Once the weather begins to dry out, the leaves become fibrous and dry, unsuitable for eating. If you want to make fermented-fireweed tea, you can continue to harvest in August, as long as the leaves are tender enough to be bruised.

Look-Alikes

Goldenrod and false Solomon's seal could both be growing alongside fireweed and look similar in this stage of growth. There are a few ways to tell them apart: Fireweed shoots, when broken, should exude a clear substance that is slimy, like okra. You can also look at the leaf arrangement, which should be whorled up the stem. Fireweed leaves are perfectly lance shaped, without lobes, whereas goldenrod have small lobes on the edges. Solomon's seal leaves have parallel veins, and fireweed leaves have normal, netted veins.

TOP: Fireweed shoots emerging in late May near Snoqualmie Pass
BOTTOM: A bountiful harvest, while leaving behind ample shoots for the plant to thrive

Sustainability

When harvesting fireweed shoots in a smaller patch, avoid harvesting every shoot. Harvest no more than half of the shoots

FERMENTED-FIREWEED TEA

Makes 2 to 4 cups of dried tea leaves

This Eastern European tea, also known as Ivan chai, serves as a tasty, caffeine-free alternative to black tea. It's considered to be a digestive tonic, probably because of the astringent and mucilaginous compounds that can reinforce and soothe digestive tissues. The process of fermenting fireweed leaves is relatively simple, involving activating the enzyme by bruising the leaves, much like how black tea is made. Harvest fireweed stalks just before they bloom, for best results, removing the top half of the plant. The lower leaves tend to be older and drier and the top leaves a bit more moist and therefore better for this recipe.

10 stalks of fireweed

Wilt the fireweed stalks in the sun for 1 to 3 hours, until they are wet and rubbery. Don't wilt for so long that they start to dry.

Remove all the leaves from the stalks and discard the stalks. Put the leaves in a large pile.

With clean hands, working over a large bowl, rub the fireweed leaves between your hands in batches, bruising them thoroughly until they darken and become soft. Place the bruised leaves in the bowl. This step breaks the cell walls and activates enzymes that begin reactions that will change the flavor profile. Some people like to carefully roll the leaves into balls, much like gunpowder green tea. This is not required but can make it seem fancy.

Once all the leaves are rubbed, put them into a clean, airtight glass container and seal it well. Leave them out of direct sunlight in your kitchen for 2 to 5 days without opening the container. The longer you leave them to ferment, the more novel flavor compounds will develop. However, the risk of mold also increases the longer you let them sit. When you open the container after fermenting, you should smell a sour, floral smell. If you see mold, discard the batch.

Now it's time to dry the fermented leaves and stop the enzymatic processes. This can be done out in open air (out of direct sunlight), in a dehydrator, or in a warm oven (170 degrees F or less). Spread the leaves out without them touching, as much as possible. If you have a big batch where there is a lot of overlap, you may need to turn them frequently to prevent moisture pockets from growing mold.

They are dry when they crunch easily in your hand. Store them in a jar.

To make a cup of tea, steep 1 tablespoon of dried leaves in 8 ounces of hot water for about 5 minutes.

ICED FERMENTED-FIREWEED TEA *Makes ½ gallon*

This is my favorite way to enjoy fermented-fireweed tea. I especially like to use lavender-infused honey to sweeten it, as the flavors combine very well. Even unadventurous eaters enjoy this tea!

½ cup (½ ounce) fermented-fireweed
  tea leaves
4 cups boiling water
3 to 4 tablespoons honey or sugar
4-plus cups ice

Place the tea leaves in a quart mason jar (or other 4-cup or larger heatproof vessel). Pour the boiling water carefully over the tea leaves. Mix in the honey with a spoon while the tea is still hot. Let it sit on the counter for 30 to 60 minutes.

Strain the warm tea through a fine-mesh, metal strainer into a ½-gallon mason jar or pitcher. Fill the rest of the pitcher up with ice. Let sit for a few minutes, allowing it to cool down, then serve.

Store leftovers in the fridge for up to 3 days.

that you find. That is a higher percentage than I would normally recommend, but fireweed is a fairly aggressive grower, so it should send up new shoots to replace the old ones. If harvesting where it is super abundant (like a burn site), then harvest as much as you'd like. There will be enough for the deer and the bees.

Grow Your Own

Fireweed is very easy to grow in your garden, though it can be a bit unruly, making it a better choice for a more wild type of garden style. Once planted, it should come back year after year and even spread by seed and rhizome. Fireweed readily grows from seed—either purchased or collected from the wild. Keep in mind that fireweed seeds don't stay viable long, so don't save them for later. You can also buy potted plants and bare-root plants at some nurseries and some online purveyors. The flower stalks can grow 6 feet or taller, so plant it somewhere

> ### Cautions
>
> Fireweed shoots and leaves contain oxalates, which can irritate the kidneys and gastrointestinal tract when eaten in large quantities (see sidebar "What Are Oxalates?" in Part One). Consume them in moderation and consider parboiling them before eating to remove some of the oxalates (see Cooking with Fireweed).

that is ready for that kind of height. Fireweed can sometimes be outcompeted by weeds, so keep its base clear from competitors.

Cooking with Fireweed

Fireweed shoots have a tangy, astringent, sour flavor, and a satisfying snap when raw. They can be cooked much like you would cook asparagus. I lightly sauté them with olive oil and garlic and top with a bit of lemon juice. You can also blanch them or serve them raw in salads. Keep in mind that they are mucilaginous, like okra, and some people don't care for it.

If you're sensitive to oxalates, parboil fireweed shoots before eating: Bring a large pot of water to boil over high heat. Reduce the heat to medium and plunge the fireweed into the boiling water. Boil for 1 to 2 minutes and strain and rinse in a colander in the sink. Cool, and squeeze out excess water, then use in the recipe.

Fireweed has unique, cross-shaped pistils

The other way to enjoy fireweed is to ferment the leaves and dry them to make tea. This is a tradition that comes from Eastern Europe, especially Russia, where it is called Ivan chai and thought to be a digestive tonic. The tea tastes a bit like black tea and is similarly astringent but does not contain caffeine (see recipes).

Hairy Cat's Ear

Hypochaeris radicata
Asteraceae (sunflower family)

If you have a lawn, you likely have hairy cat's ear growing in it. Named for its hairy leaves, hairy cat's ear is a relative of dandelion and a close look-alike. The leaves are edible and much less bitter than dandelion. In most counties in Washington State, this plant is considered a noxious weed. Concerted efforts have been made to eradicate it from our endemic prairies, where it has thrived and crowded out more sensitive endemic species. Be aware that this plant is a common target for chemicals, both by nature-conservation organizations trying to restore native habitats and by those seeking a weed-free lawn.

Where to Find It

Hairy cat's ear was introduced from Europe, where it grows abundantly in many different climates. It is a favorite wild green in Greece. In the Pacific Northwest, it is incredibly common on both sides of the Cascades. It can also be found in most other states.

TOP: Hairy cat's ear at the edge of a community garden path **BOTTOM:** A late summer harvest of hairy cat's ear leaves

Its preferred habitat is lawns, prairies, and any grassy areas. Hairy cat's ear is also known as flatweed because of its tendency to grow flat to the ground, nicely avoiding lawnmower blades. I have found that the best way to eradicate it from your lawn is to develop a taste for it.

How to Harvest

Harvest hairy cat's ear leaf in the spring (February through April) before the flower stalks emerge from the center. To harvest, lift up some leaves to get access to the taproot. Insert a knife or scissors into the soil underneath the rosette and cut the taproot, freeing the whole plant. Shake off dirt and insects and pick off any brown or yellowing leaves.

You can also selectively harvest the tender new leaves as they emerge, harvesting just a few from each plant.

The young flower stalks have a short harvest window, starting in late May and into the first few weeks of June. They are best when just emerging from the center of the rosette and get more fibrous as they get larger. Harvest the top 4 to 5 inches.

Dig the roots with a trowel or Japanese digging knife in the fall, winter, or spring. Spray the dirt off with a hose and then scrub them thoroughly with a scrub brush.

Look-Alikes

See the Dandelion entry for a full discussion on look-alikes.

Sustainability

This plant is extremely abundant and non-native, so you can harvest as much of it as you want. Chances are you can find someone nearby who would be delighted for you to remove it from their lawn. Please do not propagate or spread the seeds of this plant.

Rabbits enjoy hairy cat's ear flower stalks.

WILD GREENS WITH OLIVE OIL AND GARLIC   *Makes 2 servings*

This is a simple way to prepare an assortment of wild greens. The lemon juice and garlic can help cover up the bitterness of certain greens such as hairy cat's ear and dandelion. These greens are very tasty served with mashed potatoes and chicken.

6 cups wild greens (such as hairy cat's ear, dandelion, nettle, mallow, or sow thistle)
2 tablespoons extra-virgin olive oil
3 cloves garlic, minced
Salt, to taste
¼ cup chicken or vegetable broth
Juice of ½ a lemon

Wash all greens and remove stems, dead leaves, and bugs.

Bring 6 cups of water to boil in a large pot on medium-high heat. Once boiling, plunge the greens into the water, starting with the most fibrous greens (like hairy cat's ear), and saving more delicate leaves until last. Boil the greens for 5 to 20 minutes, until softened to your liking.

Strain through a metal strainer and rinse with cold water. Once greens are cool enough to touch, wring the excess water out with your hands. Chop the greens finely.

Heat oil over medium heat in a cast-iron pan. Add the minced garlic and cook until just brown, about 1 minute.

Add greens and season with salt. Stir and cook for about 5 minutes. Add the chicken broth and cook for a minute or two more, then remove from heat. Squeeze fresh lemon juice on top before serving.

Cooking with Hairy Cat's Ear

All parts of the plant are edible, though the leaves are the most commonly used. Hairy cat's ear leaves can be eaten raw, but it is rather fibrous and a bit hairy, making it a better cooked green. To hide the hairiness, I slice it finely, combine it with other greens, and cook it with ample garlic and olive oil (see recipe).

The budding flower stalks can be eaten as well, if harvested when young and tender as you would asparagus.

The roots can be roasted as a coffee substitute, like dandelion and chicory roots (see Roasted Chicory Coffee recipe in the Chicory entry), and in fact, can be used medicinally much like dandelion root.

Hawthorn

Crataegus monogyna, C. douglasii
Rosaceae (rose family)

Two main species of hawthorn grow in the Pacific Northwest: black hawthorn (*Crataegus douglasii*) and one-seed hawthorn (*Crataegus monogyna*). Black hawthorn is native to this area, with a long history of use by local Native groups. One-seed hawthorn was introduced from Europe, where it is used heavily as a hedgerow plant to prevent livestock from wandering neighboring land.

The *haw* in hawthorn is the old name for the fruit, and *thorn* refers to its woody and very sharp thorns.

Black hawthorn trees have dark-red to purple-black berries that ripen much earlier than one-seed hawthorn berries, though they don't produce as many berries as one-seed hawthorn. The berries' black color indicates the presence of anthocyanins, the antioxidant found in blueberries.

The one-seed hawthorn bloom is something to behold: all the trees in a given area bloom at the same time for only about a week in early May. The entire tree is covered in small white

A young one-seed hawthorn tree

LEFT: Ripe oneseed hawthorn berries in October **RIGHT:** A handful of perfectly ripe black hawthorn berries in July

blossoms! Because of this timing, their flowers are associated with the pagan holiday of Beltane and May Day. They are also called whitethorn in Britain, which is the English equivalent of the Italian name *bianca spina*.

A thicket of one-seed hawthorn trees will typically have mostly white and some pink flowers. The pink color can be faint or almost magenta, depending on the tree. This is a form of genetic diversity, which helps plants have a better chance at success.

You may notice that hawthorn flowers smell like rotten fish, which attracts flies to pollinate it.

Where to Find It

One-seed hawthorn grows mostly on the west side of the mountains in Oregon and Washington and occasionally on the eastern slope of the Cascades. It also grows in Northern California down into San Francisco. It is common in grassy open fields, farmland, parks, and roadsides. I often find it in local parks, which is a great place to harvest the berries. One-seed hawthorns sometimes grow in forest environments, but they don't thrive there and don't produce good berries.

Black hawthorn is less common but more widely distributed. It grows in western and eastern Washington (except for the Columbia Basin), western Oregon, the west coast of Northern California, and all over northern Idaho. Find it in sunny areas at the edges of forests, in open fields, and especially, near water.

Picking leaves and bugs out of a black hawthorn berry harvest (Photo: Lukas Speckhardt)

How to Harvest

One-seed hawthorn berries are ripe in October, around the time of the first frost, and can be harvested as late as November. They turn red in September, but they take a while to fully mature. Frost often does the job, converting the final complex starches into simple sugars. The flesh should squish between your fingers and be yellowish rather than green or white. Ripe berries taste bland and sweet, but not astringent. They contain more pectin when they are less ripe, which means that they may turn into gel when you are cooking with them if you harvest too early.

If you have the choice of many trees, find the tree with the largest and darkest berries. The smaller berries are mostly seed and don't have much flesh on them. Try to avoid berries with a thin coat of visible black mold on the outside, which will increase as the wet weather of fall intensifies. Spiders and other insects like to live in the clusters, so steer clear of spider webs and insect holes.

Take a bucket and harvest the berries in clusters using hands or scissors. You can remove the leaves and stems later.

Black hawthorn berries ripen in July—much earlier than one-seed hawthorn berries. They should be harvested when soft and dark in color.

Hawthorn flowers and young leaves are harvested to eat in small amounts, and these can be harvested when the flowers bloom in early May.

Look-Alikes

Pacific crab apple could be mistaken for black hawthorn before the berries ripen, as their irregularly lobed leaves are very similar. Chokecherry and serviceberry have very similar berries. The key to identifying hawthorn is to look for the thorns, which can be hard to see at first glance. One-seed hawthorn has much shorter thorns, often located at the ends of branches. Black hawthorn has much larger, obvious thorns that are about an inch long!

Sustainability

Despite being non-native, one-seed hawthorn berries provide a wonderful source of winter forage for local birds. I once witnessed a whole flock of cedar waxwings gorging themselves on hawthorn berries in January. Black hawthorn berries are also a favorite of birds when they ripen in July, especially robins.

HAWTHORN FRUIT LEATHER

Makes one 10" to 15" sheet

This is a recipe I learned from the BBC show Grow Your Own Drugs, hosted by the wonderful James Wong. The key is to separate the berry pulp from the seeds, which is best done with a food mill, as pictured.

4 cups fresh or frozen hawthorn berries
½ cup apple juice

Put the berries and juice into a large pot and cover. Bring to a boil, then lower the heat and simmer until they squish easily under a spoon, 10 to 15 minutes.

Let cool for at least 15 minutes, then spoon the mixture in batches into the food mill with a bowl below to catch the pulp. Periodically scrape the pulp off the bottom with a spatula and remove the seeds and compost them.

Set your oven on the lowest setting (usually around 170 degrees F) and line two baking trays with parchment paper or silicone baking mats. (Alternatively, if using a dehydrator, line your dehydrator trays.) Use a spatula or the back of a wooden spoon to spread the mixture on the parchment paper until it is 4 to 5 millimeters thick. Spread it as evenly as possible so it will all dry at the same speed.

Put the trays in the oven, leaving the door cracked open. Let the fruit leather sit in the oven for a few hours, or until it is nice and leathery and easily separates from the parchment paper. Slice the fruit leather and store in a sealed plastic container. You can use pieces of parchment paper to keep it from sticking together, if you need to.

Thankfully, the berries at the top of the tree are naturally unreachable to humans, ensuring we leave enough for the birds.

One-seed hawthorn is often considered invasive, partly because it prevents the natural flow of livestock on rangelands. If your city is making efforts to eradicate one-seed hawthorn, write letters to the appropriate departments to let them know that you are harvesting from and using them, as many are not aware that they are edible.

Cautions

Herbicide plugs, which look like small bullets and are nailed into the base of a tree, are used to kill one-seed hawthorn trees and other hard-to-eradicate trees like holly. Especially when harvesting in city parks, check the base of the tree before you harvest the berries. The herbicides are injected into the tree tissue to be absorbed and distributed systemically, meaning we should not consume any part of the tree once the plug has been installed.

Grow Your Own

Black hawthorn trees are a great option for those wanting to introduce more native plants into their landscape. They typically grow as a shrubby bush or a small tree, depending on how they are pruned. They are typically 8 to 12 feet tall and can reach 20 feet in the right conditions.

A robin enjoys a black hawthorn berry near Cle Elum, WA.

Cooking with Hawthorn

Hawthorn berries have large seeds in the middle and a bland taste, making them unsuitable for eating raw. They are best cooked, with the seeds removed and some sugar added. Some may not think they are worth the bother, but studies have shown that hawthorn berries have more antioxidants than most other fruits and are beneficial for heart health.

Various species of hawthorn berries and flowers have long been used as a food and medicine in Europe, the Middle East, and China. China, in particular, really embraces hawthorn berries. The species that grows in China has much larger berries, the size of small plums, which are much easier to cook with. They make all different kinds of sweet confections with them, the most common of which is hawthorn flakes, which are round disks made of hawthorn berries and sugar.

Most of my cooking experience is with the red berries of one-seed hawthorn, as they are much more abundant. I usually make hawthorn-berry ketchup or chutney, which are savory-sweet sauces that combine well with meat. On the rare occasions that I cook with black hawthorn berries, I enjoy their more complex flavor and dark color. They make fantastic syrups and sodas.

One-seed hawthorn combines well with strawberry and rose. See the strawberry entry for a fun recipe idea using this combo. Pomegranate and apple are also quite good with one-seed hawthorn berries. Black hawthorn combines very well with blueberry.

The most important thing you need to know about preparing hawthorn berries is how to remove the seeds. The easiest way to do this is to simmer them with water and then process them using a food mill (see recipe), which pushes the pulp through small holes, filtering out the seeds and leaving only the pulp. Those who don't have a food mill usually use a fine-mesh, metal sieve, pushing the pulp through with the back of a spoon. Having tried the sieve method, I can tell you it's a huge bother and you should just buy yourself an inexpensive food mill. You can also use it to make applesauce without having to peel or core your apples (see Easy Slow-Cooker Applesauce).

Hazelnut

Corylus cornuta, C. avellana
Betulaceae (birch family)

Our native species of hazelnut is called beaked hazelnut (*Corylus cornuta*) because the husk makes a little beak (actually a modified leaf) that covers the shell of the nut. The nuts are much smaller than the cultivated hazelnut, but equally delicious. Like other nuts, the edible part is encased in a hard shell that you'll need to crack with a light whack of a hammer or a nutcracker.

These can be very hard to find due to their popularity among squirrels. I often think I've found one, but the nut inside has not properly developed, explaining why it was left by the squirrels. When you are lucky enough to find a few, though, they are incredibly tasty.

You may also occasionally find European hazelnut (*Corylus avellana*) growing wild, usually left over from old homesteads or escaped from cultivation. These trees bear more nuts than our native beaked hazelnut, and the nuts are larger, so they can be a very lucky foraging find.

European hazelnuts are also known as filberts, especially in Oregon. Parts of Oregon are very well suited for growing filberts, such as the Willamette Valley, where you will see miles of filbert farms along the roadside.

Ripe beaked hazelnuts drying and curing on a flat bamboo basket

HAZELNUT

Where to Find It

In the Pacific Northwest, beaked hazelnut grows mostly west of the Cascades, with quite a few on the eastern slope of the Cascades and occasionally east of the Cascades in riparian habitats. They love to grow in open forests where they can find a bit more sunlight, and resprout quickly from the root stock after low-intensity burns. Beaked hazelnut also grows in the Northeast and pockets of the Midwest.

European hazelnuts can sometimes be found at old homestead sites or abandoned farms. Much like apple trees, hazelnut trees can continue growing without human care and naturalize to a certain extent. Sometimes I come upon them in the park growing among native trees and shrubs.

How to Harvest

To find a good patch of beaked hazelnut, look in places where the trees get good sun and water, as these trees will bear more nuts. To beat the squirrels, be sure to show up as soon as the nuts ripen, which may involve monitoring and checking your patch.

Beaked hazelnuts are ready to harvest in late July and August, which is slightly earlier than some other nuts. Wait until the leafy covering on the outside starts to yellow or even brown, and the nuts turn tan and begin falling out of the husk. It is important to wear gloves when harvesting beaked hazelnuts, because the husks are covered in spiky hairs that can embed themselves in your fingers. Pluck off the entire nut (husk and all) and

The sprawling, straight trunks of a beaked hazelnut tree in a Bellevue, WA park.

ROASTED HAZELNUTS

Makes 1 to 2 cups

Roasting shelled nuts in the oven enhances their flavor and makes them much easier to crack and remove from their shells. You can do a light roast or heavy roast, depending on your preference. Use the roasted nuts in salads or eat them as a snack. Feel free to add salt or other seasonings if you wish.

1 to 2 cups shelled hazelnuts

Line a baking tray with parchment paper. Lay the shelled hazelnuts out on the baking tray in a single layer.

Put the baking pan in the oven and set the oven to 300 degrees F. Let roast for about 20 minutes. They usually release a lovely roasted scent when they are ready.

Cool the nuts for about 20 minutes, and then set up three bowls—one for the unshelled nuts, one for shells, and one for the shelled nuts. Using your nutcracker, crack each nut carefully and remove the nut inside, placing it in its respective bowl.

Once cool, store in an airtight container for up to 3 months. Store in the freezer for up to 2 years.

---

collect in a bag or container. Leave some for the squirrels (even though they won't leave any for you).

Avoid picking nuts that have brown spots on the husk, as this is usually a sign they have been infested with insects, such as the filbertworm or the filbert weevil. The shell will have a hole bored into the top or a brown, branched pattern. If you crack one open, you may find a larva inside.

Nuts with holes like this have been infested and can be discarded.

Note that European hazelnuts ripen a bit later, with most harvest occurring in September in the Pacific Northwest. The nutshell is more visible in this variety because the husk is different, so you can watch for the shell to turn tan or brown to indicate they are ready to harvest. They will begin dropping to the ground as well.

Look-Alikes

Before fruiting, beaked hazelnut trees could be mistaken for red alder (*Alnus rubra*) or mountain alder (*Alnus alnobetula*). Thankfully, hazelnut leaves have a velvetlike fuzz, whereas alder leaves are hairless and smooth. Witch hazel (*Hamamelis* spp.) also has a similar habit and leaf shape but does not have hair on its leaves.

Sustainability

Be sure to leave some for the squirrels, and feel free to bury a few ripe hazelnuts a few inches underground nearby.

Something else you can do to care for your wild hazelnut trees is to prune dead or dying branches. Use a clean pruning saw and cut at an angle. Trees benefit from this kind of care as dead parts of the tree can be a vector for disease entry.

Grow Your Own

Beaked hazelnut is a great shade-tolerant, native, shrubby tree to plant in your garden. Like vine leaf maple, it has multiple thin trunks and loses its leaves in the fall. Hazelnut trees tend to be about 10 feet in diameter and 10 to 15 feet tall when mature. However, if you really want a hefty hazelnut harvest, I recommend planting European hazelnut instead, since it bears far more nuts per tree.

Cooking with Hazelnuts

Processing hazelnuts is a multiple-step and fairly tedious process, which is one reason hazelnuts are so expensive. However, the flavor of a freshly roasted and shelled hazelnut is unparalleled. More than any wild food I've eaten, my first taste of fresh, wild hazelnut made me question the quality of food that's been stored in warehouses and shipped halfway across the world. It is my experience that our bodies know fresh food, and it is deeply satisfying to eat. You don't need to forage them—this level of freshness can also be accessed by buying farm direct, unshelled hazelnuts.

Beaked hazelnuts can be used in the same ways that European hazelnuts are used in baking, salads, snack mixes, and more. Just keep in mind that it can be hard to accumulate a large amount of them.

When you get your harvest home, lay the nuts out to dry in a single layer on trays or flat baskets. Put them somewhere that animals can't get to and where they won't be in sunlight. Leave them out for 1 to 2 weeks. If drying in a moister climate, it is wise to rotate the nuts and be sure to dry them on something porous to prevent mold.

Once completely dry, don your gloves and peel off the leaflike outer covering to expose the shell. The coverings should peel off easily when they are sufficiently dried, though if you have picked some prematurely, they may require more work. Store the dried nuts in glass jars away from heat and light. Well-dried nuts still in the shell will store for about a year, perhaps more if stored well.

It is best to roast the nuts before starting to shell them, as they are much easier to extract whole after roasting (see Roasted Hazelnuts recipe). I also recommend using a nutcracker that can crack the smaller size of beaked hazelnuts. Some people just rest the hazelnut on a flat rock and crack it with another rock. Whatever your method, crack the nut gently, to avoid crushing the inside, and remove the nutmeat from inside.

After shelling the nuts, dry them fully in a basket for a few days and then store them in a glass jar in the cupboard for no more than four months.

Shelled nuts (roasted or raw) can be stored in a sealed bag in the freezer for up to 2 years.

Beaked hazelnuts can be used in the same way as cultivated hazelnuts. You can roast them, put them in salads, make hazelnut milk, grind them and add them to baked goods, or just eat them as a snack.

Like most nuts, hazelnuts go rancid after a certain amount of time because of their fat content. Many people are not aware of this and store their nuts for long periods. In fact, many store-bought nuts are rancid. When rancid, they taste more bitter and a little tangy, and they have a sour smell to them. Be sure to store them properly to avoid this.

Immature beaked hazelnuts have a green outer covering, sometimes with streaks of red, and often grow in clusters of 2–6 nuts.

Huckleberry

Vaccinium spp.
Ericaceae (heath family)

Huckleberries are one of the most quintessential and widely known edible plants of the Pacific Northwest. At least twelve different species grow here, all with delicious edible berries. These native shrubs thrive in the moist, acidic soils here.

Huckleberry was once one of the primary subjects of cultural burning, which Native people used to increase berry production by burning away competing shrubs and trees to increase the shrubs access to sunlight. Huckleberry bushes vigorously resprout from root crowns after these fires and create copious new growth and berries. It is therefore no surprise that huckleberry populations have been affected greatly by decades of fire suppression. Though low-intensity fires are helpful for huckleberry growth and production, higher intensity fires (which are becoming more commonplace) may kill the shrubs, and it can take many years for them to reestablish from seed.

Only recently is cultural burning being allowed once again, with some controversy. Not only is it important to allow Native groups to continue long-held cultural land-management practices, but the reintroduction of these practices will be crucial in creating fire-resilient forests in the future.

The spring leaves of huckleberry are used as a medicinal herb in teas and other preparations to help regulate blood sugar. Huckleberries themselves are also considered an herbal medicine due to their incredibly high concentration of antioxidants. The wild berries have even higher levels of these than the cultivated variety.

A harvest of multiple types of huckleberry

OPPOSITE, TOP: Oval-leaf blueberry has slightly frosted berries, unlike its close look-alike tall huckleberry. **MIDDLE:** The delicate flowers of Cascade blueberry bloom low to the ground as the snow recedes. **BOTTOM:** Tart, red huckleberries are the first to ripen in the Pacific Northwest.

A native species of cranberry, small cranberry (*Vaccinium oxycoccos*) is also a member of this genus, though I have not included it here as it is somewhat rare and bears only a few fruits for each small plant.

Where to Find It

Most huckleberries in the Pacific Northwest grow at elevation, except for red huckleberry and evergreen huckleberry (*Vaccinium ovatum*; see next entry). Each species has a slightly different habitat and range, but they grow mostly along the Pacific coast and in the Cascade, Olympic, and Sierra Nevada mountain ranges. That is to say that they rarely grow in the drier parts of our region. I have included only the most common species here.

Red huckleberry (*Vaccinium parvifolium*) is the first to ripen of the year because it grows at low elevations. It produces small bright-red berries in July that are quite tart. Red huckleberry grows in western Washington, western Oregon, the western part of Northern California, and all throughout the Sierra Nevada range. This is probably the most commonly occurring species, and you have probably seen it on a forest walk if you live in those areas.

Cascade blueberry (*Vaccinium deliciosum*) is my favorite species of huckleberry, growing at elevations between 2000 and 6000 feet. You usually have to hike a bit to get these. The bush itself is relatively short, from 6 to 18 inches tall. The berries are so flavorful that they actually make my jaw ache a little sometimes. They ripen a bit later than the others because they grow in places that have snow in the wintertime, so look out for them in August and September.

Grouseberry (*Vaccinium scoparium*) looks like a mini version of red huckleberry, growing to about 1 foot tall with tiny red berries and tiny bright-green leaves. I think the berries are much tastier than red huckleberry, though their habitat is more specific and harder to reach. This is perhaps the

Oval-leaf blueberry
Vaccinium ovalifolium

Ripe berry

Classic urn-shaped flower occurs in all members of the blueberry family (*Ericaceae*)

Flower cross section

Flower

Leaf spray

Red huckleberry
Vaccinium parvifolium

Berry spray

Flower

The pentagonal crown reflects the flower shape

Ripe berry

Leaf front and back

Tall huckleberry
Vaccinium membranaceum

Leaf front and back

Ripe berry

Berry spray

least abundant member of the *Vaccinium* genus included here, but where it grows, it is very abundant. It shares habitat with Cascade blueberry in higher elevation areas in the Cascades, Olympics, Rockies, and other mountain ranges in the western states. Definitely worth knowing for backpackers and high-elevation hikers. They also ripen in August and September.

Oval-leaf blueberry (*Vaccinium ovalifolium*) grows in the mountains in Oregon, Washington, British Columbia, and southern Alaska. Their range starts at lower elevations than Cascade blueberry, so start looking on any mid-elevation hike in a coniferous forest. These berries look very similar to store-bought blueberries, with their frosted blue skin and small round crown. They ripen in July and August.

Tall huckleberry (*Vaccinium membranaceum*) has almost the same habitat range as Alaska huckleberry, though it is slightly more abundant on the east side of the Cascades, extending into Idaho and Montana. They often grow side by side and look quite similar, but tall huckleberry has

Red huckleberry growing in its preferred habitat: the top of a nurse log

shinier and darker berries and serrated, waxy leaves. These also ripen in July and August.

How to Harvest

Huckleberries ripen from July to September, depending on the specific species. See Where to Find It for details on when to harvest each species and their specific habitats.

The best berries are to be found in places where sunlight can filter through the trees or in open meadows. Sometimes the purple-blue huckleberries can look ripe before they are, so be sure to check the area where the stem is attached to the berry—if it is still tinged red, the berry is not yet ripe. Unripe berries will be more sour, astringent, and less sweet and tender. Harvest huckleberries into a sealed plastic container to prevent bruising during travel.

Harvesting red huckleberries on the trail

Look-Alikes

False azalea (*Rhododendron menziesii*) is the most convincing look-alike I have seen, resembling tall huckleberry and Alaska huckleberry, and the three of them often grow together. Thankfully, false azalea does not have edible berries, but rather it has a dry brown seedpod that you would not mistake for a berry. However, if you want to harvest huckleberry leaves, you will need to be sure of your ID.

Sustainability

Bears, rabbits, mice, birds, foxes, chipmunks, and other animals rely on huckleberries as a late-summer food source. In

HUCKLEBERRY SORBET

Makes about 1 quart

When I was young, my mother used to make a small batch of huckleberry or blackberry sorbet every year. It was so flavorful, all you needed was a small scoop of it. I would savor each precious bite on my tongue and then lick the bowl carefully to be sure I hadn't missed anything. This recipe is a re-creation of her very simple method.

1 cup water
1 cup sugar
1 teaspoon fresh lemon juice
4 cups fresh or frozen huckleberries (any species)

Combine the water and sugar in a saucepan over medium heat. Stir until the sugar has dissolved. Remove from the heat and let cool for about an hour.

Combine the cooled syrup, lemon juice, and the berries in a blender and blend until smooth. If you like chunks of huckleberry in your final product, blend for less time, and if you like a smoother sorbet, blend for more time. Pour the mixture into a sealable glass or plastic container and chill the mixture in the refrigerator for at least 2 hours.

Pour into an ice cream maker and continue according to the manufacturer's instructions. Alternatively, if you don't have an ice cream maker, put the mixture in the freezer and stir every 30 minutes or so to form a soft sorbet, scraping the frozen sides each time. Using a metal container can make the process go more quickly, just be sure not to use metal utensils to scrape it. Store in a sealed, labeled container in the freezer and consume within a month.

the mountain habitats where huckleberries mostly grow, sugar sources are more scarce, making huckleberry an important food source. The leaves of huckleberries are also a favorite of deer, elk, and other browsing species.

Huckleberries are heavily harvested for commercial sale in our region. Commercial huckleberry harvest has several negative impacts, including depriving wildlife of an essential food source through overharvest, damage to shrubs done by harvest rakes, and removal of seed stock needed to propagate. Wild huckleberries are not currently cultivated on a large scale, which means that any huckleberry products for sale are harvested in the wild. More awareness is being spread about the negative impacts of the commercial harvest of forest products, but there is still a lot that is hidden from the public. It is important to purchase sustainably/ethically harvested huckleberry products on the market, so avoid the lineup of huckleberry products in gift shops.

Because of all this, we need to be extra aware of our impact when we harvest huckleberries. A few guidelines to go by: harvest only what you will use, tread lightly, and be sure to leave some of the berries for wildlife.

Grow Your Own

Growing wild huckleberries in your yard can be difficult, so I recommend selecting a variety that grows in your area. For those residing in the lowland areas of western Washington, Oregon, and Northern California, red huckleberry and evergreen huckleberry (see next entry) are going to be your species of choice. Cultivated blueberry, known officially as high-bush blueberry (*Vaccinium corymbosum*), grow very well in the same areas. If you have a boggy place on your property, you might also consider growing the cultivated cranberry (*Vaccinium macrocarpon*). For those who live in mountain areas above 2000 feet in elevation, consider growing tall huckleberry or Alaska huckleberry, which you can purchase at a native plant nursery or transplant from the wild. Cascade blueberry and mountain huckleberry have too specific a habitat to grow well under cultivation, so please leave those in the wild.

Cooking with Huckleberries

Huckleberries are used in much the same way that cultivated blueberries are, though the wild ones tend to be much more flavorful. They can be used in sauces, jams, jellies, syrups, sorbet (see recipe), ice cream, candies, pie, crumbles, cakes, and more.

If you are not going to use them immediately, you can freeze them. I wash and dry them, pick out leaves and stems, and then spread them out on a baking sheet and freeze. Once frozen, you can pour them into a labeled resealable plastic bag to store them in the freezer for up to a year. This process keeps them from freezing into one large mass, making them easier to work with.

Huckleberry, Evergreen

Vaccinium ovatum
Ericaceae (heath family)

The small dark-blue berries of evergreen huckleberry are more firm and less juicy than other huckleberries, but they ripen much later, making them a great cold-season treat. I have harvested these berries as late as January, and often in November. More so than other berries, these shrubs seem to ripen on their own time, varying widely from bush to bush and year to year.

Evergreen huckleberry has white-and-pink, urn-shaped flowers that bloom from April to August, which accounts for its extended fruiting season. Urn-shaped flowers are characteristic of the heath family, which includes all huckleberries, salal, heather, uva-ursi, and Pacific madrone. The heath family is locally abundant due to its preference for acidic soils, which our conifer forests provide.

Many people are surprised to learn that evergreen huckleberry is edible. Its waxy evergreen leaves resemble boxwood more than its blueberry kin. The other members of the huckleberry genus lose their leaves in the fall and are much more delicate in construction. This is why I chose to feature evergreen huckleberry in its own entry, separate from the other huckleberries.

Evergreen huckleberries beginning to ripen in early fall, a process that continues sometimes as late as January

Berries

Leaves back and front

Flower cross section

Flower cluster with leaves

Berry cluster with leaves

Leaf cluster

Native people traditionally ate fresh evergreen huckleberries with animal fat, and the berries were sometimes stored in animal fat to preserve them. With the high-antioxidant content of huckleberry and the anti-inflammatory fats of wild meats, that would be a very nourishing combination. Though this may not

Drying Evergreen Huckleberries Without a Dehydrator

Evergreen huckleberries are much less juicy than other berries and thus lend themselves perfectly to drying, much like salal berries. This recipe details how to dry them in open air, without the help of an oven or dehydrator. If you prefer to dry them in an oven, use the method described in the Salal entry.

I avoid washing things that I am going to dry, if possible, but some people really like to wash everything they eat. If you wash your berries, just dry them thoroughly with a paper towel or clean dish towel without crushing them. You could even line a basket with a towel and roll them around in there.

I use wide, flat baskets for drying berries. Baskets made with natural materials are porous, absorb excess moisture, and have holes for air circulation. You can also lay them out on a bedsheet or put them in a tiered, mesh herb-drying rack. Spread them into a single layer with space in between to maximize air circulation to each fruit and minimize crowding, which can allow moisture to collect and mold to grow.

For the best results, put a fan near your berries, turn it on low, and point it in the direction of the berries. The more air circulation, the faster the berries will dry. The faster they dry, the less likely they are to mold.

The time it takes for the berries to dry fully will vary, but expect it to take at least a week. During the drying time, turn them every 1 to 2 days to ensure the air accesses all sides of each berry. When fully dried, they will feel a lot like a raisin (but smaller). They should be leathery, but should not expel any juice when squeezed. They should not be moldy (look for white or blue fuzz) or smell like yeast (putting fruit out like this is actually a way to foster natural yeasts for bread and alcohol fermentation).

I don't recommend drying them outside. Every time I get a wild hair and think that's a good idea, ants get into them.

Store them in a dark, dry place and consume them within a year. A glass jar in the pantry is a great option. Note that if they are not fully dry, they will mold in storage, so I usually let them dry a bit longer than I might think they need.

---

sound very tasty to someone from an industrialized culture, traditional foods like this are far more nutrient dense than most modern food.

Huckleberry leaf tea (made from the leaves of any member of the *Vaccinium* genus) lowers blood sugar and can be used for gout as well.

Where to Find It

This plant has an affinity for the temperate, coastal forests of our region. In Washington, I see it most often growing among Sitka spruce, western hemlock, Douglas-fir, and western red cedar. In California, it grows in the understory of misty redwood forests. Its range runs from Vancouver Island down to Southern California, hugging the coast. It can sometimes be found in the Cascades and some of the ranges in California, but it is sparse there. It often shares a habitat with other berries such as red huckleberry and salal, which also thrive in the coastal forests.

How to Harvest

Evergreen huckleberries are slow to ripen and remain on the bush for much longer than other berries. In Washington and Oregon, evergreen huckleberries can be found from October to January. In California, they will begin to ripen earlier, in late August or September.

The berries can survive several frosts. In fact, they are rumored to be sweeter after the first frost, which is also true of other berries, such as rose hips and hawthorn berries. Colder temperatures trigger stored starches to be converted into simple sugars, making them sweeter to taste. Because these berries are less resistant to rot, they are good ones to dry or store.

A November evergreen huckleberry harvest

The best berries will be found at the edges of forests, in openings where the sun can reach them, and in exposed areas (especially those exposed by logging). Evergreen huckleberry shares a habitat with red huckleberry (see previous entry).

Look-Alikes

Evergreen huckleberry could be mistaken for the ornamental shrub sweet box (*Sarcococca confusa*), which has evergreen leaves with the same alternate-leaf arrangement and dark berries that ripen at a similar time. Thankfully, sweet box does not grow in the wild and thus can be distinguished by habitat. Sweet box berries are not necessarily toxic but are not considered edible, so the mistake would only get you a mouthful of yucky berries.

Oregon boxleaf (*Paxistima myrsinites*), which does grow wild in our region, could also potentially be mistaken for evergreen huckleberry. The two plants have very similar waxy leaves with a slight serration on the edges. The difference lies in the leaf tips: Oregon boxleaf's are rounded, whereas evergreen huckleberry's are pointed. However, Oregon boxleaf does not bear fruit, so a mistake ID is harmless.

Sustainability

Evergreen huckleberries provide late-season forage for birds, squirrels, and bears, so try not to take more than 50 percent of the berries from a bush, especially if there are fewer berries than usual that year. Like all fruiting plants, there will be abundant years and light years, depending on the rainfall and temperatures during the spring and summer.

Grow Your Own

Evergreen huckleberry is well suited to gardens as it is a fairly well-behaved and shade-tolerant shrub. It is also great because the foliage stays green all year long. Instead of planting boxwood or sweet box, try evergreen huckleberry instead. Keep in mind that most blueberry-family plants like acidic soil, so it may enjoy growing under a conifer tree. You might even consider underplanting it with Oregon wood sorrel! This plant is a staple of native plant nurseries, so you shouldn't have trouble finding it.

Cooking with Evergreen Huckleberry

These berries are less sweet than other huckleberry species, but they're flavorful and rarely sour. They are delicious when eaten fresh off the bush, or you can use them in jams, cakes, and other desserts. I think these berries lend themselves best to drying as they don't have a lot of moisture in them, and drying concentrates their mild flavor (see Drying Evergreen Huckleberries Without a Dehydrator).

Indian Plum

Oemleria cerasiformis
Rosaceae (rose family)

Indian plum, also known as osoberry, is one of the very first plants to bloom in the spring, sometimes blooming as early as February. Its emerging lime-green leaves stand out against the brown background of winter. I see it as the first sign of spring. It has edible leaf buds and berries, which make a great trail snack for hikers.

Where to Find It

Indian plum grows exclusively west of the Cascades in Washington and Oregon and in a section of Northern California. It also grows up into British Columbia. It likes open, moist forests and can sometimes be found in riparian zones and forest edges. I see it growing among Douglas-firs, red alders, and bigleaf maples, with sword fern, low Oregon grape, and salal growing underneath.

How to Harvest

The tiny edible leaf buds are one of the first things to emerge from Indian plum in February. You can pluck them off with your fingers and eat them; I usually don't eat leaves that are more than an inch long.

Most flowering plants have male and female parts on the same flower. However, Indian plum is dioecious, which means that some trees are male and some trees are female. Roughly

LEFT: Ripe Indian plums with identifiable red stems and orange unripe berries RIGHT: Indian plum is shrubby, sometimes sprawling, and often pruned into strange shapes by hungry deer.

INDIAN PLUM

LEFT: Wart-like lenticels on the bark of an Indian plum branch
RIGHT: Harvesting ripe Indian plums from an abundant tree (Photo: Abby Laden)

75 percent are male trees, which bear pollen, and the other 25 percent are female trees, which bear fruit. That means that 75 percent of Indian plum trees you encounter will not bear fruit, which makes harvesting the berries a bit tricky.

Indian plum is one of the first berries of the season to ripen, typically in June, along with salmonberry. The best berries are found in trees that have access to sunlight, so look on the edges of the forest or in openings in the tree canopy. Harvest the ones you can reach and leave the rest for the birds.

Look-Alikes

You are unlikely to mistake this tree for anything else while in flower or berry, but early in the season, it may resemble a red elderberry (*Sambucus racemosa*), which often grows nearby and has a similar habit. To confirm your ID, look at the leaf edges: red elderberry has serrations on the edges of its leaves, while the edges of Indian plum's leaves are smooth.

Sustainability

Animals are very interested in Indian plum fruits. I once witnessed a squirrel and a robin battle over a particularly abundant patch in Discovery Park, causing quite a stir. It's probably because they are one of the first berries to ripen in the spring that they are so in demand. For this reason, it is especially

INDIAN PLUM SHRUB

Makes about 1 cup

Indian plums have a unique flavor that is much less sweet than many other fruits and with a hint of cucumber. This is a small batch because it's rare to find a lot of Indian plums at once. If you find more, then definitely double the recipe! I like to add the shrub to a glass of sparkling water and ice, but you can also use it to make mocktails and cocktails.

1 cup fresh Indian plums
½ cup sugar
½ cup apple cider vinegar or champagne vinegar

Rinse the plums and shake dry. In a small bowl, combine the Indian plums with the sugar and mash with the back of a wooden spoon or squish them with clean hands. Cover the mixture with plastic wrap and store in the fridge for 12 to 24 hours.

Add the fruit-sugar mixture to a 16-ounce mason jar with a plastic lid. Add the vinegar, put the jar lid on, and let sit for 2 more days in the refrigerator.

Pour the mixture through cheesecloth into a clean bottle or jar to strain out the pits, and store in the fridge for up to 4 weeks. Check for mold before using.

Use 1 to 2 tablespoons of the shrub in mocktail or cocktail recipes.

important to leave them for the wildlife. This is a berry that I harvest only if I find a particularly abundant patch, which does happen occasionally.

Grow Your Own

Indian plum is very easy to find in local nurseries and is a great shade-tolerant shrub to plant in your yard. It can handle some sun too, and will produce more berries in that case. Only the female bushes bear fruit, and one in four is female in the wild, so plant several bushes to ensure you have at least one fruit-bearing shrub. Also note that deer do love Indian plum, so if there are a lot if deer in your area, it is wise to protect it in its early years.

Early spring sun filters through bigleaf maple branches onto emerging leaves of Indian plum, one of the first plants of the season to awaken.

Cooking with Indian Plum

The leaf buds of Indian plum are best for a snack on the trail, though I am curious about using it to flavor bitters or other mocktail items. In general, though, the leaf buds cannot be consumed in a large amount, and the flavors are pretty strong, so enjoy it as an occasional trail snack rather than as an ingredient.

The fruits are the real prize. Like cherries, Indian plums have a single large pit inside. They are definitely not as sweet as cherries, having a unique cucumber like taste that I find quite refreshing. I first encountered Indian plum at an herbal-conference cocktail competition, where someone had made an Indian plum syrup and served it with sparkling water. Yum!

Aside from eating them fresh while out on a walk, most people make small batches of syrup or shrub—a combination of vinegar and sugar infused with fruit that is used to make beverages. Because of their large pits, Indian plums aren't the best candidates for pies or jams.

Cautions

As Indian plum leaves mature, they accumulate cyanogenic glycosides, a toxic compound that is present in many rose-family plants. Consume only the very young, tender leaves and avoid the more mature leaves.

Japanese Knotweed

Fallopia japonica, F. x bohemica, F. sachalinensis
Polygonaceae (buckwheat family)

Japanese knotweed is an invasive weed with edible shoots that was introduced from East Asia. It grows in nearly all states in the US and is considered noxious or invasive in many of them.

There are three species colloquially known as Japanese knotweed that grow in Washington State. The first is the official Japanese knotweed (*Fallopia japonica*), which is the smallest of the three species and the most common in Japan. The second is giant knotweed (*Fallopia sachalinensis*), which is less common but still equally problematic in its aggressive growth pattern. The leaves of giant knotweed are much bigger, and the plant itself grows 13 to 16 feet tall (more than twice the height of Japanese knotweed). The third species, bohemian knotweed (*Fallopia x bohemica*), is actually a hybrid of the first two. Its leaf size (5 to 9 inches) and height (6 to 13 feet) are in the middle of the two

TOP: A thick stem of bohemian knotweed **BOTTOM:** A patch of bohemian knotweed in a suburban stream with sandy, moist soil—ideal conditions for knotweed

Bohemian knotweed
Fallopia x bohemica

Leaf

Flower

Flower cluster and leaves

Flower spike

Shoot

species. Bohemian knotweed is gaining traction and is quite aggressive, though thankfully, because it is a hybrid, it does not always produce seeds. When harvesting, distinguishing the three is unnecessary as they are all equally edible. The thick shoots of bohemian knotweed are the best for harvest, in my opinion.

Knotweed is a hugely problematic invasive weed in Washington and Oregon that is very difficult to eradicate—herbicides being the method of choice. It can cause damage to the concrete foundations of structures, and it crowds out valuable riparian habitat. If you drive along the Snoqualmie River near Duvall, Washington, you can see vast sections of the riverbanks that have been entirely taken over by this plant.

While doing fieldwork for this book, I went out with some folks from Oxbow Farm to research plots on which they have been testing some nonchemical removal methods for Japanese knotweed. One of the methods involves covering the patch with black plastic for a year or more, and the other requires a weekly mowing regime, both of which show promise. Unfortunately, these methods take far more time and diligence than herbicides do.

The entire plant dies back every fall, leaving a sea of brown and hollow stalks that are visible in the wintertime. It is actually quite amazing that this plant grows from nothing to 15 feet tall every single year. What vigor! Some claim that it grows so fast you can actually watch it grow.

On a lighter note, bees love the white flowers, which emerge starting in July. Knotweed-flower honey is dark and very unique tasting. It is purported to have unique health benefits as well, so it's certainly worth tracking down from a local beekeeper to try.

Bees and other pollinators adore the abundant flowers and nectar of knotweed.

The young shoots, which taste like rhubarb, are edible. And the roots of Japanese knotweed are used in herbal medicine. It is a lesser used and very specific remedy, used for some complex infections associated with Lyme disease and some viruses.

Where to Find It

Japanese knotweed can grow in a variety of habitats, including forests, streams, meadows, pastures, sidewalks, and vacant city lots. However, it especially thrives on the banks of rivers and near freshwater streams. It spreads easily in this environment: leaves or stem fragments fall into the water, float downstream, and establish new patches. I especially see it thriving in the sandy alluvial soils on the banks of some of the lowland rivers in my area. It is a problem in that environment because it encourages erosion and does not create a suitable habitat for fish and wildlife that rely on the river.

It grows mostly in the moist parts of our region, including the Idaho panhandle. You will find it only occasionally on the east side of the Cascade Range.

How to Harvest

The young shoots of Japanese knotweed are edible and taste much like rhubarb. Harvest them in April or May, depending on your location. Select shoots with leaves barely unfurled, still reaching straight up to the sky, and cut about 3 inches above the ground. The stem should be easy to cut, like cutting a cooked potato. The fatter, younger shoots are better—some shoots are thin and extremely difficult to peel, and older stems are too fibrous and will be more difficult to cut.

As you carry your harvest home, be sure not to drop *any* stems or leaves. These could propagate and turn into a new patch, thereby spreading this extremely aggressive weed.

Finding a patch of Japanese knotweed that has not been sprayed with chemicals can be challenging. Most knotweed patches on public land have been sprayed, including those near creeks and rivers. Glyphosate is the herbicide of choice for eradicating knotweed, either sprayed or injected into the crown. Theoretically, glyphosate has a half-life of less than a year and as little as a day, which means it should be broken down by microorganisms in that time frame. But other chemicals are

Visiting a bohemian knotweed patch in late April. This patch will tower over my head in a month's time. (Photo: Ann Norton)

BLUEBERRY AND JAPANESE KNOTWEED PIE

Makes 1 (9-inch) pie

This is a wild twist on the classic blueberry-rhubarb pie, using Japanese knotweed instead of rhubarb. When you prepare the knotweed, be sure to discard any leaves, skin, and overly fibrous sections. The filling also works great in a cobbler recipe.

3 cups peeled and chopped knotweed
3 cups blueberries or strawberries
¾ cup sugar
4 tablespoons cornstarch
1 tablespoon fresh lemon juice
1 teaspoon cinnamon
1 homemade double pie crust, or 1 store-bought bottom crust

Preheat oven to 400 degrees F.

Toss the knotweed, blueberries, sugar, cornstarch, lemon juice, and cinnamon together in a large mixing bowl until everything is evenly coated.

Prepare the bottom pie crust and place in a pie pan. Pour the filling over the top. If you're using a homemade crust, arrange the top crust and crimp the sides. For a premade crust, add a crumble topping (see Note) or skip the topping altogether.

Bake for 20 minutes, then reduce the temperature to 350 degrees F and bake for another 25 to 30 minutes, until the filling is bubbling and the crust is golden brown.

Cool for 2 hours to allow the filling to set. Slice and serve. Store leftovers in the fridge for up to 1 week.

Note: If using a premade bottom crust, make a crumble topping by using a pastry cutter to combine ½ cup (1 stick) of cold, unsalted butter with ½ cup sugar and 1 cup flour until the mixture resembles granola. Sprinkle over the top of the pie and follow baking instructions.

Photo: Ann Norton

used along with glyphosate that can also be harmful to human health, such as surfactants that help coat the leaves, and some of which have longer half-lives. There is conflicting evidence and opinion about whether it is safe to consume the plant after the half-life window.

Cautions

Japanese knotweed contain oxalates, which can irritate the kidneys and gastrointestinal tract (see sidebar "What Are Oxalates?" in Part One), and should not be eaten raw. No part of the mature plant should be consumed, as the oxalate content increases as it matures and becomes much more fibrous.

I first learned about eating Japanese knotweed shoots in Japan, where I volunteered at a tea plantation and we harvested shoots from the fields.

The best way to find an unsprayed patch is to find some on private land. The county (or other municipality) must ask for permission to spray glysophate on privately owned landwill. Confirm with the landowner that it has not been sprayed for at least five years.

All that said, once you have found a good patch, you can return to it year after year. Harvesting the shoots can discourage the plant, especially if all the shoots are cut each year.

Sustainability

Please do the world a favor and do *not* try to grow this plant at home. Not only is it illegal, but it can lower your property value.

When all you have seen is a tame patch in your neighborhood, you may not understand why this plant captures such animosity. Trust me on this one: There are patches the likes of which you have never seen. Imagine forests of it extending as far as the eye can see.

If you have it in your yard, I do recommend keeping it controlled, especially if it is anywhere near a structure. It is known to crack foundations with the power of its roots. A lot of online resources address how to control and eliminate it.

Look-Alikes

All three species of mature knotweed have such large leaves and stature that it's unlikely to mistake them for anything else. Even knotweed shoots are quite unique in their habit and appearance. However, broadleaf dock (also listed in this book) shares a family with knotweed and has some similar stem and leaf patterns. However, broadleaf dock leaves are smooth, and the plant is significantly smaller. Also, broadleaf dock stalks are not hollow and juicy like those of knotweed.

Cooking with Japanese Knotweed

Knotweed is related to rhubarb, though not quite as sour, and is used similarly in the kitchen. Japanese knotweed shoots are excellent when used in place of rhubarb in sweets, such as pies (see recipe), crumbles, bars, and chutneys.

Peeled Japanese knotweed shoots are also excellent pickled and used as a condiment.

I originally learned about eating Japanese knotweed in Japan, its original home, where we harvested shoots from the tea fields. We took them home, peeled them, sprinkled salt on them, and let them sit for a few hours. We then added some to a salad. According to my sources in Japan, the salt is supposed to remove the *aku*, or toxicity; though they eat only a little at a time because it can be upsetting to the stomach.

Lady fern

Athyrium filix-femina
Athyriaceae (lady fern family)

A fiddlehead is the emerging coiled shoot of any fern. Many species of fern produce edible fiddleheads, but the best fiddleheads in the Pacific Northwest come from lady fern.

Another lovely species in the same genus is called alpine lady-fern (*Athyrium distentifolium*), grows only at high elevations in the mountains in rocky talus fields. It is nearly identical, except that it is much smaller than lady fern. Though it also has edible fiddleheads, it is best not to harvest alpine lady-fern due to its sensitive habitat and limited range.

Where to Find It

Lady ferns grow in rich soil in wetlands or near streams. They like the dark, leafy mud in boggy parts of forests, and often grow alongside skunk cabbage. The ferns grow in lowland areas and all the way up in montane habitats.

Lady fern unfurling on a streambank in spring

How to Harvest

In the very early spring, lady fern fiddleheads emerge in a cluster around the crown of a single plant. The fiddleheads are coiled into a spiral shape, ready to unfurl into a fern frond. They are insulated from the cold weather by leaf duff and papery fuzz that the fern makes. It is best to harvest the fiddleheads before the leaves develop, usually when the fiddlehead is about 3 inches tall. Once they get older and the leaves start jutting out the sides of the spiral, the texture and taste change for the worse. Sometimes you have to pull some of the protective duff aside to reach the fiddleheads inside the crown.

TOP: Lady fern growing among thimbleberry, salmonberry, and young red alder trees
BOTTOM: Ferns reproduce through spores, which they release in July and August

Use your fingers to gently pluck the tender stems or use a clean knife or scissors. Harvest about one in every five fiddleheads you encounter. Store them in a hard-sided plastic container to avoid bruising them during transport.

The best patches of lady fern are in low spots in the woods that accumulate moisture and thick, dark-brown mud. In such places, it is common to see a hundred or more lady fern plants in an area. Step lightly when walking in these patches off-trail as there may be other plants below your feet that have yet to emerge. Also, the mud can suck your shoes off.

Avoid fiddleheads that are brown or black, contain insect holes or signs of slug predation, or have an off-putting smell. Because of their wet habitat and early sprouting time, they sometimes rot or get diseases.

Look-Alikes

Some people might mistake bracken fern and lady fern, but their growth habit sets them apart easily. Lady fern has five or more fronds per plant, all of which radiate out from a central crown like a feather duster. Bracken ferns, however, shoot up a solitary stalk. Furthermore, lady fern fiddleheads are one perfect spiral, and bracken fern fiddleheads look more like a fist with many little spirals.

Sustainability

Fiddleheads are quite a popular wild food among chefs and foragers, and I often see the signs of overharvest. It is common for people to cut off all the fiddleheads from a single plant, which is definitely harmful to the plant and not a sustainable harvesting practice. Please take no more than 20 percent of the fiddleheads from each plant. If you see signs of harvest already in a patch,

FIDDLEHEADS WITH BUTTER AND GARLIC *Makes 2 to 4 servings*

This simple and classic way to cook fiddlehead ferns reduces the mucilaginous texture that fiddleheads can take on when prepared in other ways. These sautéed fiddleheads are great served with pasta, on a salad, or with egg dishes. The dish comes together quickly, so be sure to prepare these just before serving.

2 tablespoons unsalted butter
3 cloves garlic, minced
2 cups lady fern fiddleheads
Salt, to taste

Gently heat the butter in a large skillet over medium heat until it begins to bubble. Add the garlic and sauté for about 30 seconds, until it begins to brown and let off its aroma.

Add the fiddleheads and sauté, stirring occasionally, for about 10 minutes. To check for doneness, cut one to see if it is soft all the way through, much like you would test broccoli. Turn the heat down if you are getting too much browning or if the garlic is burning. Season with salt and serve immediately.

please refrain from harvesting there and find another patch. If you'd like to gather a lot, find yourself a good patch where the ferns are abundant, usually in a boggy area in the forest.

Cooking with Lady Fern

The papery brown hairs should be removed before eating lady fern fiddleheads, if only because they have a strange texture that is off-putting to the average eater. Use a spoon, a bristled

Cautions

Don't eat lady fern fiddleheads raw, as they contain toxic compounds that can cause gastrointestinal upset.

brush, or your fingers to scrape them off. It can be difficult, so just do the best you can.

The fiddleheads should be cooked before eating, partly because they contain toxic compounds that are destroyed by cooking and partly because of their bacteria-rich, boggy habitat. They can be cooked by boiling or steaming for 7 to 10 minutes or by sautéing them in oil or butter.

Lady fern fiddleheads have a strange texture that some adore and others struggle with. For those who struggle, I recommend trying a recipe like fiddlehead ravioli, where they are pureed or cut up into small pieces. For those who love it, sauté them whole with garlic and butter (see recipe). You can use them in most contexts where you would use asparagus.

Fiddleheads are eaten frequently in many East Asian countries in noodle soups, pickled, and in stir-fries.

Lambsquarters

Chenopodium album
Amaranthaceae (amaranth family)

Not only are the young greens of lambsquarters just as tender and delicious as spinach, they are also exceptionally nutritious. They contain both more protein and more calcium than spinach.

The leaves of lambsquarters have a unique powdery coating, a type of wax that the plant produces to protect its leaves from sunlight and water. This makes it easy to spot from far away, as it has a white-blue tinge.

Most populations of lambsquarters come from genetic stock introduced to North America from Europe, though populations native to North America exist in the Midwest.

Where to Find It

Lambsquarters thrives in the rich, disturbed soils of gardens, farms, and in weedy waste areas. It grows in most places in our region, and across the United States for that matter, save for the highest elevations and the driest climates. It even grows in Alaska!

How to Harvest

Harvest lambsquarters in the spring and early summer before the plant flowers. Find plants that have abundant, large, tender leaves and are still low to the ground. At this point, you can eat the tender stems too. Snip the whole plant just under the leaves. Harvest more than you think you'll need as the leaves will reduce in volume when you cook them, like spinach does. I recommend harvesting the greens into plastic bags,

Lambsquarters ready to harvest, growing in the rich soil of a community garden plot

170

THE PLANTS AND RECIPES

which will keep them from wilting during transport.

Later in the season, the plants will get taller, the stem more fibrous and woody, and the leaves smaller. You can pluck individual leaves off, but they are definitely not as nice at this stage.

Many farms have a lot of lambsquarters growing in their tilled fields, so you could try visiting a local organic farm and asking for permission to harvest lambsquarters. You may even find other wild edible weeds while you are there, such as dandelion, mallow, and purslane.

Look-Alikes

Lambsquarters is best distinguished from look-alikes such as pigweeds (*Amaranthus* spp.) and smartweeds (*Persicaria* spp.) by the powdery coating on the leaves and the arrow-shaped leaf. However, close relatives may share these traits. Many other species in the *Chenopodium* genus (colloquially known as goosefoots) resemble lambsquarters and are edible but generally more fibrous. The closely related *Atriplex* genus (known as saltbush) also has similar leaf shapes and silvery sheens. There are many edible saltbush species, though certain species contain more oxalates and some saponins and shouldn't be consumed in large amounts.

Lambsquarters is most easily set apart by its habitat, which is disturbed soil. Many of the other species grow in sensitive coastal or sagebrush steppe ecosystems and not in disturbed areas. If you are unsure of your ID, use an app and/or an internet forum to help with this one.

TOP: Lambsquarters growing in a scrubby vacant lot like this one tend to be drier and more fibrous than ones that grow in rich, moist soil, and thus less good for eating.
BOTTOM: Lambsquarter leaves have a white powdery coating, which is made up of tiny wax particles that protect the plant.

Sustainability

Lambsquarters is a non-native weed that is rather abundant, so you can harvest as much as you'd like.

WILD LAMBSQUARTERS RICOTTA TART

Makes 4 to 8 servings

I love anything that comes in a pie shell, savory or sweet. This bright-green tart is so stunning to behold, and so simple. It can be made with spinach and kale if wild greens are out of season. If you use a homemade pie crust, you'll need to prebake the crust since the filling doesn't require much baking time. Prebaking can also make the bottom crust a little less soggy. If you're sensitive to oxalates, parboil the greens ahead of time (see Cooking with Lambsquarters for instructions).

- 1 homemade or store-bought bottom pie crust or tart crust
- 1 (15-ounce) container of ricotta cheese
- 4 cups (10 ounces) lambsquarters, stems removed
- 4 cups mixed wild spring greens (such as lambsquarters, miner's lettuce, nettle, dandelion) or spinach, stems removed
- 3 eggs
- ½ cup grated Parmesan cheese
- 1 bunch parsley, leaves chopped and stems removed
- 2 to 3 tablespoons fresh thyme leaves, stripped from the stem
- 2 fresh scallions, chopped
- 1 teaspoon salt
- ¼ teaspoon pepper

Preheat the oven to 375 degrees F.

If you're using a homemade crust, prebake the shell. Place a layer of parchment paper atop the crust with pie weights on top—this is so the center doesn't bubble up and the sides don't sink down. (I don't own pie weights, so I just use a slightly smaller pie dish with a layer of parchment paper underneath.) Bake with the weights on for 15 minutes at 375 degrees F, then remove the weights and bake for another 5 to 7 minutes, until it turns golden. Remove from the oven to cool while you prepare the filling.

Add the ricotta, lambsquarters, greens, eggs, Parmesan, parsley, thyme, and scallions to a blender, season with salt and pepper, and process until smooth. If the mixture is too thick for your blender, try using a food processor or an immersion blender.

Pour the filling into the prepared pie shell. Bake for about 35 minutes, until the center no longer jiggles when jostled. Let cool for at least 10 minutes before serving.

Cautions

Though lambsquarters does contain oxalates, it actually has less than spinach, so it is not as much of a concern. That said, oxalates can interfere with calcium uptake, so if you want to absorb the calcium in lambsquarters, parboil the leaves first (see Cooking with Lambsquarters). Sensitive individuals, such as those with kidney stones, may still want to avoid this plant.

Grow Your Own

Though lambsquarters is a non-native weed, you can easily grow it in your garden by scattering seeds in a newly tilled area of your yard in the fall. It is an independent vegetable, though it will be much more tender and leafy with a bit of water and compost.

If you prefer to seek out Pacific Northwest native species, there are several related species to choose from. I recommend growing maple-leaf goosefoot (*Chenopodium simplex*), which is closely related and is also edible. It will thrive in some of the drier areas of the Pacific Northwest.

Cooking with Lambsquarters

Lambsquarters can be eaten raw or cooked, but it is usually cooked. Its flavor and consistency are very similar to spinach, so you can replace the spinach in most recipes with lambsquarters. You can use lambsquarters in pesto, quiche, ravioli, spanakopita, saag, dips, spreads, and stir-fries.

If you are sensitive to oxalates, parboil the lambsquarters before use: Bring a large pot of water to boil over high heat. Reduce heat to medium and plunge the leaves into the boiling water. Boil for 1 to 2 minutes and strain and rinse in a colander in the sink. Cool, and squeeze out excess water, then use in the recipe.

Mallow

Malva neglecta, Malva sylvestris
Malvaceae (mallow family)

Several species from the mallow family grow in the Pacific Northwest, but I have chosen to feature common mallow (*Malva sylvestris*) and dwarf mallow (*Malva neglecta*). Neither of these species is native, both having been introduced from Europe. Dwarf mallow in particular is rather abundant and weedy and a great species to harvest. Also, the leaves of both of these species lack fuzz, making them much nicer to eat than some of their fuzzier relatives.

Though other edible species in the mallow family grow here, including all the checker-mallows (*Sidalcea* spp.), it is prudent to identify them and check their relative abundance before harvesting, as some are rarer or even threatened (see Sustainability).

Interestingly, hollyhock (*Alcea rosea*) is closely related and has mucilaginous roots and flowers. Marshmallow (*Althaea officinalis*) is also closely related and is the most common species used in herbal medicine for its mucilaginous roots, which can be made into a tea to soothe gastrointestinal inflammation and sore throats. However, both of these species have hairy leaves, making them less desirable edibles.

Where to Find It

Dwarf mallow has a very weedy habit, growing in lawns, disturbed areas, ditches, vacant lots, and gravel roads. It grows in most parts of Washington and Oregon and a small section of Northern California.

LEFT: Dwarf mallow flowers are white with lateral, pink lines in each petal. (Photo: iNaturalist)
RIGHT: Common mallow's magenta flowers have reddish dots in the center of each leaf.

MALLOW

Dwarf mallow
Malva neglecta

Seed pod

Flower

Leaves

Flowers and leaves

Common mallow
Malva sylvestris

Flower

Seed pod

Leaf

Look-Alike ⚠️
Shiny geranium

Whole plant

Similar leaf shape, but lobes are cut much deeper

Leaf

Common mallow is more elusive. I have found it mostly near the sea in wet grassy areas. It is much more common along the coast in California than it is in the northern parts of the Pacific Northwest.

How to Harvest

Keep in mind that common mallow is, ironically, not so common here, so harvest it more lightly and only pluck a few leaves from each plant.

Dwarf mallow, on the other hand, is quite abundant in some areas. Because its leaves are much smaller, I sometimes harvest the whole plant, since harvesting leaves individually can be more time consuming. Leaves are most tender in the spring and early summer.

LEFT: Dwarf mallow growing on a sidewalk in Portland, OR
RIGHT: Common mallow growing along a fenceline in Sequim, WA

Look-Alikes

Dwarf mallow especially resembles several geranium species that grow wild in the region, including shiny geranium (*Geranium lucidum*) and dovefoot geranium (*Geranium molle*). However, dwarf mallow has a unique red dot in the middle of the leaves, and its white-pink flowers are distinct from the darker pink-purple flowers of most geranium species.

Ground ivy (*Glechoma hederacea*) has a similar leaf shape to mallow but is a much smaller plant and has distinctly shaped purple flowers in the mint family.

Sustainability

Harvest dwarf mallow to your heart's content. Common mallow, despite not being native, has

SAUTÉED MALLOW GREENS WITH GARLIC

Makes 2 servings

Mallow grows abundantly around the Mediterranean and is used as a wild green in soups and simple dishes like this. Eating mallow greens is excellent for gut health, as they contain soothing mucilage. Thinly slicing the leaves can improve the texture to appeal to more palates. I sometimes mix in other greens from my garden, such as hairy cat's ear or dandelion. This dish pairs well with chicken and rice or noodles.

2 tablespoons extra-virgin olive oil
2 cloves garlic, finely minced
4 cups rinsed and thinly sliced mallow leaves
Pinch of salt
Dash of pepper
Juice of ½ a lemon

Heat the olive oil in a large sauté pan over medium heat. Add the garlic and gently brown for a minute or so, until the aroma from the garlic is released.

Add the mallow leaves with a tablespoon of water and sauté for 5 to 7 minutes, until the leaves are soft and easy to crush with your fingernail. Add another tablespoon of water if needed. I cook mallow leaves a bit longer than I would more delicate greens, as their texture is better when thoroughly cooked. Add salt and pepper and more water if needed, and cook for 1 to 2 minutes more, sampling a bit to see if they are soft enough for you.

Remove from the heat and squeeze lemon juice over the top before serving.

become a beautiful and noncompetitive wildflower in some places. To me, that warrants being a bit more conservative in our harvest, taking only a few leaves and/or flowers from each plant.

Other mallows you encounter may be rare, such as the native bristly-stem checker-mallow (*Sidalcea hirtipes*), which is classified as threatened in Washington State. Please do not harvest these.

Grow Your Own

When selecting species for your garden, I recommend seeking out a native species if possible. Oregon checker-mallow (*Sidalcea oregana*) is a great choice. You can buy seeds online—search by scientific name to ensure you're getting the right species—or you might be lucky enough to find a start at a local native plant nursery. Plant it in a wet area of your garden, perhaps at a low spot that is a little more green than the rest of your yard. It's a great pollinator species!

Cooking with Mallow

Like its close relative okra, all mallows have a slimy texture. When chewed, the leaves feel slippery, so an entire salad full of mallow leaves might be a little much for the average eater. Cooking reduces this somewhat, but not entirely. The young leaves are consumed widely in the Mediterranean and Middle East, where they are often cooked with garlic and olive oil.

Marshmallows were once made with the root of the marshmallow plant (*Althea officinalis*), though modern marshmallows no longer contain it. You can find online recipes for making marshmallows at home using marshmallow root.

Mallow flowers are edible and mild tasting, making them great for flower garnishes on cakes or salads.

Miner's Lettuce

Claytonia perfoliata, C. sibirica, C. rubra
Caryophyllaceae (pink family)

Miner's lettuce, so named because it was eaten by miners during the California Gold Rush to stave off scurvy, is an excellent and very abundant wild green.

I like to harvest three species of miner's lettuce: miner's-lettuce (*Claytonia perfoliata*), Siberian miner's lettuce (*Claytonia sibirica*), and red miner's lettuce (*Claytonia rubra*). Note that miner's lettuce is both the name of the group of plants and the common name of the single species *Claytonia perfoliata*. In this entry, I refer to *Claytonia perfoliata* as miner's-lettuce (with a hyphen) to distinguish it from the group name miner's lettuce, so look sharp.

The leaves of all species of miner's lettuce share a tender, almost succulent-leaf quality. They have a slight iridescent sheen, which comes from the oxalic-acid crystals in the leaves. The flowers of most *Claytonia* species are white to pink and five-petaled, with a notch in each petal. You will likely notice a pattern when looking at the visuals in this entry.

Ten or more other species in this genus grow in the Pacific Northwest, many of which are beautiful wildflowers, but they are mostly too rare and special to want to harvest or disturb. Among these, my favorite is alpine spring-beauty (*Claytonia megarhiza*), which likes to grow in subalpine talus fields. I encounter this plant in summertime on approaches to alpine rock climbs, where it steals the show with its magenta flowers and tenacious

TOP: Miner's-lettuce (*Claytonia perfoliata*)
MIDDLE: Siberian miner's lettuce (*Claytonia sibirica*)
BOTTOM: Red miner's lettuce (*Claytonia rubra*)

Red miner's lettuce
Claytonia rubra

Leaf lineup

Whole plant

Flower

presence where not much else will grow. This is a good example of a plant that should not be disturbed by us foragers due to its sensitive and limited habitat.

Where to Find It

Miner's-lettuce (*Claytonia perfoliata*) is especially common in California but grows abundantly all throughout the Pacific Northwest, except in very dry areas such as the Columbia Basin and the John Day area in Oregon.

Miner's-lettuce likes moist, rich, soft soil and has a very weedy habit; it loves to grow in unkempt patches of grass. The biggest patch of miner's-lettuce I ever encountered was growing in the grass underneath well-manicured Douglas-firs in a park near my house. It was interspersed with dandelion, chickweed, sheep sorrel, and dead-nettle, which are common associates.

Red miner's lettuce grows in pine forests, sandy soils, and open fields. It mostly grows in the drier parts of the region, such as the eastern slope of the Cascades and the Columbia Basin, though it can also be found in some of the rain shadows in the San Juans.

Siberian miner's lettuce has a slightly different habitat, occurring mainly in the coastal part of our region—west of the Cascade Range and on the coast in Northern California. It is a forest-understory plant, mostly found growing underneath Douglas-firs and bigleaf maples. You will find it alongside other forest-understory plants, such as bleeding heart, sword fern, stinging nettle, and foam flower.

How to Harvest

When it grows in mild, wet climates, miner's-lettuce usually has two seasons of new, tender growth: spring and fall. Like chickweed,

---

WILD-GREEN SOUP *Makes 3 to 4 servings*

This blended soup is a great way to incorporate wild greens into your diet. Be sure to limit the amount of greens that shouldn't be consumed in large quantities, like sheep sorrel and dock (see Note), and feel free to mix in spinach and kale for some or all of the greens, if desired. Make it vegetarian by replacing the chicken broth with vegetable broth.

- 2 cups mixed wild spring greens (such as chickweed, sheep sorrel, dandelion, hairy cat's ear, dock leaf, chicory, or stinging nettle)
- 1 cup miner's lettuce leaves and stems
- 2 tablespoons extra-virgin olive oil or unsalted butter
- 1 small onion, diced
- 2 stalks celery, diced
- 3 cloves garlic, minced
- 3½ cups chicken broth
- 1 (15-ounce) can chickpeas or white beans, drained and rinsed
- 1 teaspoon salt
- ¼ teaspoon ground black pepper
- 1 tablespoon minced fresh thyme leaves
- 1 teaspoon minced fresh rosemary
- Sour cream, for serving

it loves cool, moist weather. Even in a warmer winter, you may encounter a delicious flush of green miner's-lettuce.

Siberian miner's lettuce can be harvested in the early spring, around the same time as stinging nettle. Red miner's lettuce is also best harvested in the early spring, preferably before it flowers.

For any of these, harvest with scissors into a plastic bag; I like to use a gallon-size resealable freezer bag. Snip the top 4 inches off, like you're giving it a haircut. The stems and leaves are equally edible and are best when harvested before flowering or just after it begins to flower. They get fibrous if you wait longer than that.

Look-Alikes

Miner's lettuce has no close look-alikes, though the flowers may look like others in the pink family, such as spring-beauty (*Claytonia virginica*) and chickweed (*Stellaria media*).

Wash and sort the greens and pick out stems, dead leaves, and insects. Trim off and discard fibrous stems. Set aside.

In a medium stock pot, heat the olive oil over medium heat. Add the onion and sauté until clear and slightly brown, about 5 minutes, then add the celery and garlic and sauté until the garlic starts to release its aroma, about 1 minute.

Add the broth, chickpeas, salt, and pepper. Bring to a simmer and cook for 10 minutes, until the celery is soft and translucent.

Add the washed and chopped greens and the thyme and rosemary and simmer gently for another 3 minutes. Remove from the heat and let the soup cool a bit.

Use an immersion blender to puree the soup until it is roughly blended. I like a chunkier puree, but prepare it as you see fit. If you do not have an immersion blender, let the soup cool considerably before blending it in small batches in a blender, to avoid having it explode upward and spurt out of the lid. Pour it back into the pot to heat through.

Serve with a dollop of sour cream or a garnish of wild greens.

NOTE: For dock leaves, nettle, or any other green that must be parboiled first, bring a large pot of water to boil. Plunge all the greens into the water for 1 minute. Strain in a colander in the sink, rinse with cold water, and squeeze out excess water. If you're sensitive to oxalates, you'll want to parboil all the greens first.

Sustainability

Miner's-lettuce is abundant and will regrow readily after snipping, so you can harvest freely. Siberian miner's lettuce grows less abundantly and in a more specific habitat, so the typical "harvest one-in-ten" foraging rule applies. Red miner's lettuce is also incredibly abundant in some areas, including in my yard, though I don't harvest more than 50 percent in order to let some go to seed and maintain the patch.

Cooking with Miner's Lettuce

Miner's-lettuce and red miner's lettuce are watery, delicate, and mild, and all the aboveground parts can be eaten raw and cooked. I like them best as salad greens as they have great texture.

Siberian miner's lettuce is noticeably tangier than miner's-lettuce and can also have a funny aftertaste (partially because of how many oxalates it contains), so I recommend including it with a mix of other greens in a salad.

If you are sensitive to oxalates, parboil Siberian miner's lettuce before use: Bring a large pot of water to boil over high heat. Reduce heat to medium and plunge the greens into the boiling water. Boil for 1 minute and strain in a colander in the sink. Cool, and squeeze out excess water, then use in the recipe.

> ### Cautions
>
> Like spinach, these species contain oxalates, which can irritate the kidneys and gastrointestinal tract when eaten in large quantities (see sidebar "What Are Oxalates?" in Part One). Miner's-lettuce and red miner's lettuce contain relatively low levels of oxalates (less than spinach), but Siberian miner's lettuce contains quite a bit more. So, it is important to consume Siberian miner's lettuce in moderation and consider parboiling the leaves first (see Cooking with Miner's Lettuce).

Mountain Ash

Sorbus sitchensis, S. scopulina, S. aucuparia
Rosaceae (rose family)

Though the berries of mountain ash are not a favorite of foragers due to their bitterness, they're worth mentioning simply because of their abundance in some areas. Mountain ash berries grow in clusters much like elderberries so it is easy to harvest a lot at a time. Most people make jams or chutneys with them, adding other ingredients and sugar to improve the flavor.

Three main species of mountain ash grow in the Pacific Northwest: Sitka mountain-ash (*Sorbus sitchensis*), western mountain-ash (*Sorbus scopulina*), and European mountain-ash (*Sorbus aucuparia*). The three species closely resemble each other: they all have a pinnate leaf (which has a central stem with several pairs of leaflets), five-petaled white flowers that form in a cluster, and red berries that resemble tiny apples. European mountain-ash, which is the only non-native of the three, is the easiest to pick out with its central trunk and upright growth pattern. This species tends to get much taller than the other two, which are more shrub-like.

Mountain ash bark resembles the bark of cherry trees, with its gray horizontal lines and small lenticels (oval-shaped dots in the bark). Lenticels are pores that help with gas exchange between the inner part of the tree and the air and can be found on many other trees, such as blue and red elderberry.

Historically, local Native groups did not eat these very often, as there were many other tastier berries to focus on.

Sitka mountain ash bearing pinkish-red fruit

Sitka mountain-ash
Sorbus sitchensis

Berries

Berry cluster

Flower cluster

Flower

European mountain-ash
Sorbus aucuparia

Berry cluster

Leaves

Berries

Where to Find It

Sitka mountain-ash and western mountain-ash favor similar habitats, which include open areas at mid- to high elevations. They thrive in post-avalanche terrain and talus fields, where there are fewer trees and plenty of sun. They often grow near mountain alder (*Alnus alnobetula*) and red elderberry (*Sambucus racemosa*).

European mountain-ash is found at lower elevations in open fields, forest edges, and meadows, where the soil is moist and disturbed, mostly in the western parts of our region, where it's wetter, but occasionally in moist areas east of the Cascades.

How to Harvest

Mountain ash berries ripen in the fall, generally in late August through September. The berries get sweeter after a frost, so try harvesting after the first frost in your area, which will vary depending on your location and elevation.

Harvest the clusters by snipping them off the tree into a bucket or basket. Leave some for wildlife. When you get them home, remove the berries from the stems and sort out the bad berries. Give them a good wash, and then either use them or freeze them.

Look-Alikes

Many trees and shrubs produce red berries like mountain ash (e.g., one-seed hawthorn, chokecherry, red elderberry), and some shrubs resemble it (serviceberry), but the pinnate leaves and clustered berries of mountain ash are very distinct. Red elderberry is perhaps the most objectively similar shrub, due to its pinnate leaves, but the berries are much smaller and the berry cluster is a different shape. Red elderberry clusters are cone-shaped (a.k.a. raceme), while mountain-ash berry clusters are dome-shaped (a.k.a. round-topped panicle).

TOP: Sitka mountain ash is shrubby with no central trunk, unlike European mountain ash.
BOTTOM: The base of mountain ash berries resemble apples, which are also in the rose family.

CLASSIC ROWANBERRY JELLY *Makes about 4½ cups (4 half pints plus ½ cup)*

In Europe, mountain-ash is called rowan. You can use any of the three mountain-ash species featured in this entry for this recipe. This jelly is perfect on buttered toast or served with game. The recipe comes from chef Alan Bergo, author of The Forager Chef's Book of Flora and creator of foragerchef.com—the largest culinary resource online for wild mushrooms. He was also a contestant on the Chefs vs. Wild reality-TV cooking competition on Hulu, and his foraging and cooking show Field, Forest, Feast won the James Beard Award in 2022. For the apples, Alan says, "You want apples that have a good amount of natural pectin here, so use green ones like Granny Smith or slightly unripe apples. For a 100 percent wild version, use crab apples."

- 2 pounds green apples, such as Granny Smith
- 1 pound rowanberries
- 4 cups water
- 1 tablespoon chopped fresh ginger (optional)
- 3 to 4 cups sugar
- 2 teaspoons fresh lemon juice, or ¼ teaspoon citric acid

Top photo: Alan Bergo, Bottom photo: Mathew Hintz

In a wide 3- to 4-quart pot, gently mash the rowanberries with a potato masher or fork.

Cut the apples into pieces and add them to the pot, including the skins and seeds.

Add the water and ginger and bring to a simmer over medium-high heat. Stir, turn the heat to low and cook uncovered for 20 minutes, stirring occasionally. Don't mash the apples.

Line a fine-mesh strainer with a double layer of cheesecloth or a jelly bag and set atop a large heatproof bowl. Carefully pour the mixture through the strainer and allow to drain for a few hours. Don't squeeze the liquid from the cheesecloth unless you're okay with cloudy jelly. Discard the spent apple-berry mix.

Put a small metal bowl, or similar, in the freezer for later.

Measure the reserved liquid and transfer it back to the pot; you should have 3 to 4 cups. Stir in 1 cup sugar for each cup of liquid and cook over high heat, stirring until the sugar is completely dissolved. Once the liquid reaches a boil, turn the heat to medium, and cook until the temperature starts to hover around 220 degrees F. Keep an eye on the liquid and lower the heat as needed to avoid overflowing. (Cleaning up jelly overflows is sticky and not fun.)

Pull the bowl from the freezer and pour a teaspoon of jelly into it. Once you can see a gentle wrinkle on the top when it cools, it's ready. Beat in the lemon juice or citric acid and pour the jelly into sterilized jars (see sidebar "How to Sterilize Jars"). Screw on lids and rings and allow to cool. The jars will naturally seal themselves.

If you have more than will fit in the jars, store that in the fridge and use right away. Store sealed jars in a cool, dark place for up to 2 years.

Cautions

Many species of mountain ash contain cyanogenic glycosides like chokecherry and other rose-family members do. These compounds can turn into the poison cyanide. Their presence is easy to detect as they smell and taste like almond extract. In general, the compounds are quickly metabolized and your body expels them, but care should be taken not to consume too much at one time.

Certain parts of the plant tend to contain more of the compounds, like the seeds and the bark. Also, more cyanogenic glycosides are made by trees growing at higher elevations, especially 3000 feet and above. These compounds are toxic only in large amounts, so don't let this deter you from enjoying some berry jelly on your toast. The real concern is eating large amounts of raw berries, leaves, or bark. The compounds are destroyed by heat, so cooking decreases them dramatically.

Sustainability

Be sure to leave some berries on the bush for wildlife. Mountain ash is an important winter forage for wildlife, as the berries remain on the bush into fall and early winter when many of the tastier berries have gone.

A native butterfly enjoying a Sitka mountain ash flower at Snoqualmie Pass

Cooking with Mountain Ash

Mountain ash berries should be cooked before eating. It's okay to eat a few berries raw (though they don't taste great), but they can be toxic in large amounts (see Cautions).

In Europe, where mountain ash is known as rowan, it's common to make a rowanberry jam or jelly, which is served with roast meat or game (see recipe). I have also seen rowanberry-and-grapefruit jam, rowanberry chutney, and rowanberries combined with other berries in jams and syrups. It's best to combine them with sugar, other fruits, and/or spices to improve their flavor.

Nettle

Urtica dioica
Urticaceae (nettle family)

Nettle, more formally called stinging nettle, is one of the most valuable plants in our region for both food and medicine. Nettle leaves are high in protein, have a wonderful flavor, and are quite versatile, able to be used in pesto, *saag*, quiche, ravioli, cake, and more. Nettle leaves are also used medicinally, mainly as a tea for hay fever. Nettle root is commonly used as a medicinal herb for genitourinary tract and prostate inflammation. Nettle seeds are used for energy and thyroid issues. All parts of the nettle are very nutritive and high in minerals.

Brushing up against nettle's stinging hairs will give you an itchy rash. The hairs are vial-like silicate structures that break and deposit a cocktail of concentrated acids on your skin, which burn through and cause a histamine reaction. For this reason, many people are afraid to eat nettle. However, it is easy to dismantle the stings, you need only parboil it, cook it, or even just crush the plant.

Though stinging nettle (*Urtica dioica*) is native to North America, some populations of nettle growing here are a subspecies derived from Europe, which technically means this plant is both native and non-native. This is also the case with yarrow (*Achillea millefolium*).

Before the introduction of cotton to the European market, nettle stem fibers were commonly used for textiles, including clothing and linens. There is evidence to suggest that nettle

LEFT: The stinging hairs of nettle are most potent in the early spring, so wear gloves when you harvest. **RIGHT:** Nettle seeds are a medicinal food rich in essential fatty acids.

fibers have been used for thousands of years by traditional cultures in countries like Nepal, China, India, North America, and Russia.

Another species of nettle, called small nettle or dwarf nettle (*Urtica urens*), also grows sparsely in our region. I admit I have never seen it growing in the wild here, so I haven't included it in this entry.

Where to Find It

Nettles grow in lowland areas all over the Pacific Northwest, on both sides of the Cascades, as long as there is water nearby. Nettles like thick leaf duff and moist soil. They will grow near streams, in the woods, in compost piles, and especially love growing among the dead leaves under bigleaf maple trees. I find that they grow much more rarely in the higher elevations, and they also do not prefer the drier, desert, or prairie ecosystems of the region.

How to Harvest

The spring shoots of nettle are the best for eating and can be harvested from February to April. Before harvesting, check for aphids, which commonly infest nettle patches. If one plant has aphids, the rest in the patch may also.

Harvest nettle leaves before they flower because as they get older, they develop cystoliths, crystalline structures that can damage your urinary tract and kidneys if consumed in too large an amount. My teacher advised us to stop harvesting the plants for food after they grew taller than our knees.

When harvesting the shoots, I use thick gloves and scissors. Check your gloves for holes before using, and note that gloves

TOP: An abundant patch of spring nettles at the perfect stage for harvest **BOTTOM:** Nettle's needle-like, silicate hairs break upon contact and deposit a mix of irritating acids on the skin, causing a localised reaction.

NETTLE FRITTATA

Makes 4 to 6 servings

This yummy breakfast frittata can be altered to your taste and to use what you have around. You can also use many of the other wild greens in this book in addition to nettles, such as hairy cat's ear, dandelion, lambsquarters, watercress, and miner's lettuce. To prevent yourself from getting stung, wear gloves or use tongs to hold the nettles as you chop the leaves and young stems. Remove any stems that may be too thick.

1 to 2 tablespoons extra-virgin olive oil
½ yellow onion, chopped
⅓ cup roughly chopped salami, bacon, or other cured meat
1 yellow potato, sliced
2 carrots, diced
8 eggs
½ cup milk
2 to 3 cups chopped nettles
¾ teaspoon salt
Pinch of pepper
1 cup grated cheddar cheese
Chopped green onions, to top

Preheat the oven to 350 degrees F.

Heat the olive oil in a large cast-iron or oven-safe pan over medium heat. Add the onion and sauté until clear, about 5 minutes, then add the meat. Keep cooking until browned. Add the potato and carrot. Cover and cook for 10 to 15 minutes, stirring every few minutes to prevent burning, until the vegetables are fully cooked.

Meanwhile, add the eggs and milk to a medium bowl and whisk until well combined. Set aside.

Add the chopped nettles to the pan and cover to cook for 1 to 2 minutes, stirring once. Once nettles have reduced in size, stir in the salt and pepper, remove from the heat, pour the egg mixture over, and sprinkle the grated cheese on top.

Put the pan in the oven and cook for 18 to 22 minutes. To test if it's cooked through, jostle the pan and see if the center jiggles. If it does, it needs more time.

Slice and serve hot with green onions on the top.

---

with fabric on the top will not protect the top of your hands from stings.

Grab a single shoot with a gloved hand and snip it with your scissors, leaving at least two sets of leaves below the snip so the plant can keep growing. Harvest into a large paper grocery bag (check the bag for holes; you don't want to get stung through an unknown hole!).

Nettle seeds can be harvested in June and July, when they are green and shiny. Remove them like bunches of grapes, harvesting them into a well-sealed container or a ziplock bag (you don't want them leaking through holes in a basket, trust me). Though the seeds themselves do not sting, the stems that they grow on do. Dry them away from sunlight by spreading them out on a piece of thick paper or a very tightly woven basket.

Look-Alikes

It would be easy to mistake Cooley's hedge nettle (*Stachys cooleyae*) for stinging nettle before they flower. They have a similar habitat and sometimes grow side by side. If it stings, it is obviously stinging nettle, but as some may not be willing to use this uncomfortable identification technique, let's dig deeper.

First, hedge nettle leaves have thick, woolly hair all over their leaves, making them soft to the touch. Nettle's hairs are much more dispersed. Second, hedge nettle has one prominent central vein, whereas stinging nettle has three prominent veins that fork from the leaf stem. Third, hedge nettle has a very strange smell (earning it the nickname "stinky stachys"), which thankfully, stinging nettle does not share. When in flower, they are easy to tell apart: hedge nettle has tubular magenta flowers that grow in a spike at the top of the plant, and nettle has small white flowers that emerge from all leaf nodes.

Many people say that dead-nettle (*Lamium purpureum*) is a look-alike, though dead-nettle is much smaller and the leaves are a very different shape than nettle.

Sustainability

Even though nettle is common, it can still be overharvested. It is important to practice the "harvest one-in-ten" rule of foraging for this plant. Nettle is an important cold-weather habitat for aphids, which are an important part of the food chain. If they don't have a place to live in the colder months, their numbers suffer, which affects the whole food chain. I am always deeply awed by the small and unexpected ways that plants support our complex ecosystems. It is so important for us to have a mind for stewardship and ethics in our practice of foraging.

Grow Your Own

Nettle will thrive when introduced to the right spot in your garden. The leaf duff is the most important part, as nettle spreads through underground rhizomes. If you don't want a stinging plant running rampant in your garden, prepare a large barrel or bed with rich compost and a thick layer of dead leaves on the top. Transplant several spring nettles or a store-bought plant into it.

Cooking with Nettle

To prepare the nettles for cooking, wash and pick through the nettles in a large colander. Use gloves or tongs to avoid touching them and pick out any seeds and leaf duff. If the nettles were harvested in their later stages when the stem is more fibrous, you will also want to remove the leaves from the thick stems. If they were harvested when very small, you can use the whole thing.

I parboil my nettles for most purposes. To do this, bring a large pot of water to boil. In batches, use tongs to plunge the raw nettles into the boiling water, cooking for 1 minute, then

Cautions

The nettle plant is covered in stinging hairs that cause an itchy and sometimes painful skin rash.

Nettle allergies seem to be quite common. Several people I have met break out in hives when eating it. If that happens to you, avoid it. I have heard that plants harvested when older may be more likely to trigger reactions, and I know from my time being a bulk-herb buyer that many herbal distributors sell nettle harvested in seed and flower stages.

Older nettle shoots develop crystalline structures called cystoliths that can damage your urinary tract and kidneys if consumed in too large an amount, so be sure to harvest shoots before they flower (see How to Harvest).

Do not eat too many nettle seeds, as they can be overstimulating to the nervous system.

remove them with the tongs into a metal strainer in the sink. After parboiling all the nettles desired, rinse them with cold water. You can either use them directly in your dish or squeeze the water out of them, roll them into balls, and freeze to be used later.

Nettles can be used in much the same way spinach is used, though their taste is richer and more mineral. My personal favorite is making a nettle frittata (see recipe); I am also partial to nettle pesto. You can use nettle in soups, meatballs, and even cake.

You can even make beer with nettle leaves, which is actually quite delicious, and very nutritious, of course.

Nettle seeds are also edible, though only limited quantities should be consumed in a day (no more than 2 tablespoons per day is the word on this). You can dry them and make a tea or nettle-seed salt. Nettle seeds are high in essential fatty acids and are also used to boost the thyroid gland.

Though many people discard them because of their texture, the young stems of nettle are also edible and can even be eaten by themselves. One way to prepare just the stems is to chop them finely and sauté them in olive oil with garlic and salt. Nettle stems contain more fiber than the leaves and more silica, which helps in the uptake of calcium. My herbalism teacher, Cascade Anderson Geller, would use nettle stems in her bone broths.

TOP: If folded up properly, so only the upper side of the leaf is presented, nettle leaves can be eaten raw. However, I have stung my tongue doing this, so proceed with caution.
BOTTOM: Nettle flowers emerge where the leaf stems meet the main stem, indicating it's time to stop harvesting them for food.

It is best not to eat nettles raw. Some people use raw nettles in pesto and smoothies as breaking them down in this way eliminates the sting, but I find raw nettles make my throat feel strange.

Oregon Grape

Mahonia aquifolium, M. nervosa, M. repens
Berberidaceae (barberry family)

Chances are, no matter where you live in the Pacific Northwest, there is a species of Oregon grape near you. It is well known for its medicinal bark, but it also produces edible, tart, blue-purple berries that are incredibly high in vitamin C. Some people really love the slap-in-the-face sour flavor of the berries raw, but most make Oregon grape jelly or other sweetened preparations.

Three species of Oregon grape grow in the Pacific Northwest: tall Oregon grape (*Mahonia aquifolium*), low Oregon grape (*Mahonia nervosa*), and creeping Oregon grape (*Mahonia repens*). You may see some cultivated varieties around as well, which share the yellow flowers and spiky pinnate leaves. The berries of all of these are equally edible, with slight differences in flavor.

Oregon grape bark contains berberine and other antimicrobial compounds. It is used as an herbal remedy for various bactrcial and fungal infections, usually as a tea or tincture.

TOP: Low Oregon grape flower spikes
BOTTOM: Tall Oregon grape flower spikes

Where to Find It

Each of the three species have different habitat preferences, but there are some areas where all three grow.

Tall Oregon grape (*Mahonia aquifolium*) is the largest of the three species, reaching heights of 10 to 15 feet, and thus produces the most berries. It is very drought tolerant and grows abundantly in gravel, prairies, and open fields. It is also frequently used in landscaping and native plant restoration projects because of its resilience, so you may find some growing

in your neighborhood park, or even in the grocery-store parking lot.

Low Oregon grape (*Mahonia nervosa*) is a forest-understory plant. Each plant produces one clump of berries, and plants in very shady areas of the forest may not produce at all, so these can be a bit harder to harvest. Look for larger patches near the edge of the woods or in an open area in the canopy.

Creeping Oregon grape (*Mahonia repens*) is very common in the dry eastern parts of our region. It grows in sunny, open woods and will thrive in much drier areas than the other two species. It is the smallest of the three species and is harder to find, so the berries can be hard to collect. I suggest that you not

Low Oregon grape
Mahonia nervosa

Inflorescence

Pinnately compound leaves

Low habit

Berries

harvest creeping Oregon grape berries and stick to the other species of Oregon grape.

How to Harvest

Harvest berries soon after ripening, in July and August, as birds and bugs will get into them. The berries of all Oregon grape species grow on stems much like grapes, hence the name. You can pluck whole clusters by seizing the stem and pulling, which is much faster and less messy than picking berries individually. If the stems do not readily come off, use scissors or garden clippers to snip them off into your bag or basket.

I find the berries from tall Oregon grape to be the most delicious, making it an obvious first choice for harvest. That said, low Oregon grape can sometimes produce a prolific crop, if you can find a large patch that has good exposure to sunlight.

TOP: Low Oregon grape laden with ripe berries, growing in its preferred habitat in a forest understory
BOTTOM: Tall Oregon grape with ample berries, growing in a garden

Look-Alikes

Holly (*Ilex aquifolium*) is often confused with Oregon grape because the leaves have a very similar shape. Thankfully, holly berries are red, so it is unlikely you would mistakenly harvest their slightly toxic berries. Another good way to tell them apart is the leaf arrangement: holly has an alternate-leaf arrangement, and Oregon grape has a pinnate-leaf arrangement (which means pairs of leaves will be right next to each other on the stem).

Sustainability

As with other berries, the only sustainability concern here is to be sure to leave some for the birds. This plant relies on birds to disperse its seeds.

OREGON GRAPE OXYMEL

Makes about 1 cup

The large amount of vitamin C in Oregon grape berries is what makes them so sour, but unfortunately, cooking destroys a significant amount of the vitamin C in foods. An oxymel—a mixture of vinegar and honey often infused with herbs and berries—is a great preparation to fully capture it. The vinegar helps soften and extract the berry goodness without cooking, and the honey and vinegar help to preserve it. Because of the acid, use a plastic top on the jar rather than metal. I buy plastic mason jar tops with silicone rings that last years and seal well. Use the oxymel in mocktails and sodas or take it by the spoonful.

½ cup honey
½ cup apple cider vinegar
1 cup Oregon grape berries, washed and sorted

Add the honey and vinegar to a glass bowl or measuring cup and mix well with a spoon until dissolved. This may take a while, as honey is slow to dissolve.

Put the berries in a jar and squash them with a spoon or large pestle. Pour the honey and vinegar mixture over the berries until the liquid is about a half inch below the rim of the jar. Cover it with the plastic lid and give it a good shake, then label it well with the date and contents.

Store in a cool, dark place for 2 to 3 weeks, until the liquid is dark purple, shaking it a few times. Strain the liquid through cheesecloth, squeezing well. Compost the strained berries and keep the oxymel in a bottle in the fridge. Some oxymels made with dried berries or herbs are shelf stable, but because of the large amount of water introduced by the fresh berries, this oxymel isn't necessarily shelf stable. It will keep for a year or more in the fridge.

Grow Your Own

Of the three native Oregon grape species, the best to grow in your yard is tall Oregon grape. It tolerates the most varied habitats and is drought tolerant. It will do best in well-drained soil in full sun. Potted plants should be available at most native plant nurseries, but you can also grow it from seed or propagate it with cuttings.

If you have a forested yard shaded with Douglas-firs, then low Oregon grape might be a good choice for you. Creeping Oregon

LEFT: Tall Oregon grape isn't so tall when it grows in a harsh mountain environment. **RIGHT:** The emerging leaves of all Oregon grape species are edible, and a little tart.

grape is a good choice for anyone who lives east of the Cascades and has a gravelly, dry yard.

Cooking with Oregon Grape

Oregon grape berries are so sour they literally make your entire face pucker if you eat them raw. This is because they contain loads of vitamin C. They also have large seeds in them, so they are not eaten raw or unprocessed. Generally, they are cooked or infused, seeds removed, and sugar added.

Oregon grape jelly is the most popular preparation to make with the berries. See my book *Medicinal Plants of the Pacific Northwest* for a recipe.

Pineapple Weed

Matricaria discoidea
Asteraceae (sunflower family)

This plant is a close relative of chamomile, showing many similar traits, including the flavor, except that pineapple weed has a fruity, pineapple-like overtone that is delicious. Because of its fibrous texture, it's more of a flavoring plant than an edible plant, but I love it so much I had to include it here.

There is some debate over whether pineapple weed is native to the Pacific Northwest or not. The consensus seems to be that it is indeed native to the Pacific Northwest, but introduced and weedy in other areas. It does grow like a weed, and alongside many weeds like plantain (*Plantago* spp.) and knapweed (*Centaurea* spp.), so I can see where the confusion comes from.

TOP: Pineapple weed loves compacted gravel, and lush patches can often be found on pathways, driveways, and gravel roads. **BOTTOM:** Pineapple weed looks a lot like its close relative chamomile, except it lacks the white ray flowers surrounding the yellow center.

Flower | Leaf | Whole plant in flower

Where to Find It

Pineapple weed loves gravel and compacted soils in general, and it is a bit of a specialist in that regard. You will most often find it in gravel driveways, gravel roads, on paved roadsides, and along hiking trails and waste lots. Basically, places where you are likely to drive in it or step on it. You will occasionally find it growing in softer soils, but I haven't seen that much.

How to Harvest

Pineapple weed is best harvested between April and June, while it is in flower. Note that the flowers don't have petals, per se, so it can be a bit hard to tell. The best way to tell if it's ready for harvest is to crush a bit in your fingers and smell it. If it smells fragrant, pungent, or delicious to you, it will make great tea or flavoring. Snip off the top of the plant with scissors, leaving a leaf or two on the bottom so the same plant can continue to grow.

Once the flower heads have gone to seed, the plant turns brown and gets much less aromatic, and the season is over.

DRIED PINEAPPLE WEED TEA *Makes about 10 cups*

This chamomile-like tea is fruity, aromatic, and slightly sour. You will need to dry the pineapple weed for the best tea results. In general, dried plants make for better tea because the hot water can penetrate the plant material more effectively, allowing for better extraction. However, if you want to make it from fresh plant material, just add a bit more material to get the flavor you want.

2 cups fresh pineapple weed

To dry the pineapple weed, spread it out on a flat basket (make sure it's made of natural material) or a flattened paper bag, so there is as little plant material touching as possible. Leave it somewhere dry and away from direct sunlight for 1 to 2 weeks, flipping over the sprigs occasionally to ensure even drying. Leave out until the plant crumbles easily in your fingers; the timing will vary depending on the temperature and humidity in your house.

Store the fully dried pineapple weed in a glass jar, resealable plastic bag, or paper bag. I have had pineapple weed mold when put too early into a jar because the plant still had a bit of moisture in it. You can avoid that by storing it in a paper bag. Some people store the plant pieces whole; others like to cut or break it up into smaller pieces for easier steeping.

To make a cup of tea, use about 2 tablespoons of dried pineapple weed for one mug of tea. Put the plant material into whatever tea infuser you have. I recommend the metal infusers that nest in the cup, as pictured. Pour 8 ounces hot water into the mug and cover. Let steep for 5 to 10 minutes, strain, and drink. It tastes great with honey too!

Look-Alikes

Before pineapple weed's flowers emerge, its lacy leaves look similar to several other plants.. Yarrow (*Achillea millefolium*) has basal leaves that are nearly identical to pineapple weed, except that they are much longer. Yarrow also has a peppery scent that is different than the sweet, fruit scent of pineapple weed. False chamomile (*Tripleurospermum inodorum*) is a weedy plant in our region that looks very similar to chamomile, has leaves that are much more wiry and fuzzy-looking. Unfortunately, false chamomile is not scented like chamomile and thus doesn't have the same culinary and medicinal uses.

Sustainability

The idea of sustainability is an interesting quandary for a plant that seems weedy but is actually native. I always fall back on this rule of thumb: don't harvest more than 10 percent of a given patch. It's important to let some of the plants go to seed and propagate themselves to ensure the patch continues to thrive. You could even help your patch out by sprinkling the seeds around in mid- to late summer when the seeds are ripe, or establish a new patch by bringing some seed home to a gravelly or compacted area.

Cooking with Pineapple Weed

The strange texture of the flowers and fibrousness of the stems makes me hesitant to advise you to consume the plant itself, so I recommend extracting the flavor instead. You can boil pineapple weed in water or milk or steep it in hot water, syrup, or milk. I love drinking pineapple weed tea (see recipe), which has similar digestive and calming properties to chamomile. You can also use it to flavor jams, syrups, and other flavor-filled things. A friend of mine made strawberry and pineapple weed jam once that was just divine!

As with any aromatic plant, overcooking it can ruin the delicious flavor you're going for, as the aromatic flavor molecules are heat sensitive. I recommend covering the pot when boiling or doing a covered hot infusion (see recipe for instructions).

Purslane

Portulaca oleracea
Portulacaceae (purslane family)

Purslane is one of the few succulent wild edibles in our region and is prized for being very nutritious. Its range extends across North America, South America, Europe, Africa, and the Middle East, and it is eaten in most of those places. It has a pleasing snap and bright flavor when raw, making it a wild food staple. It's a real shame that most people think it's a weed and poison it or pull it out of their yards—if only they knew!

The current belief is that it was introduced to North America from Europe, but there are arguments suggesting it could have existed in North America before European colonization.

Where to Find It

Purslane loves sidewalk cracks, though that is not where you would want to harvest for eating. In fact, it can be difficult to find it growing somewhere other than in a crack in the pavement. I find the best purslane for eating growing in vegetable gardens where the soil is disturbed, soft, rich, and well moistened. It also loves gravel, though when growing in drier habitats, its leaves are much smaller and sometimes even red, making it harder to identify and not as tasty.

The yellow flowers of purslane emerge in mid-summer.

You could try asking local organic farms if you can harvest purslane from their fields. You can also sometimes find purslane sold by the bunch at farmers' markets.

How to Harvest

Harvest purslane in May, June, and July, before it flowers, as its stems are not fibrous at that stage of growth and can be eaten along with

Whole plant

Flowers

Leaf back

Flower

Look-Alike Spurge

the leaves. Use scissors or your fingers to snip off the leafy tips of the long tendrils of the plant.

Avoid harvesting in places that could have been sprayed with herbicides. I have seen neighbors spray the purslane growing in their curbs with herbicides, and I also know many cities use herbicides to kill weeds.

Look-Alikes

Ridge-seed spurge (*Euphorbia glyptosperma*) is perhaps one of the closest look-alikes and often grows alongside purslane. However, purslane leaves are succulent, while ridge-seed spurge

The black seeds of purslane form in capsules.

leaves are flat and include a colored marking in the middle. On top of that, ridge-seed spurge leaks milky white sap when cut, whereas purslane leaks clear when cut, like aloe.

Prostrate knotweed (*Polygonum aviculare*) also looks somewhat similar but lacks the succulent leaves of purslane. Another way to tell them apart is that prostrate knotweed has a membranous protective sheath attached at the spot where the leaf stem meets the main stem. This sheath is called an ocrea and is a unique characteristic of the buckwheat family to which prostrate knotweed belongs.

Sustainability

Purslane is a common weed that is often removed by gardeners and city landscapers, so harvest to your heart's content.

GREEK SALAD WITH PURSLANE

Makes 4 to 6 servings

Mediterranean cultures make good use of this humble wild vegetable. In Greece, locals add purslane raw to salads, such as the following one, or they cook it with olive oil, garlic, salt, and lemon juice to eat by itself or to add to stews. In Turkey I had delicious pickled purslane with soft cheese and bread.

You can use both the leaves and young stems for this salad, but omit the stems if they are too fibrous. The salad could also be made with chickweed and miner's lettuce if it's too early for purslane.

1 block of feta cheese (7 to 10 ounces)
1 cup grape tomatoes
1 cup chopped purslane leaves and stems
¼ of a red onion, finely chopped
2 cloves garlic, finely minced
3 to 4 sprigs fresh oregano, chopped
3 tablespoons extra-virgin olive oil
Salt and pepper, to taste
½ a lemon, squeezed over the top (optional)

Break up the feta cheese into chunks with a fork and put into a salad bowl.
Add the tomatoes, purslane, onion, garlic, oregano, and olive oil and season with salt and pepper. Toss together to coat.
Squeeze lemon over the top, if using, and serve fresh.

Grow Your Own

Purslane is very easy to grow in your garden—it grows in sidewalk cracks after all. Collect seeds from wild plants or order them online and scatter them in a forgotten corner of your garden.

Cooking with Purslane

Purslane is a well-loved vegetable in many areas of Europe, especially the Mediterranean. You can find it in Greek salads, and I even once encountered delicious pickled purslane in Turkey. It can be eaten raw, cooked, or pickled.

Purslane growing in one of its favorite habitats: a sidewalk crack (Photo: iNaturalist)

Some people don't care for the texture of purslane, which has a sliminess to it, akin to okra. For this reason, add only a limited amount in a salad when eating it raw. If you do cook it, it is best to cook it into soups rather than in something like a stir-fry, where the mucilaginous quality will dominate more.

Purslane could be classified as a superfood because of its nutrient profile, which includes a large amount of alpha-linolenic acid, an essential fatty acid. It is rare to find essential fatty acids in leafy greens. It also contains large amounts of vitamins C and E.

Wrap extra purslane in a paper towel and store in a sealed container or plastic bag in the fridge for 3 to 5 days. It's convenient that this plant can last a little longer in the fridge than other greens because it is a succulent. Discard when it starts to turn black or when it gets too droopy.

Rose

Rosa gymnocarpa, R. nutkana, R. rugosa
Rosaceae (rose family)

The enchanting aroma of wild rose petals can add floral depth to beverages and desserts. Roses are associated with romance and the heart and are considered by some to be an aphrodisiac. The fruit of rose, which develops from the flower after pollination, is called a hip. Rose hips tend to be very sour and are high in vitamin C and antioxidants. Rose-hip tea is commonly consumed in Eastern Europe for vitality and beauty.

Of the approximately eight species of rose that grow in the Pacific Northwest, there are a few I recommend seeking out for harvest.

Nootka rose is one of the most strongly scented of our local roses and definitely worth your time to harvest. In areas of the Puget Sound, San Juan Islands, and Gulf Islands, Nootka rose (*Rosa nutkana*) dominates roadsides and open fields, growing in epic tangles of thorny canes.

Rugosa rose (*Rosa rugosa*) is non-native but commonly used in landscaping and naturalized in some places in the Puget Sound area. It is the easiest to harvest, has the largest and most numerous petals per flower, and has the largest and juiciest hips. This is typically the species I work with.

The flowers of non-native dog rose (*Rosa canina*) don't have a strong scent or taste, but its hips tend to be abundant, easy to

LEFT: A bumblebee pollinates a Nootka rose flower at a park in West Seattle
RIGHT: Nootka rose hips in November in Victoria, BC

harvest, and persist into early winter. They are some of the hardest rose hips you'll come across and the best for using in flower arrangements and decorations. The flesh won't soften into a paste like rugosa rose hips, but they will make a nice tea or jelly.

Other local species of rose include cluster rose (*Rosa pisocarpa*), rambler rose (*Rosa multiflora*), pearhip rose (*Rosa woodsii*), sweetbrier rose (*Rosa rubiginosa*), and bald-hip rose (*Rosa gymnocarpa*). Bald-hip rose is particularly common where I live, on the eastern slope of the Cascades, but the flowers and fruits are small and sparse, so I don't typically harvest it. The flowers smell wonderful, though, and are worth a sniff if you pass by it on the trail.

Bald-hip rose hips look strange without the star-shaped sepals that other rose hips have.

All rose hips and rose petals are edible, though not all are equally delicious and easy to harvest or work with. You will need to test out your local roses to see what your favorites are. Many cultivated species of rose are a joy to cook with as well, such as Damask rose (*Rosa damascena*).

Where to Find It

Nootka rose is the most widely distributed of the three roses mentioned here. It does prefer a slightly drier climate, which means it thrives in the Puget Sound rain shadow, as well as some places east of the Cascades. It can be found in coastal ecosystems all the way up into the mountains on both sides of the Cascades. Look for it in open areas with rocky soils.

Rugosa rose can mostly be found in parks, landscaping, and gardens.

Dog rose is a bit less common than the others. It can often be found in open grassy meadows and on roadsides.

Bald-hip rose prefers the rocky, drier soils of the Puget Sound, San Juans, and eastern slope of the Cascades.

How to Harvest

Rose petals can be harvested when they bloom in the late spring. May is typically the best time to harvest rose petals, though some bushes may bloom into June and July. The best flowers

Rugosa rose
Rosa rugosa

Hip

Leaves

Bracts at the base of the leaf stem are found on all species of rose

Flower and leaves

are the most aromatic ones, usually the ones just opening and calling in the pollinators. Pull the petals off the flower, leaving the future rose hip below intact. Rose petals can be stored in the fridge for up to 3 days, though keep in mind that they will be the most aromatic when you first pick them, so use quickly.

Bees absolutely love rose flowers, so be sure to check each flower before you pick, to avoid getting stung. I have heard that if you leave one petal on the flower when harvesting, bees can still find the flower and pollinate it.

LEFT: Leaving one petal per flower while harvesting can help bees still find and pollinate the flowers. **RIGHT:** Harvesting the oblong, hard hips of dog rose, a non-native rose that is common in some parks.

Rose hips are harvested in the fall. Rugosa rose hips start ripening first, in August or September. Nootka rose hips and others often ripen later in October, or even November. Rose hips that undergo a frost will be the sweetest, though the longer you leave them on the vine the more bugs get into them, so there is a balance to strike.

Look-Alikes

There are several other local species of rose and several cultivated species of roses that are used in landscaping. All rose species are equally usable but not all are equally tasty, so follow your nose and your taste buds. Avoid using roses from store-bought floral arrangements, as chemicals are used pretty heavily on those.

Sustainability

Both rugosa rose and Nootka rose are rather abundant. Leave some flowers for the bees, and I think it polite to consider that

---

ROSE-PETAL JAM *Makes four 4-ounce jars*

Rose-petal jam, or rose confit, is a decadent treat that speaks of past eras. This version is more of a silky syrup than a firm jam, with luscious bits of petals. Enjoy it on toast, ice cream, vanilla cheesecake, or with goat cheese. This recipe is from Tonia Schemmel of Feasting at Home, a website that offers seasonal, mostly vegetarian, and very healthy recipes and sometimes features foraged ingredients in recipes. For this recipe, you'll need about 2 cups of lightly packed, fresh rose petals (or what would be a perfectly comfy fairy bed)—preferably collected at least 50 feet from roads and from a pesticide-free area—or ⅔ cup dried rose petals.

1½ cups filtered water
2 ounces wild rose petals (2 cups lightly packed, fresh petals or ⅔ cup dried)
2 cups organic cane sugar, divided
3 tablespoons fresh lemon juice
1 teaspoon pectin

Place the water and rose petals in a medium saucepan. Bring to a gentle simmer for 10 minutes, uncovered.

people walking by in a park may want to enjoy some of the flowers too. Thankfully, both of these species bloom continuously, so more will likely bloom after your harvest. Harvest dog rose hips to your heart's content as the plants are thorny and sprawling, crowding out natives in some areas. In my experience, bald-hip rose has such tiny, scarce blooms and such tiny little hips that I generally don't harvest it except to taste a single hip or smell an individual flower.

Grow Your Own

If you would like to plant a native rose in your yard, Nootka rose is a great choice. Not only is it tolerant of most climates in our region, but its flowers are deliciously aromatic. Bald-hip rose is also a great option for those living in drier areas east of the Cascades.

Though not native, rugosa rose is a great choice for someone looking for a fast-growing and hardy rose. Its petals are abundant, aromatic, and not too astringent. Rugosa rose is a good choice for folks who are looking for a hedge plant, as it has thicker greenery than other rose species and grows quickly.

Add 1¾ cups of sugar to the simmering petals. Stir to dissolve the sugar crystals.

Add the lemon juice and observe the gorgeous vibrant color that emerges. Simmer for 10 minutes over low heat.

In a small bowl, combine the remaining ¼ cup sugar and pectin. While stirring the jam in the saucepan, sprinkle in the pectin-sugar mixture a little at a time to ensure the pectin incorporates without clumping.

Simmer gently for 20 more minutes. The mixture may seem quite loose for jam, but it will firm up a bit as it sets.

Pour it into sterilized jam jars (see sidebar "How to Sterilize Jars"), and let the jars cool to room temperature. Once cooled, seal them and store in the fridge for up to 2 months or in the freezer for up to a year.

All photos: Sylvia Fountaine

You might also consider the heavily scented cultivated species Damask rose, which is the species bred for perfumes and grown in Europe and the Middle East for centuries.

Cooking with Rose

Not all varieties and species of rose lend themselves to cooking. Some rose petals are less aromatic or more astringent, making them less desirable in recipes. And the hips of ornamental rose varieties, like the ones you buy at a flower shop on Valentine's Day, are so hard and sour that you would not want to cook with them. All in all, rugosa rosa and Nootka rose have both aromatic flowers and fairly tasty hips, which is why I seek them out when foraging. Avoid dog rose, whose flowers are bland and astringent.

The delicate floral flavor of rose petals is actually quite challenging to capture. Not only is the rose aroma sensitive to heat, but the petals also have a bitter, astringent flavor that can leach out and spoil the delicate flavor. For this reason, it is common for chefs to use rose water, which is a distillation of rose that contains water and the aromatics. Also known as rose hydrosol, rose water is made using a similar type of still as distilled alcohol. Rose petals and water are heated, and the steam is captured and condensed into a liquid. This is also the initial step in making a steam-distilled essential oil. This process can be done at home using a crude homemade still, though it is not as efficient as using a commercially made still. You can also purchase rose water, but note that modern store-bought rose water often contains artificial rose flavoring.

Because the aromatics of rose are fat soluble, one simple trick is to infuse it into milk or cream. A cold or slightly warm infusion is the best way to ensure that the aromatics are captured

> ### Cautions
>
> The seed hairs inside rose hips can cause gastrointestinal (GI) irritation. See Cooking with Rose for instructions on how to properly remove the fibers.

without the astringent compounds. To do this, fill a jar with fresh rose petals and then pour the milk or cream over it. Put it in the fridge and leave it overnight. Strain it well in the morning through several layers of cheesecloth. The milk can be used in various beverages or desserts, including ice cream, whipped cream, hot chocolate, and tea. Just be sure not to heat it too much or the aromatics may evaporate. If you want a very strong flavor, you can repeat the infusion process with a new batch of fresh rose petals. Rose makes a very nice flavoring in dishes like crème brûlée and custard. I use this milk-infusion technique with other delicate aromatic flavors, such as Douglas-fir tips.

Another great way to harness the rose flavor without the astringency is to make a rose-petal-infused honey. Similar to the preceding method, simply pour honey over a jar packed full of fresh rose petals and let infuse for 12 to 24 hours. Taste the honey to see if it's infused to your liking, then pour the now thinner honey through a fine-mesh strainer, letting it drip for a while. You can also use dried rose petals for this, but you will need to heat the honey by putting the jar into a hot-water bath for 3 to 4 hours. For this I use a slow cooker on the lowest setting (warm or low).

Rose petals can also be made into jam; the sugar helps cut the astringency of the petals (see recipe).

Rose hips are very high in vitamin C and bioflavonoids (a type of antioxidant) and have a lovely sour, fruity flavor that is best with a little sweetener. Combine them with other fruits, like strawberry, hawthorn, apple, or pomegranate for a complex taste. You can make rose-hip jelly, rose-hip fermented soda, rose-hip kombucha, rose-hip iced tea, or even rose-hip ketchup. I also put some rose hips in my herbal chai recipe to add depth to the flavor—something I learned while I was formulating teas for Rainbow Natural Remedies in my youth.

Rose hips contain hairs around the seeds that can irritate the GI tract and thus are best scooped out and discarded. To do this, first cut each hip in half. Then use a tiny spoon or the blunt end of a butter knife to scrape out the seeds and hairs. Finally, soak them in water; the remaining hairs should rise to the top. It is difficult to remove all the hairs, but do the best you can. If making jam or tea, you can also strain out the hairs using cheesecloth or a very-fine-mesh strainer.

Salal

Gaultheria shallon
Ericaceae (heath family)

Salal berries grow in the moist forests west of the Cascades. They are related to blueberries and have a very similar taste and nutrient profile. Interestingly, they are also closely related to wintergreen (*Gaultheria procumbens*). Though salal berries and wintergreen berries don't taste much alike, their shape is very similar, with a large star cut into the base of the berry.

Salal flowers are white and urn shaped, characteristic of the heath family. They bloom from May through June (perhaps earlier or later depending on elevation and how far north or south you are in the region).

Because salal leaves are evergreen and stay fresh long after cutting, salal leaf sprays are collected commercially and shipped all around the world to use in floral arrangements. This multimillion dollar industry is notorious for underpaying their collectors and for illegal collection and overharvest. Compared to people harvesting small amounts for personal use, these commercial wild-harvesting operations have a much larger impact on plant populations. It is important to be aware of other pressures present for the

TOP: A nice, juicy crop of salal berries **BOTTOM:** Ripe salal berries overlooking the Pacific Ocean in Oregon

plants we harvest from. Thankfully, collecting the berries has a relatively low impact.

Of the other native species in the same genus (*Gaultheria*), the tiny western teaberry (*Gaultheria ovatifolia*) is the most abundant. The leaves of western teaberry closely resemble salal in their shape and arrangement, but the plant is only 3 to 5 inches tall! Its red berries are quite tasty, though hard to find. I see them most often when hiking at higher elevations on the western slope of the Cascades. Look for the same star pattern at the base of the berry.

Where to Find It

Salal is found west of the Cascades, especially in the moist forests of the Pacific coast. It can be found growing all over the bluffs and headlands of the Pacific Ocean. When growing further inland, it is a forest-understory plant, growing in acidic, conifer-dominant forests with Sitka spruce (*Picea sitchensis*), western red cedar (*Thuja plicata*), hemlock (*Tsuga heterophylla*), Douglas-fir (*Pseudotsuga menziesii*), and redwoods. Other understory plants that grow alongside it are evergreen huckleberry (*Vaccinium ovatum*), red huckleberry (*Vaccinium parvifolium*), oceanspray (*Holodiscus discolor*), beaked hazelnut (*Corylus cornuta*), sword fern (*Polystichum munitum*), and vine maple (*Acer circinatum*).

TOP: Salal growing at a local park, planted as part of restoration project
BOTTOM: Salal's white, urn-shaped flowers show it's in the blueberry family.

As with other berries, the best salal berries are often found where the bush has access to sun and good moisture. Bushes that grow in dense forests bear few fruits. After tree thinning or removal, such as on a timber site, salal often thrives and bears a lot of fruit. However, before harvesting salal berries from a recent clear-cut, check with the land manager about herbicide applications as they are sometimes used on salal to prevent it from outcompeting young tree seedlings.

How to Harvest

Salal berries begin to ripen in mid-July and continue through to mid-September. They are very abundant in some areas and often overlooked.

Salal berries are difficult to remove from the stems without squishing them, so they are often harvested in clumps like grapes. Test the berries for ripeness and harvest when the whole clump is ripe. As they age, the berries get wrinkly and sometimes have insects, so check for that.

Wash and remove from the stems before using or freezing.

Look-Alikes

Salal's larger leaf size sets it apart from closely related huckleberry species, especially evergreen huckleberry (*Vaccinium ovatum*), which often grows alongside salal. Oregon grape also has waxy evergreen leaves and blue berries, but its leaves have spikes on the edges. Cherry laurel and other species of laurel could be mistaken for salal, though in general, they get much bigger, have more elongated leaves, and the berries have a single large pit in the middle, whereas salal berries have many small seeds inside, much like blueberry. For that reason, it can be helpful to break open a berry to see how the seeds are arranged to help confirm your ID.

Sustainability

Salal berries are very abundant in our region. However, note that many birds and bears rely on this species for food, so don't strip your patch completely clean.

Salal is a great native to grow in your garden. It is a shrubby groundcover, averaging about 2 to 3 feet tall, and makes a great slope stabilizer.

Grow Your Own

Salal can grow in partial or full shade (note that it will bear more fruit in partial shade). This plant is a lover of wet coastal forests and will not do well in the dry climate east of the Cascades. Like many other members of the blueberry family, it likes acidic soils, so it will thrive under conifer trees. When happy, salal can spread and cover a whole area, so give them some room. You should be able to find salal in most native plant nurseries.

Cautions

Many years ago, I went to a workshop led by John Kallas, a wild foods researcher and author (see Resources). He claimed that the berries from a small number of certain salal bushes can make you nauseous when cooked. I have not seen this from any other sources, but I felt it important to note, in case you encounter this phenomenon.

OVEN-DRIED SALAL BERRIES

Makes about 2 cups

Drying berries is a great way to preserve them for later seasons. Many of the berries in this book are much too juicy to be good for drying, but salal berries are an exception. Traditionally, berries would have been dried in the sun on a clear summer day. This recipe uses an oven to not only speed up the process but to reduce the likelihood of birds and insects enjoying your haul. I have also dried salal berries effectively in my sunroom, which gets very warm on summer days.

4 cups salal berries

Wash the berries in a colander, shaking off as much water as possible. Then spread them on a paper towel and gently pat them dry. Be careful not to smash them.

On a baking sheet covered with parchment paper or a silicone baking mat, spread the berries out so that they touch as little as possible. Use a second baking sheet if you need to. Spend a moment picking out leaves, stems, and bad berries.

Set the oven to the lowest possible temperature (usually around 170 degrees F), and turn on the oven fan if your oven has one. My oven actually has a dehydration setting, so use that if you have it. Leave the oven door cracked open to prevent the berries from cooking, and let sit for 6 to 12 hours. Every 3 hours or so, take the trays out, mix the berries around so that new surfaces are exposed to the air, and put them back in. Leave in the oven until they crunch when eaten.

Let the berries cool and then store in an airtight container at room temperature for up to a year.

Cooking with Salal

Salal berries are not as popular as other berries as they are less juicy and can be mealy and hairy on the outside. However, these traits make them suitable for drying and making fruit leathers. Salal berries also make great jams, jellies, and sauces. For something like a pie, I would combine them with other berries because their texture might be overpowering by themselves. You can also bake them into scones; their drier texture prevents the gooeyness that fresh blueberries can often cause in baked goods.

Like other dark-purple berries, they contain loads of antioxidants. In fact, they contain more antioxidants than blueberries and many other commonly consumed berries. So yes, they are definitely worth our time.

Salmonberry

Rubus spectabilis
Rosaceae (rose family)

Salmonberry is one of my *favorite* native berries. The berries are less sweet than others, have a bright flavor, and are very refreshing. Like raspberries, salmonberries have a hollow core, much like a thimble.

The berries are polymorphic, which means they come in different colors: darker purple-red and lighter orange-red. The different-colored berries taste generally the same, and there is debate among scientists about the evolutionary purpose of the two different berry colors.

Salmonberry leaves, like raspberry leaves, are used to make a medicinal tea for female reproductive health.

Where to Find It

Salmonberry grows exclusively west of the Cascades in the moist parts of our region. It grows as far north as the southern part of Alaska, and in California it grows along the northern coast. It also appears in small patches in Idaho, where there are some pockets of moist habitats. Salmonberry can be found growing near water sources such as creeks and swamps, mostly in forests. It often grows alongside bleeding heart, red elderberry, sword fern, nettle, Indian plum, and bigleaf maple.

LEFT: Salmonberry's magenta flowers sometimes face downward to stay dry in the spring rains.
RIGHT: All of these salmonberries are ripe; they are just different genetic phenotypes. Scientists don't know what role the different colors play.

Leaves
Berries
Flower sideview
Spray
Flower

How to Harvest

Harvesting salmonberries

Salmonberries are among the first berries of the season to ripen, from early May to late July. They often ripen right after Indian plum, which may be found nearby. Harvest berries into a hard-sided plastic container to avoid bruising these sensitive fruits.

The best salmonberries are found near open spots in the trees (like a bike trail, for example) with good access to a water source, such as a river or stream. In other words, sun exposure plus water access makes nice juicy berries.

PAVLOVA WITH SALMONBERRIES

Makes 6 servings

Pavlova is a delicious dessert that I had never heard of until the fateful day when my partner's mom made it for a birthday party, and I was immediately in love. It is a baked meringue topped with whipped cream and berries. I cannot think of a better setting than this for our beloved salmonberry, whose bright flavor contrasts perfectly with the sweet, gentle cream and soft crunch of the meringue. The recipe is simple, but it takes a lot of time to bake the meringue, so think ahead. This version is adapted from a recipe from Bernice Speckhardt, my partner's mom. You can easily make this dessert dairy free by using a premade dairy-free whipped cream.

FOR THE MERINGUE
3 egg whites
¼ teaspoon cream of tartar
½ teaspoon vanilla extract
¾ cup white sugar

FOR THE TOPPING
1 cup chilled heavy cream
2 tablespoons white sugar
2 cups fresh salmonberries

To make the meringue, preheat the oven to 225 degrees F. Line a baking sheet with parchment paper.

Using an electric mixer or a handheld eggbeater, beat the egg whites with the cream of tartar until they are foamy (about 1 minute), then add the vanilla. Gradually beat in the sugar a spoonful at a time. Once it's all been added, keep beating until the meringue forms stiff peaks, 2 to 3 minutes.

Use a spatula to spread the meringue onto the baking sheet into your desired shape. I like to do a classic disk shape with a bit of an indent on the top to hold the whipped cream.

Put in the oven and bake for 90 minutes. Turn off the heat and leave the meringue in the oven with the door closed for 1 hour. *Do not open the oven!* After the hour has passed, take it out of the oven and let it cool to room temperature before putting the whipped cream on top, or the whipped cream will melt and run off the sides.

When the meringue has cooled fully and you're ready to serve, make the whipped cream. Beat the heavy cream and sugar with an electric mixer until stiff. Spread the whipped cream onto the top of the meringue base right before serving (if added too early, it will partially liquify the meringue). Arrange the fruit on top and serve immediately.

Look-Alikes

When not in flower or berry, the leaves of salmonberry resemble the leaves of many related trifoliate berry species, such as trailing blackberry (*Rubus ursinus*) and blackcap raspberry (*Rubus leucodermis*). Salmonberry stems set them apart as the bark of the older stems becomes papery and brown. Once they bear fruit, salmonberries are easy to tell apart from the others by their color.

Sustainability

Salmonberries are an important early-season berry for birds, so leave the hard-to-reach berries for them.

Grow Your Own

Salmonberry likes moist, well-drained soils and will grow in full sun or partial shade. It will not grow well east of the Cascades, so this is one for folks on the west side. I have seen it produce a lot of fruit on just one bush when planted in native gardens in full sun. Single bushes reach about four feet wide and six or more feet tall. The plant likes mulch, such as leaves or bark chips, so replenish that every few years. You should be able to find salmonberry in most native plant nurseries.

TOP: On older woody salmonberry canes, the bark peels and there are no thorns.
BOTTOM: On younger woody canes, there are small, breakable thorns.

Cooking with Salmonberry

Salmonberries are best eaten raw due to their subtle flavor. Eat them with fresh cream. They can be challenging to harvest in large amounts, so sometimes I just eat them as a trail snack and don't take any home. The berries are quite seedy, so keep this in mind when eating and cooking with them.

Serviceberry

Amelanchier alnifolia
Rosaceae (rose family)

Serviceberry is a small tree with edible blue fruits that resemble blueberries. These fruits are an important food for many Native groups. It is known by other names as well, including saskatoon berry and juneberry.

Where to Find It

Serviceberry grows abundantly in western Washington and Oregon and in the less dry parts east of the Cascades. It grows all over British Columbia, up into the Yukon and the Northwest Territories, and in a small slice of Alaska. There are several pockets in other states as well, including all over North and South Dakota.

This shrubby tree seems to like rocks, as it grows in canyons and along rocky fields. You can also find it in some open meadows and prairie environments, again usually in rocky soil. I have found the trees on the eastern slope of the Cascades, where I live, to be a great place to harvest as there seem to be fewer diseases, and they often get a lot of sun.

A lone serviceberry tree growing in the South Puget Sound Prairies

LEFT: Ripe serviceberries in abundance near Cle Elum, WA **RIGHT:** Like blueberries, serviceberries have a frosty, protective coating of yeast on the outside.

Berry cluster

Leaves

Flower

Flower cluster

Berries

How to Harvest

The dark-purple fruits of serviceberry are ripe anytime from June to early August depending on your location. Harvest when berries are dark purple and squishy, avoiding the red ones. The fruits are a bit delicate, so harvest into a bucket or hard-sided container to protect them during transport. Remember to leave some for the birds!

Look-Alikes

The species name of this plant—*alnifolia*—means "alder leaf." Indeed, the leaves slightly resemble alder because of their serrations, but they are much smaller than alder leaves and do not have a waxy coating on the surface.

The berries and flowers also look fairly similar to those of black hawthorn. However, black hawthorn trees have inch-long thorns, and their leaves have shallow, irregular lobes. Black hawthorn berries (also edible and featured in this book; see Hawthorn entry) have larger seeds and are not as sweet as serviceberries.

Sustainability

Because of this tree's propensity for acquiring a fungus called cedar-apple rust, please avoid ripping off branches and exposing the inside of the tree. Also, if you are going to prune them, use clean tools (see Grow Your Own for more information).

When harvesting the berries, always leave some for the birds, who disperse the seeds far and wide.

Grow Your Own

Serviceberry trees are commonly available at native plant nurseries and sometimes even regular nurseries. They are a great small tree for a native landscaping project.

When buying, check to make sure it's our native species *Amelanchier alnifolia*. You may also be able to find some that are disease resistant.

Unfortunately, serviceberry is susceptible to many tree diseases. One of the ones I see most often is cedar-apple rust, which is a fungus that creates a bright-orange coating on the berries and orange spots on the leaves. Because of the prevalence of this disease in the areas I've lived, I have not gotten the chance to harvest large amounts of these berries.

TOP: Serviceberries infected with cedar-apple rust
BOTTOM: A fungal disease creates strange protrusions from serviceberry leaves.

Cedar-apple rust actually needs two hosts to complete its life cycle: one rose-family host and one juniper. You can help to prevent the disease by planting your serviceberry at least 200 yards away from any juniper species. It also helps to keep the soil well moistened, avoid top-watering, and remove any contaminated leaves or branches from the tree or the ground immediately.

SERVICEBERRY FRUIT LEATHER

Makes 1 large sheet (14 by 18 inches)

This fruit leather recipe is a breeze as you don't have to cook the berries or strain the seeds like you do for the hawthorn-berry fruit leather (page 131). Serviceberries make a good base for fruit leather because they have so much pectin. You can certainly add huckleberries, strawberries, salal berries, or other berries that don't need the seeds removed. I don't recommend fruits like blackberry and salmonberry, as the seeds can be annoying when eating, if they aren't strained out first. This recipe uses an oven to dehydrate the fruit leather, but you can use a dehydrator with square trays (the ones with donut-shaped trays are much more challenging). The dehydrator method also ensures the berries retain the vitamin C, as temperatures need to remain under 140 degrees F.

2 cups serviceberries
¼ cup honey (see Note)
2 teaspoons fresh lemon juice (see Note)

In a food processor, puree the berries with the honey and lemon juice until smooth, about 1 minute. If you don't have a food processor, you can mash the mixture with a pastry cutter or use an immersion blender, but a food processer is the superior tool for the job. Most blenders will not work for this recipe because the mixture is so thick, though a Vitamix could work.

Preheat the oven to 170 degrees F or the lowest setting. Line a large baking sheet with parchment paper or a silicone baking mat. Use a spatula to carefully spread the mixture evenly onto the parchment paper, about 3 to 4 millimeters thick. The more evenly you spread it, the chewier and more uniform your fruit leather will be.

Put the pan into the oven, leaving the door open. Leave it for 4 hours, checking every hour. The sides will dry first, and the center will take the longest. Check for doneness by pressing your finger in the center: If you can easily dent it, then it needs more time. It will be ready when the center is firm.

Remove the pan from the oven, pull the fruit leather gently off the parchment paper, and cut the leather into strips. Layer the strips in an airtight container with parchment paper between them, and store at room temperature for 1 to 2 months, or in the fridge for several months.

NOTE: The honey and lemon help preserve the fruit leather store longer without molding. If you omit these, consume it more quickly. You can also substitute an equal amount of sugar for the honey, if desired.

I counted seven species of birds eating berries from this serviceberry tree, a good reminder to leave fruit for the birds when you harvest.

Tree diseases can be spread from tree to tree from contaminated clippers, so always clean your tools between uses, especially when cutting trees and shrubs and definitely when you are cutting a visibly contaminated plant.

Cooking with Serviceberry

Serviceberries can be used just as you would blueberries. They are slightly less sour than blueberries, having a fairly smooth and sweet taste. You can make jam, bake them into muffins, add them to fruit leather (see recipe), and more. Though they are good raw, I think they are best cooked. Like blueberries, they contain small seeds that are edible and unobtrusive.

Sheep Sorrel

Rumex acetosella
Buckwheat family (Polygonaceae)

Sheep sorrel is a common weed with edible sour leaves that taste a lot like wood sorrel. They have a unique shape, making them easy to ID. Because this non-native species is very abundant, it is a great alternative to harvesting the harder-to-find wood sorrel.

This plant is in the buckwheat family, which is the same family as yellow dock, broadleaf dock, and Japanese knotweed. Because of that, you may notice similarities, such as the membranous sheath (called an ocrea) found at the leaf nodes. Like these other buckwheat family members, sheep sorrel contains oxalates, so it is important not to eat too much of it, especially raw (see Cautions).

An interesting historical note: Sheep sorrel is one of four ingredients in a famous herbal Essiac formula, which was based on an Ojibwe formula and popularized in the early 1900s to detoxify the blood and promote health. The four ingredients are sheep sorrel, burdock root, slippery

TOP: The unique shape of sheep sorrel leaves resemble a sheep's snout and ears. **BOTTOM:** It's harder to notice sheep sorrel until its red-tinted flower sprays emerge.

235

SHEEP SORREL

WALDORF SALAD WITH SHEEP SORREL

Makes 6 servings

The refreshing crunch of Waldorf salad is one of my favorites. The tart leaves of sheep sorrel add to the interplay between sour and sweet in this classic recipe. Note that wood sorrel leaves could also be used here.

2 cups diced apples
1 cup sheep sorrel leaves
1 cup celery
2 cups red grapes, halved
½ cup toasted pecans (or use beaked hazelnuts, if you have them)
⅓ cup dried cranberries or raisins

FOR THE DRESSING
¼ cup mayonnaise
1 tablespoon lemon juice
⅛ teaspoon salt
1 tablespoon maple syrup

Wash the fresh produce, including the sheep sorrel leaves. Carefully dice the apples and celery, halve the grapes, and chop the pecans. Thinly chop the sorrel leaves. Put everything into a bowl and add the cranberries.

Combine the dressing ingredients in a separate bowl and stir. Pour onto the salad and mix with a spoon to coat. Let the salad sit for about 10 minutes to let the dressing soak in before serving.

---

elm bark, and turkey rhubarb root. As an herbalist myself, I've never understood the role of sheep sorrel in this formula, but the other three are still commonly used herbs for healing the gut and detoxifying the kidneys and liver.

Where to Find It

Sheep sorrel is a weedy plant that loves growing in lawns, disturbed areas, meadows, prairies, fields, and sometimes even forests. I often see it growing with narrow-leaf plantain and hairy cat's ear. This is a plant that often grows clustered in patches. For this reason, you can spot it easily once it blooms, as red swaths become visible among the grass and weeds. I love to spot them along the highway on road trips while whizzing by—but remember not to harvest it there. It grows in most places in our region, except the driest areas, such as the Columbia Basin and elevations above about 4,000 feet.

How to Harvest

Sheep sorrel is best before it blooms, so harvest in March or April (or later for higher elevations or northern climes) before the red flower stalks emerge in the middle of the plant. You can harvest the whole plant and pick off the leaves later or harvest leaf by leaf. I store it in a resealable plastic bag while harvesting to keep it from wilting. Some patches will have larger, juicier leaves than others, especially where it has access to richer soil and more water. Plants that grow in dry, gravelly areas will have much smaller leaves that are much less satisfying to harvest.

Sheep sorrel (like many members of the buckwheat family) has a papery sheath, called an ocrea, where the leaf stem meets the main stem.

Look-Alikes

When very small in the spring, sheep sorrel can sometimes look like narrow-leaf plantain (*Plantago lanceolata*), which it often grows with, but they can be easily

Cautions

Sheep sorrel contains oxalates, which can irritate the kidneys and gastrointestinal tract (see sidebar "What Are Oxalates?" in Part One). Consume them in moderation; I recommend limiting your daily intake to twenty leaves or less. A good way to limit your intake is to combine it with other wild greens, thus diluting it. Luckily, it often grows alongside several other edible greens, such as chickweed, miner's lettuce, dandelion, and hairy cat's ear. Oxalates can be reduced by parboiling the leaves first (see Cooking with Sheep Sorrel).

distinguished by leaf shape. Sheep sorrel has its characteristic arrowhead shape with arms, plantain has lance-shaped leaves with no lobes.

Sustainability

Sheep sorrel is non-native and extremely common, so harvest as much as you'd like.

Cooking with Sheep Sorrel

Sheep sorrel can be eaten raw or cooked. The leaves have a very sour flavor, which some people absolutely love. It is used in much the same way as lemon sorrel, as a sour flavoring in soups, salads, sauces, and sometimes even ice creams. The leaves can be added to salads, stir-fries, or green sauces in combination with other greens. It works well in light, creamy soups to add a sour component, and pairs nicely with white fish. I recommend looking for French recipes that include sorrel and substituting sheep sorrel for it.

If you're sensitive to oxalates, parboil the greens before use: Bring a large pot of water to boil over high heat. Reduce heat to medium and plunge the leaves into the boiling water. Boil for 4 to 5 minutes and strain and rinse in a colander in the sink. Cool, and squeeze out excess water, then use in the recipe.

Sow Thistle

Sonchus arvensis, S. oleraceus
Asteraceae (sunflower family)

I was initially dubious of sow thistle, but once I learned how to identify this common wild edible and prepare it correctly, it has become a favorite. This plant is a non-native weed introduced from Europe that grows all over our region and may even be growing in your yard.

Identifying sow thistle can be tricky. Because there are many closely related plants that look similar, I recommend reading the Look-Alikes section in depth, where I discuss some of the most common ones.

There are three species of sow thistle found in the Pacific Northwest: common sow thistle (*Sonchus oleraceus*), field sow thistle (*Sonchus arvensis*), and prickly sow thistle (*Sonchus asper*).

All of these sow thistles have yellow composite flowers that turn into fluffy seed heads, much like dandelion (but much smaller). They also all have lobed leaves that hug the stalk and branched flower stems bearing multiple flowers. And they all have spineless stems.

Because of the huge variety in leaf shape and stem color from plant to plant and the fact that sow thistle easily hybridizes (the species mix with each other), this plant is pretty hard to ID down to the species. Luckily, they are all equally edible, so as long as you can figure out that it's sow thistle and not a look-alike, you're golden.

TOP: Sow thistle's basal rosette emerges in early spring. Though harder to ID at this stage, the leaves are nice and tender. **BOTTOM**: A sow thistle growing in my garden

Where to Find It

All three sow thistle species mentioned in this entry grow in disturbed soil, which could include yards, vacant lots, wastelands, farms, and the edges of forests. They grow in most places in the United States, so foragers everywhere can rejoice.

Sow thistle is often found in areas that you may not want to harvest from, like sidewalk cracks or roadsides. Harvest plants only in areas where you feel confident about the safety. Local farms or yards may be the best place to look.

How to Harvest

Harvest the leaves from March to June. As the plant flowers and goes to seed and as the weather gets drier, the leaves get more insect ridden and sometimes mildewy, so be selective about the leaves you

Common sow thistle growing in the cement seam in front of a garage

TOP: A prickly sow thistle leaf clasping the stem
BOTTOM: Common sow thistle leaves also clasp

harvest later in the growth cycle. I harvest individual leaves by hand into a plastic bag or hard-sided container. You can also harvest the whole aboveground portion of the plant when it is younger. Once it sends up a central flower stalk, the stems will become fibrous and unpalatable.

Look-Alikes

Sow thistle ID can be tricky, so please review this section closely and consider using some additional tools, such as a plant ID app, and checking out some of the species listed on the Burke Herbarium Image Collection (see Resources section). There are three main look-alikes that are important to be aware of.

The first is wild lettuce (*Lactuca* spp.), including species such as prickly lettuce (*Lactuca serriola*) and great lettuce (*Lactuca virosa*). The young leaves of prickly lettuce are considered edible, though in my opinion they are far too bitter for casual eating. Great lettuce is not considered edible. Both of these species are characterized by a line of sharp uniform spines down the central leaf vein.

Second, various species of thistle (*Cirsium* spp.) can also resemble sow thistle, such as Canadian thistle (*Cirsium arvense*). A few key differences can help us tell them apart: Sow thistle does not have spines on the stem, whereas thistle (*Cirsium* spp.) and wild lettuce (*Lactuca* spp.) do. Also, sow thistle exudes white, milky sap when cut, and thistle does not. Finally, sow thistle leaves clasp or hug the stems, while thistle and wild lettuce are attached to the stem normally. Thankfully, most thistles are considered edible, though many are too prickly to eat.

The third of the look-alikes are certain plants in the groundsel genus (*Senecio* spp.), such as common groundsel (*Senecio vulgaris*). It is especially important not to accidentally harvest groundsel, as plants in that genus are toxic to humans. Both groundsel and sow thistle leak white sap when cut, have yellow

BOILED SOW THISTLE LEAVES

Makes 2 servings

This is a classic cooking method for wild greens that you will see mentioned throughout this book. It involves two steps of cooking, which seems like an unnecessary bother, but is key when preparing wild greens, as the water can remove a lot of the less palatable flavors. Keep in mind that most greens reduce in volume significantly when you boil them, so gather more than you think you will need. Be sure to pick through the leaves ahead of time to remove any insects and discard any browning or mildewy leaves, then wash the leaves in a colander.

4 cups sow thistle leaves
1 tablespoon extra-virgin olive oil
Dash of salt

Put the sow thistle leaves in a large pot with at least 6 cups of water, cover, and bring to a boil over medium heat.

Reduce the heat to low and simmer for 30 to 40 minutes, stirring occasionally. Test a leaf for softness by squishing with a fingernail or chewing on it. More fibrous leaves should be cooked longer.

Once you are satisfied with the level of doneness, strain through a colander, giving the leaves a bit of a squeeze to remove excess water. Chop them roughly with a knife and put into a serving dish. Drizzle with the olive oil and add salt. Serve hot.

flowers that form white fluffy seed heads, have leaves that clasp the stems, and have smooth, spineless stems. Because of these similarities, we have to look a bit closer at these plants. The leaf shape is the best indicator. Groundsel leaves are more lobed and shaped differently than sow thistle's. Groundsel is also never prickly, while sow thistle tends to be at least a little prickly.

Sustainability

Sow thistle is a non-native weed and can be harvested to your heart's content. Neighbors may appreciate it if you top it, so it doesn't go to seed and spread onto their land.

Cooking with Sow Thistle

Sow thistle leaves are slightly bitter, much like dandelion, and certain species are a bit prickly. They also can be a bit fibrous if harvested later in the season. I was a bit dubious about eating this plant until I came across an account that mentioned that the Greeks harvest it even when it's fibrous and boil it for long periods to soften it for eating—which I had not yet tried. I harvested sow thistle leaves from a plant already going to seed in summer and boiled them for 30 minutes, and I was immediately impressed! The boiling not only removed the bitterness but also softened the fibrous stem and prickles very nicely. The flavor is mild, much like kale or spinach. Once you try it, you may wish that this weed grew in your yard!

The boiled greens can be eaten as a side dish (see recipe) or added to soups, stir-fries, curries, wild-green pies, ravioli filling, and more.

Strawberry

Fragaria virginiana, F. vesca, F. chiloensis
Rosaceae (rose family)

Wild strawberries are some of our most delicious wild berries, found in various habitat types throughout the Pacific Northwest. The berries are smaller and much more flavorful than store-bought strawberries, making them one of the best trailside treats out there.

Strawberry leaves are used medicinally, mostly dried in herbal teas. They are used in much the same way raspberry leaf is, as a tonic for the uterus. They are also astringent, making them a good wound wash or mouthwash. I also sometimes substitute fresh strawberry leaves for grape leaves in my pickles or sauerkraut—the astringent compounds help keep the veggies crunchy during fermentation.

Where to Find It

We have three native strawberry species in the Pacific Northwest: woodland strawberry (*Fragaria vesca*), mountain strawberry (*Fragaria virginiana*), and beach strawberry (*Fragaria chiloensis*). They are all equally edible and delicious, so there is no need to memorize the differences between the species unless you are, like me, a nerd.

Mountain strawberry is the most common of the three species and has the widest range of habitats. You will find it in the mountains as well as in the lowland prairies south of Puget Sound and down into the Willamette Valley in Oregon. It actually grows all across the northern states, thriving anywhere

LEFT: Woodland strawberry's upright berry clusters set it apart from other species, which bear fruit low to the ground.
RIGHT: Beach strawberry growing in the sand on the California coast. (Photo: iNaturalist)

Mountain strawberry
Fragaria virginiana

Berries

Leaf

Flower

Whole plant in flower

Woodland strawberry
Fragaria vesca

Whole plant in flower

Berry

Flower

Leaf

LEFT: Mountain strawberry leaves have a slight blue tint, causing some to call it blueleaf strawberry.
RIGHT: Woodland strawberry leaves are lighter green than the other two species.

that is open to the sun with gravelly soil. I harvest this species the most of the three, usually up in the mountains in gravelly/sandy meadows with plenty of sun.

Woodland strawberry is the second most common species, found at low- to mid-elevations in particularly moist woodlands and near streams, especially in sandy soil. This species is easily distinguished from the other two because it has multiple berries per stem and the leaves are not silver underneath as they are on the other two species (the silver comes from small hairs). This species has a very wide distribution, basically growing in all the northern climes of the Northern Hemisphere.

Beach strawberry, as its name suggests, is found near bodies of salt water all over the region—along the Puget Sound, on the Gulf Islands of British Columbia, and all down the Pacific coast. These plant communities are very exciting for plant nerds, as there are all kinds of unique plants that have carved out an ecological niche for themselves in the harsh wind and salty air. The leaves of beach strawberries are dark green, shiny, and a bit waxy—the smallest of the three species.

How to Harvest

Wild strawberries ripen from May to July, depending on the species and the location. They ripen later at higher elevations in our region and earlier at lower elevations. The berries are typically about the size of a kidney bean and sometimes hide under leaves, so you may need to get down to the ground to spot them.

Wild strawberries are soft and fragile when ripe, so handle them gently while picking. They will travel better if you pick them with the stem and green fringe on the top. I recommend storing them in a small airtight plastic container—less room for them to crash around—especially if you are on a hike. Be aware that the more they are jostled, the more they will get squished. Personally, I eat them in the field, as I think they are tastiest that way.

ROSE AND STRAWBERRY KANTEN
Fills a standard 8½" x 4½" loaf pan

For this classic fruit, I chose a unique recipe, one that I developed many years ago when I was very deep into experimenting with Japanese ingredients from my travels. Agar powder is a gelatin-like thickener, made of a type of red algae or seaweed, used to make kanten, a Japanese dish that is similar to Jell-O. This kanten recipe is a celebration of the flavors of rose and strawberry. Agar powder can be purchased online or at most East Asian or Southeast Asian grocery stores. You can substitute store-bought strawberries if you aren't able to get 2 whole cups of wild strawberries.

- 2 teaspoons agar powder
- 4 cups apple juice, divided
- 1 cup fresh or dried hawthorn berries
- 2 cups fresh or frozen strawberries
- 2 tablespoons sugar
- 1 tablespoon rose water (preferably Sadaf brand)

Soak the agar powder in 2 cups of the apple juice in a large saucepan. Set aside.

Put the remaining 2 cups of apple juice into another medium saucepan with the hawthorn berries. Simmer for 10 to 20 minutes, until the hawthorn berries can be squished with the back of a spoon. Strain out the hawthorn berries and discard, then pour the juice back into the pot after rinsing the pot. The juice should be brownish red from the hawthorn.

Add the strawberries to the strained hawthorn-apple juice and mix. If the strawberries were frozen, heat the liquid briefly to warm the strawberries through, but fresh strawberries need not be cooked.

Pour the mixture into a blender or use an immersion blender to puree the strawberries with the hawthorn-apple juice until smooth. Set aside.

Bring the apple juice and agar mixture to a rolling boil over medium heat and cook for 2 minutes, constantly stirring. This is to activate the agar. Remove from the heat and stir in the strawberry slurry. Finally, stir in the sugar and rose water.

Pour the entire mixture into a small glass Pyrex dish or a silicone Jell-O mold. Let cool at room temperature for several hours until set. Unlike gelatin, agar-agar sets most evenly at room temperature, so don't put the kanten in the fridge to cool. Once set completely, slice and enjoy. Store in a sealed container in the fridge for 1 to 2 weeks.

Look-Alikes

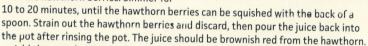

Mock strawberry (*Duchesnea indica*) is the only strawberry look-alike that could fool you, though it is not common in our region. Mock strawberry can be distinguished from strawberry by its yellow flowers and its berries facing upward. The fruits of mock strawberry are edible, so it wouldn't be a deadly mistake. Their fruits are much less sweet and taste like watermelon.

Sustainability

Wild strawberries are fairly common in our region, but it is always a good idea to leave some for wildlife when you harvest.

Grow Your Own

Mountain strawberries and woodland strawberries grow well in Pacific Northwest gardens. They spread through runners that creep over the ground, and they grow enthusiastically when given sun and sandy soil. They don't fruit as much as garden strawberries, but they make a very effective and fast-growing ground cover. You can find mountain strawberry and woodland strawberry on the internet and at native plant sales. Unless you live in the mountains, I would plant both and see which thrives in your garden. They can also be transferred from the wild by digging up a plant. Dig it up with a 2-inch block of soil and try to keep it moist during transit.

Mountain strawberry loves to grow in lawns and would make a great addition to a meadow lawn. Meadow lawns involve replacing the grass with low-growing native plants and grasses. This practice is becoming popular because it requires less water, less mowing, and increases local biodiversity.

Beach strawberry is harder to find and has a more specific habitat, but those gardening on the Pacific coast and Puget Sound may find it in local native plant nurseries that specialize in coastal species.

Cooking with Strawberry

If you are able to harvest enough of these berries to get them home, you can use them however you would use cultivated strawberries. Be sure to gently wash them and remove their green caps before use. I love to eat these, and any other wild berries I'm able to find, with fresh whipping cream or vanilla ice cream. You can also add them to fruit leathers, jams, and other desserts.

Thimbleberry

Rubus parviflorus
Rosaceae (rose family)

The juicy red berries of thimbleberry are a summer treat not to be missed. Thimbleberry is a native shrub that grows abundantly in the Pacific Northwest.

Where to Find It

The diversity of habitats in which thimbleberry can be found is actually pretty impressive. It grows on both sides of the Cascades in forest understories, near rivers, and on alluvial plains. It can also be found equally at low and high elevations. In addition to growing all along the Pacific coast, it grows in the Rocky Mountains and in the Great Lakes area.

As with all berries, you will find the most fruit on bushes that get a lot of sun (think openings in the tree canopy, meadows, riparian areas, and fields).

How to Harvest

The bright-red, juicy berries of this plant begin to ripen in late June and continue through July. They typically dry up by August. They are easily squashed by hasty fingers, so pluck

Thimbleberries ripen one-by-one in each cluster, spreading out the season.

What Are Aggregate Fruits?

Like blackberries and salmonberries, thimbleberries are referred to in botany as an aggregate fruit. All berries of this type are edible, and there are many in our bioregion. An aggregate fruit is a single fruit made up of a group of smaller units, which in this case are referred to as drupelets. Each drupelet contains an outer skin, a fleshy interior, and a single seed in the middle, much like a plum. Indeed, plums and cherries are considered single drupe fruits. The conical white center of the fruit to which all the drupelets are attached is called the receptacle. When picked, thimbleberries detach from the receptacle to reveal, as the name suggests, a thimble-shaped berry. Conversely, blackberries come off with the receptacle when picked, and the receptacle is eaten along with the fruit.

The flowers of thimbleberry require a unique type of pollination called buzz pollination, or sonication. A bee grabs onto the flower and uses its wings to vibrate the pollen out of it, collecting it in their pollen baskets. This uses roughly the same principle as a jackhammer, using vibration to dislodge things more effectively. If you walk by thimbleberry while it's blooming on a dry spring day, listen for a distinct low buzz.

Thimbleberry leaves are perhaps the best forest toilet paper available. They are quite large and soft to the touch. Thimbleberry shoots and leaves, though not edible to humans, are an important food source for elk, deer, and other browsing mammals. The berries are eaten by birds and bears.

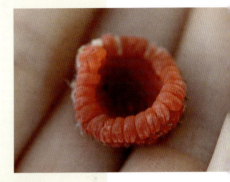

Like raspberries, thimbleberries separate from the inner core when picked, creating a thimble shape.

lightly or you'll be licking thimbleberry mush off your fingers. Their seeds are a bit smaller than salmonberry's and thus get stuck between your teeth less, which is nice.

Because these berries are fragile, they don't travel well, and I personally prefer to eat them on the spot rather than try to take them home. If you would like to take some home, harvest them into a nonporous plastic container and try not to jostle the container too much as you travel. Use or freeze them immediately upon getting home.

Look-Alikes

Thimbleberry leaves, which resemble maple leaves in their shape, set them apart from most look-alikes and close relatives.

Flower

Berry

Berry cluster

Flower and leaf cluster

Leaf

Immature green thimbleberries forming

Salmonberry, for example, has a trifoliate leaf structure that is closer to trailing blackberry. On top of that, thimbleberry leaves have stiff hairs all over the leaves, making it hard to mistake.

Sustainability

Thimbleberries are abundant and easily dispersed by birds who love the berries. Definitely leave some for the birds, though I am more concerned about the birds leaving any for you.

Grow Your Own

Thimbleberry is an incredibly easy native edible to grow in your garden, but be aware that it can spread by rhizome quite aggressively, so plant it somewhere you don't mind it taking over. The benefit of planting thimbleberry over raspberries and blackberries is that it does not have thorns. Purchase plants from a local nursery online or dig up a start from the wild.

THIMBLEBERRY MUFFINS

Makes 12 muffins

Move aside blueberry muffins because there's a new muffin in town—thimbleberry muffins! I cannot think of a better venue for these juicy, flavorful berries. I suggest freezing the delicate berries for this recipe, so they don't get smooshed as you mix them in. You can swap out the flour for an all-purpose, gluten-free mix and use dairy-free milk for the regular milk, if you like. You can also use a mix of berries or swap out the thimbleberries altogether; I have tried this same recipe with many wild berries, and the muffins have all been phenomenal.

1¾ cups all-purpose flour
½ cup sugar
2 teaspoons baking powder
½ teaspoon baking soda
¼ teaspoon salt
1 large egg
1 cup whole milk
⅓ cup vegetable oil
1 teaspoon vanilla extract
1 cup frozen thimbleberries

Preheat the oven to 375 degrees F. Line a muffin pan with paper or silicone liners or grease the cups.

Combine the flour, sugar, baking powder, baking soda, and salt in a large bowl and stir together.

In a separate, medium bowl, whisk the egg, milk, vegetable oil, and vanilla until well mixed. Gradually add the wet mixture to the dry ingredients, folding gently with a spatula to combine. Avoid overmixing, as that can cause your muffins to become less light and more gummy. Gently fold in the berries, until just incorporated.

Fill the muffin cups about three-quarters full. Bake for 20 to 25 minutes, until the muffins are golden on the top and a toothpick inserted into the center comes out clean.

Let cool for 5 to 10 minutes, then transfer to a cooling rack to cool completely. Store in an airtight container on the counter for up to 3 days, or in the fridge for up to 1 week. You can also freeze the muffins for up to 3 months.

Cooking with Thimbleberry

Thimbleberries can be used in much the same way as raspberries; they are simply less sour and sweeter. You can make jam with them, bake them into cakes and muffins, eat them on ice cream, et cetera. As mentioned, they do not store well, so freezing them immediately is your best bet if you're not going to use them right away. I have a bag in my freezer and add to it gradually as I find thimbleberries on hikes.

Violet

Viola glabella, V. sempervirens, V. adunca
Violaceae (violet family)

More than twenty-four species of violet grow in the Pacific Northwest, 75 percent of which are native. All have edible leaves and flowers. The flowers are typically either purple, yellow, or white. Some of these species are rather scarce, so please stick to the abundant species when harvesting.

Stream violet (*Viola glabella*) is the best species to harvest, as it often grows in large patches and is fairly common throughout the region. The leaves are large, tender, and good for eating.

Early blue violet (*Viola adunca*) is also quite common, though it tends to grow in more sensitive habitats, so I avoid harvesting it. However, it is still an exciting plant to encounter. Early blue violet is one of the species of violet that has a special adaptation to ensure it bears seeds even if the flowers are damaged by a hard frost or weather event. It creates closed, self-fertile flowers—called cleistogamous flowers—that bloom under the soil and then bear seeds. Though this process does not include cross-pollination and thus does not contribute to genetic diversity, it can still help maintain population numbers during adverse events.

For an interesting taste experience on the hiking trail, keep an eye out for the evergreen violet (*Viola sempervirens*), which has leaves that give a hint of wintergreen as you chew them. Its leaves are evergreen, which means they persist throughout winter.

A spring rain dampens the leaves of these evergreen violets under a canopy of western hemlocks.

Sweet violet
Viola odorata
Flower — Flower, sideview — Leaf

Nuttall's violet
Viola nuttallii
Leaf — Flower

Violet is also a medicinal plant. Most violets are mucilaginous and anti-inflammatory, and the leaves and flowers are used topically and internally for eczema and other inflammatory conditions.

Where to Find It

For the most part, violets like moist, meadowy habitats. They spread by rhizome to form small patches.

Stream violet is common along streambanks and moist forest floors. In my wanderings in the Cascades, I find a lot growing with

lady fern, Siberian miner's lettuce, bleeding heart, devil's club, and sometimes even Scouler's corydalis.

Early blue violet grows in open meadows and especially in prairies. It can reach from sea level up to the subalpine. It grows all the way from Alaska to California.

Evergreen violet grows in small openings on the forest floor of coniferous forests. You will often find it growing underneath Douglas-fir, western hemlock, western red cedar, Sitka spruce, redwood, and giant sequoia. It can be found growing among sword fern, foam flower, trailing blackberry, and red huckleberry.

How to Harvest

Violet flowers have a short window of blooming, usually in March or April. Some even bloom in February. However, you can sometimes find flowers into July or August, especially at higher elevations. Choose an abundant patch and leave about half of the flowers. Harvest flowers into a small container or jar to keep from bruising them during transport.

Violet leaves can be harvested for eating in early to mid-spring. The young leaves are more tender and thus make the best harvest. Use scissors to harvest several leaves at once or pluck them one at a time. Stream violet is the best species to harvest as it has the largest and fullest leaves.

FROM TOP TO BOTTOM: The lavender flowers of marsh violet decorate the sides of a trail; A thriving patch of Nuttall's violet grow in an open prairie remnant; Sweet violet has both dark purple and white flowers; Stream violet growing near a forest stream

Look-Alikes

False lily of the valley (*Maianthemum dilatatum*) has heart-shaped leaves, like violets, and often grows alongside stream violet. But false lily of the valley have parallel veins, while stream violet leaves have netted venation. Be sure to check when harvesting.

Wild ginger (*Asarum caudatum*) can also sometimes grow alongside stream violet. Toxic wild ginger leaves also have netted veins, but the plant is very thick, uniquely aromatic, and a little hairy. Smell the leaf if you are ever in doubt.

Sustainability

Violets are best harvested from areas where they are particularly abundant. Some plants occur in a solitary patch, which means we should leave that patch alone and let it establish itself.

Cautions

Though most violet species are edible, some species contain mild toxic compounds, such as saponins, that can cause gastrointestinal irritation if eaten in large enough quantities, and oxalates, which can irritate the kidneys and gastrointestinal tract (see sidebar "What Are Oxalates?" in Part One). Check your ID before you harvest, and if the leaves have an especially bitter or tangy flavor, limit your consumption. Most violet species contain salicylates and should be avoided by those with a salicylate sensitivity. Salicylates are compounds found in willow bark, aspirin, and other nonsteroidal anti-inflammatory drugs (NSAIDs) and in smaller amounts in some fruits and vegetables, like violet. Sensitive individuals may experience GI symptoms, congestion, skin irritations, and other symptoms.

When harvesting violet leaves, take care not to uproot the whole plant by accident, which can sometimes happen with tiny plants like these.

Also note that there are a lot of rare species of violet, such as Olympic violet (*Viola flettii*) and northern blue violet (*Viola sororia*), that should never be harvested or disturbed. This is one of the many reasons it's good to always correctly identify plants before harvest.

Grow Your Own

Violet is a must-have in your garden. Many species make great shade ground covers and bloom in the very early spring,

---

SWEET VIOLET INFUSED POT DE CRÈME (DAIRY FREE)

Makes four 4-ounce ramekins

Pot de crème is a thickened, cream-based dessert that makes a great stage for wild flavors such as fruits and delicate aromatics. The recipe is a bit fussy, as is harvesting sweet violet flowers, so pull out some patience for this one. Note that you will need to find sweet violets for this recipe, as their perfume-like aroma is what lends flavor to this dish.

For a more traditional dairy version, substitute 1 cup whole milk for the hemp milk and 1 cup heavy cream for the coconut milk. I have also made this recipe with fresh cherry blossoms, and it could even be made with roses, conifer tips, or lavender. Just infuse the cream with whatever aromatic plant you choose. Baking the ramekins in water (called a bain-marie) allows for even heating while baking, which produces a smoother texture and prevents a skin from forming on the surface.

1 cup sweet violet flowers
1 cup hemp milk
1 cup coconut milk
4 egg yolks
⅓ cup sugar
½ teaspoon vanilla extract
Pinch of salt
Optional: a few drops of natural purple (blue + red) food coloring

In a saucepan, warm the hemp milk and coconut milk over medium heat until it begins to steam. Do not boil. Remove the pot from the heat, add the fresh violet flowers, and stir well. Put the lid on the pot and let infuse for 60 minutes. Strain the milk through a fine-mesh, metal sieve or cheesecloth.

when you are most craving colorful flowers. You can get seeds or starts of several different species of violet online or at your local native plant nursery. Early blue violet is an excellent and versatile choice. Nuttall's violet (*Viola nuttallii*) could also be a great choice for folks who live in drier areas. It is a native to the prairies and grasslands of the region, growing among wild strawberry and native grasses.

With the right permits and permission, you could uproot a start of violet from the wild and transplant it into your garden. Only take starts from large patches where you will not be impacting the population very much. Avoid disturbing the roots when digging, and keep it moist during transit. The best time to do this is in the spring. Be sure to choose a species that grows in a similar climate to your garden.

Preheat the oven to 325 degrees F. Place four ramekins in a large glass baking dish.

In a saucepan, combine the infused violet milk and reheat until steaming (180 degrees F). Do not let it boil. If the infused cream is still hot, this will be a short time. Remove from heat.

At this stage, boil four cups of water.

In a medium mixing bowl, whisk together the egg yolks, sugar, vanilla, and salt. In a thin and continuous stream, slowly add the hot milk to the egg yolk mixture, whisking constantly. This process is called "tempering," which is a process of slowly heating the eggs to prevent the egg yolks from curdling and forming undesirable lumps.

Once fully combined, whisk in the vanilla extract and food coloring (if using). At this stage, if you feel there are lumps in the mixture, you can strain it through cheesecloth to ensure smoothness. Once ready, pour the hot milk and egg mixture into the ramekins. Then carefully add about a half inch of hot water to the glass baking dish, avoiding getting water inside the ramekins.

Carefully put the entire baking dish, with the water and ramekins in it, into the oven. Bake for 30 to 35 minutes, or until the cream is set and slightly jiggly in the center.

Remove from the oven and let cool to room temperature, then refrigerate for 2 hours until well chilled. Top with fresh violet flowers and provide each ramekin with a small spoon.

If you are open to a non-native species, you absolutely must try growing sweet violet (*Viola odorata*), which has beautifully aromatic flowers that are dark purple. The dark-purple flowers make beautifully colored and flavored desserts and infused liqueurs.

Cooking with Violet

Violet flowers make great garnishes for cakes and desserts. They are very neutral in taste, and some species even taste floral.

Violet leaves can be eaten raw or cooked. Some species are more mucilaginous than others, so the leaves can sometimes have a slippery mouthfeel. To reduce this effect, mix it with other wild edibles. I love mixing violet leaves with other spring forest greens like wood sorrel and miner's lettuce. You can also throw them in with a mixed wild-green *ripassata,* an Italian dish that involves blanching or boiling a mix of wild greens in water, discarding the water, and then sautéing the greens with garlic and olive oil and finishing with salt and a squeeze of lemon.

Violet leaves can also be dried to make tea. To do this, pick leaves on a dry day and spread them out on a drying rack or flat basket in a dry area of your house without exposure to sunlight. Turn the leaves every day until they readily crumble in your hands. Store in a glass jar or paper bag.

Watercress

Nasturtium officinale
Brassicaceae (mustard family)

This nutritious and classic leafy green is an elusive treat for foragers, as it can be difficult to find in a place that is clean enough to want to eat from. It loves drainage ditches, some of which receive runoff from unsavory sources like highways and sewage-treatment facilities. However, you can occasionally find it growing in a slow-moving stream or a nice clean ditch. Wherever it grows, it tends to grow in great abundance, so large harvests are possible.

Watercress was introduced from Europe, where it is a commonly eaten vegetable. It is also eaten widely in Asia.

Where to Find It

Watercress grows in most areas on the western half of the United States, save for a few counties. It can be hard to find due to its specific habitat, though in some ways it's easier because you know where to look. I find it most commonly in

TOP: Like other members of the mustard family, watercress has four-petaled flowers.
BOTTOM: Watercress grows along the edges of clean, slow-moving water.

Leaves

Shoot

Flower

Bundle

Sprig

drainage ditches next to roads, growing with cattail, creeping buttercup, and reed canary grass. You can also sometimes find it in small streams and even in agricultural irrigation and drainage ditches. It rarely grows in ponds or lakes, as it likes to have moving water.

How to Harvest

The most important thing when harvesting watercress is to make sure the water isn't tainted with sewage runoff or heavy metals. Urban waterways are often contaminated, so please be extra selective about harvest location.

You'll have to use your observations and sleuthing skills. There are several parks in Seattle that I would not harvest from, for example, because they have sewage-treatment facilities. Unfortunately, watercress seems to thrive on the extra nutrients from the runoff and tends to form tempting patches.

Most patches come back year after year, so you can keep harvesting from the same location, if you find a good one. Though you can harvest watercress year-round, it is best harvested when not in flower, which means any season but summer. Cold weather can make the leaves more tender and sweet, so harvesting newer growth in the spring and fall is best. Stalks that have gone to seed get fibrous. A caveat to this advice is that mountainous places where snow persists in the winter are too cold for winter harvests.

Watercress growing alongside cattail in an urban streambed

To harvest, take scissors and wear rain boots. Snip off leafy stalks (usually about 6 inches) one by one, or cut off bunches from a thick cluster. Younger stems are good to eat before flowering, but avoid plants that have gone to seed, which will have very fibrous stems.

Look-Alikes

Creeping buttercup (*Ranunculus repens*) often grows in similar places to watercress and can be mistaken from a distance. However, buttercup leaves have pointed lobes with a dark

> **WATERCRESS SOUP** *Makes 2 servings*
>
> *This refreshing, light, and creamy vegan soup highlights the delicate and spicy flavor of watercress well. The recipe is based on one published by the* Hungry Healthy Happy *blog, and adapted to be vegan.*
>
> 2 tablespoons extra-virgin olive oil
> 2 shallots, diced
> 1 rib celery, diced
> 6 ounces Yukon gold potatoes, peeled and diced (about 2 medium yellow potatoes)
> 1¼ cups vegetable stock
> 3 cups chopped watercress, or 1 bunch
> ¼ cup coconut milk
> Salt to taste
>
> Heat the oil in a large saucepan over medium-high heat and add the shallots and celery. Sauté until transparent and soft, about 5 minutes.
> Add the potato and stock and simmer for 10 minutes, until the potatoes are cooked through.
> Add the chopped watercress and coconut milk and simmer for an additional 3 minutes.
> Use an immersion blender to puree the soup to your desired consistency, or blend in batches in a glass blender. Taste and add salt as desired.

chevron in the middle, and the plant has tiny hairs, unlike the smooth surface of watercress. Creeping buttercup is toxic and should not be ingested.

It is also critical to avoid harvesting near water hemlock (*Cicuta* spp.), which may share habitats with watercress. Water hemlock is extremely poisonous, and if even a small bit of leaf were to end up in your watercress harvest, it could cause great harm.

Sustainability

Watercress is considered invasive in some places, so take extra care not to spread it further. This can include dislodging bits of plant, which can then float downstream and establish. You can harvest watercress freely.

Cautions

Avoid harvesting watercress from contaminated water sources, including sewage, road, and agricultural runoff.

Grow Your Own

First of all, watercress is considered invasive in the state of Oregon and is recommended for removal by some municipalities for the purpose of restoring native wetland and riparian habitats. Please do not grow it in areas that advise against it.

However, if you live outside these areas of concern, you could try your hand at growing it at home. If you have a nice clean ditch or a shallow stream on your property, you can certainly introduce some watercress to it. Some people even create aquaponics systems to grow it. You can also grow it on the kitchen counter in a bowl with a mix of gravel and soil. Definitely not a beginner endeavor, but for the right person, it could be fun.

One of the cool things about watercress is that it can be easily propagated by putting a cutting in water for a week or two. Small white roots will emerge, at which point the plant can be planted in whatever water paradise you have created for your new friend.

Cooking with Watercress

The stem, leaves, and flowers of watercress can all be eaten, though you may want to remove some stems if they are too fibrous.

Watercress is a delicious vegetable that is refreshing and a little spicy, like its mustard relatives. It makes a great addition to stir-fries and soups and even to green sauces like pesto. It combines very well with ginger and garlic and is one of my favorite ingredients in hot pot, an East Asian tradition where you cook food in a pot on the table.

Watercress is edible raw or cooked. However, aquatic species harvested in the wild have the potential for fecal contamination from the water, so it is safest to wash them well and cook them. That's not an appealing thing about foraging wild foods, but it is a practical consideration that can't be ignored.

Wood Sorrel

Oxalis oregana, O. corniculata
Oxalidaceae (wood sorrel family)

Oregon wood sorrel (*Oxalis oregana*, also known as redwood sorrel) is a native forest-understory plant. It has three heart-shaped leaves arranged like clover. The leaves are edible raw and cooked and taste sour, like a lemon, because of their oxalic-acid content.

Several other lesser-known species of wood sorrel are also edible. *Oxalis stricta* and *Oxalis corniculata* are introduced species that grow as weeds in our region. These two species are extremely similar, and distinguishing them is not necessary to harvest them, as they are both edible. However, if you are fastidious in your IDs and a little nerdy, you can check the intersections of the leaf stem and main stem for a pair of stipules (narrow, leaflike structures). *Oxalis stricta* does not have stipules there, and *Oxalis corniculata* does.

The three-lobed leaf of wood sorrel is often mistaken for clover, but sorrel has a dimple in each leaflet that forms a heart shape.

Where to Find It

Oregon wood sorrel grows in the moist western parts of our region, from British Columbia all the way to the middle of California. It prefers low- to mid-elevation forests. I often find this plant growing alongside bleeding heart, Scouler's corydalis,

Creeping wood sorrel (*Oxalis corniculata*) is often overlooked as a useless weed. This one is growing in a gravel stairway at a community garden.

deer fern (*Blechnum spicant*), sword fern, and piggyback plant (*Tolmiea menziesii*).

How to Harvest

Wood sorrel leaves are best harvested in the spring, when they are the most tender. April and May are ideal months for harvest in western Washington, though further north they may come up much later. They are edible throughout summer, but they continue to get more fibrous and sour during that time.

Use scissors to snip leaves off with about 2 inches of stem. Like asparagus, the upper stem is edible and nice, and the lower stem is too fibrous for eating. Harvesting into a plastic bag can be helpful for tender greens like this as it prevents them from wilting so quickly. Store in the refrigerator for no more than 5 days, and wash them before eating.

The flowers are also edible, though not as numerous as the leaves. Harvest no more than one in five flowers, leaving most of them to go to seed. Letting wild plants go to seed is important, not only for their own reproduction but also for the many animals (such as our native chipmunks) that rely on various wildflower seeds for their winter food stores.

Look-Alikes

It is easy to mistake red or white clover for wood sorrel as the leaf shape is the same. The leaves of Oregon wood sorrel are much larger than any clover species and have distinct flowers.

Oregon wood sorrel
Oxalis oregana
Flower
Leaf

Creeping wood sorrel
Oxalis corniculata
Flower
Leaf
Whole plant in flower

Clover also typically has a light chevron marking in the middle of the leaf, which wood sorrel doesn't have.

Sustainability

Please harvest no more than 10 percent of any patch you find in the wild. Harvest the leaves only, and use scissors to avoid pulling up the roots.

Harvest as much of the non-native, weedy species of wood sorrel as you would like.

Oregon wood sorrel growing among bedstraw, Pacific waterleaf, and lady fern in a forest

Grow Your Own

Oregon wood sorrel is one of the easiest and most attractive wild edibles to grow in your garden if you live west of the Cascades. The flowers of Oregon wood sorrel range from pink to white, with wild populations being mostly white. Cultivated species planted in gardens may be pinker. It is available at many nurseries and makes a great native ground cover in full or partial shade, though note that it can be very assertive and take over a garden bed. Wood sorrel leaves actually fold back when exposed to direct sunlight! Plant it along with bleeding heart and maidenhair fern in a shady and humus-rich area of your garden for a fairyland look. Note that all of these plants prefer the west side of the Cascades, where soils are richer and rain is abundant.

WOOD SORREL AND DOUGLAS-FIR SORBET — Makes 2 to 4 servings

This refreshing mix of wild flavors is a unique way of capturing the sourness of wood sorrel leaves. Douglas-fir tips, which are the bright-green, new growth, are typically in their prime in May. Fir tips or spruce tips can be used in combination with or in place of the Douglas-fir tips. You can also substitute sheep sorrel for the wood sorrel, which is a bit less sour and very nice. Note that this recipe is not recommended for folks sensitive to oxalates.

½ cup fresh wood sorrel leaves
½ cup fresh Douglas-fir tips
1 cup boiling water
1 cup water
1 cup sugar
½ cucumber, cubed, with skin on

Wash and roughly chop the wood sorrel leaves and Douglas-fir tips and add them to a medium sized heatproof glass bowl. Pour the boiling water over the top, cover with a pot lid or plate, and let steep for 10 minutes.

Meanwhile, prepare the simple syrup by combining the sugar and water in a saucepan and heating on low heat until the sugar has completely dissolved.

Transfer the syrup and the infusion of wood sorrel and Douglas-fir tips (without straining) to a blender, add the cucumber, and process into a smoothie-like consistency. Strain through a fine-mesh strainer or through a few layers of cheesecloth.

To freeze, pour the mixture into a metal loaf pan, put in the freezer, and scrape the sides every 30 minutes with a spatula until frozen, about 5 hours. Transfer to an airtight plastic container to store in the freezer, and consume within a month.

Cautions

Oregon wood sorrel and other *Oxalis* species contain oxalates, which can irritate the kidneys and gastrointestinal tract when eaten in large amounts (see sidebar "What Are Oxalates?" in Part One). Consume them in moderation; I recommend limiting your daily intake to ten leaves per person per day. Oxalates can be reduced by parboiling the leaves in water first (see Cooking with Wood Sorrel).

Cooking with Wood Sorrel

The leaves can be eaten raw or cooked, though they are mostly eaten raw in salads. They are very sour, which some people just love. I've noticed kids get very excited about this plant, picking handfuls to feed to all their friends.

Use the leaves as a garnish in a salad to add a sour kick. The flowers can be used as garnishes on cakes or platters. I have also seen recipes for wood sorrel ice cream, so if you are a foodie, there may be some creative ways you can use this.

If you're sensitive to oxalates, parboil the wood sorrel before use: Bring a large pot of water to boil over high heat. Reduce heat to medium and plunge the leaves into the boiling water. Boil for 5 to 10 minutes and strain and rinse in a colander in the sink. Cool, and squeeze out excess water, then use in the recipe.

Indian plum harvest

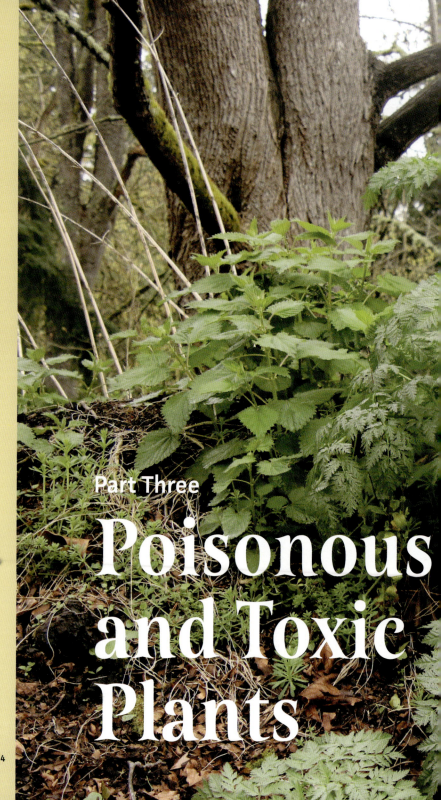

Part Three

Poisonous and Toxic Plants

Poison hemlock growing among nettle and cleavers

False hellebore growing in a high-elevation prairie.

An important rule of foraging is that you should never eat something before you are 100 percent sure of what it is. I have had friends text me with a photo of a plant, saying "I just ate some, what is it?" Please don't do this! Some plants can cause serious symptoms with just a nibble. This section is dedicated to common toxic and poisonous plants, so you can learn about them and avoid them. It's not possible to list each and every one here, so you'll have to get into the weeds a little yourself, so to speak. However, the sections that follow provide information on select plants and helpful ID photos.

First, what's the difference between a toxic plant and a poisonous plant? Poisonous plants are the ones that can kill you if you ingest even a small portion, whereas toxic plants typically cause nonlethal symptoms, such as gastrointestinal distress or accelerated heartbeat, upon ingestion. However, consuming large amounts of a toxic plant can sometimes be fatal.

Other plants, such as giant hogweed (*Heracleum mantegazzianum*), stinging nettle (*Urtica dioica*), poison oak (*Toxicodendron* spp.), and devil's club (*Oplopanax horridus*), may cause a skin reaction when touched.

The Most Poisonous Plants

Consuming even a pea-size amount of a poisonous plant could be fatal. You should also avoid handling them, if possible (especially the cut sections), as toxins can be absorbed through the skin. As an added precaution, avoid harvesting in areas where they grow, as you might accidentally collect a piece of leaf or root. Also, some plants absorb toxins from poisonous plants around them, so it is best to steer clear if possible.

These are the seven most poisonous plants in the Pacific Northwest, which we will look at in more depth in the next section:

- Columbian monkshood (*Aconitum columbianum*)
- Death camas (*Toxicoscordion paniculatum*)
- False hellebore (*Veratrum* spp.)
- Foxglove (*Digitalis purpurea*)
- Larkspur (*Delphinium* spp.)
- Poison hemlock (*Conium maculatum*)
- Water hemlock (*Cicuta* spp.)

Toxic Berries

Those seven plants aren't the only edible plants that are harmful to human health. One of the things I get asked most as a foraging teacher is "Are there any berries I can't eat?" The answer is yes, quite a few! Some will merely give you a stomachache, and others can cause more serious effects, so study the following pages carefully before you pick anything!

Toxic twin berries look very enticing.

Columbian Monkshood ☠

Aconitum columbianum
Ranunculaceae (buttercup family)

This is a Pacific Northwest native species of the genus *Aconitum*, which is famously poisonous. It gets the name monkshood from its hooded flowers. It has also been known as wolfsbane and was thought to repel werewolves. The history of this plant is steeped in magical lore and, of course, death.

It is said that when you have been poisoned by monkshood, you will feel like ants are crawling all over your body. There may also be facial numbness, weakness in the limbs, cardiovascular symptoms, nausea, and vomiting. Like other plant poisons, this is a central-nervous-system sedative that can cause asphyxiation and death with even just a little bit consumed.

Leaf

The hooded flower for which this plant is named

Inflorescence

Death Camas ☠

Toxicoscordion paniculatum, T. venenosum
Melanthiaceae (false hellebore family)

Death camas is a concern mostly in the harvest of edible camas (*Camassia quamash*) and other prairie plants. This plant is actually the reason camas is always harvested when in bloom, so that the bulbs are not mistaken for death camas. Thankfully, the flowers of death camas are white, and the flowers of camas are purple.

The poisonous alkaloids in death camas cause hypotension (low blood pressure) and are highest in the bulbs and mature leaves. Other poisoning symptoms include salivation, a burning sensation in the mouth, nausea, vomiting, difficulty breathing, low body temperature, confusion, and coma.

Flower

Inflorescence

False Hellebore ☠

Veratrum viride, V. californicum
Melanthiaceae (false hellebore family)

American false hellebore (*Veratrum viride*) is a plant of moist meadows and open woodlands. It is most common at higher elevations but can occasionally be found as low as sea level. Its range is broad in Oregon, Washington, British Columbia, and into the southern parts of Alaska. California false hellebore (*Veratrum californicum*), pictured here, is found in Washington, California (as the name suggests), southern Oregon, and in the Sierras and Rockies.

This highly poisonous plant slows heart rate, interferes with normal electrical functions in the heart, and can cause a drop in blood pressure.

Foxglove ☠

Digitalis purpurea
Scrophulariaceae (figwort family)

Strangely, though foxglove is highly poisonous, it is a popular cut flower and garden plant. You can often find entire hillsides in full bloom in June and July, which are absolutely beautiful—just give them space when harvesting nearby. Before flowering, foxglove looks a lot like mullein (*Verbascum* spp.), so take care when harvesting mullein that does not have flowers.

Foxglove is a cardiac depressant, causing slowed heartbeat and low blood pressure. Because of its marked effect on the heart, it is the original source of the pharmaceutical digoxin, a heart medication.

Larkspur ☠

Delphinium spp.
Ranunculaceae (buttercup family)

In the Pacific Northwest, there are many species of the *Delphinium* genus, and all share the common name larkspur. Flowers range from white to deep purple. This is one of my favorite wildflowers because of the shocking purple color. It grows in patches, often in open meadows, and is more common in the drier parts of the region, east of the Cascades, and in our prairies.

Larkspur is sometimes confused with monkshood. To distinguish larkspur from monkshood, note the flower shape: monkshood has a hooded flower (see Columbian Monkshood entry in this section), whereas larkspur has a characteristic spur at the back of each flower.

This plant can be fatal to humans when ingested, working similarly to its cousin monkshood (*Aconitum* spp.).

Line-petaled larkspur
Delphinium lineapetalum
Leaf / Flower / Inflorescence

Upland larkspur
Delphinium nuttallianum
Leaf / Spur-shaped flower for which this plant is named / Inflorescence

Poison Hemlock ☠

Conium maculatum
Apiaceae (carrot family)

Poison hemlock is perhaps the most aggressive and widespread of the plants featured in this section. I have seen entire hillsides growing at local parks. It grows to enormous heights of 10 feet or more, and the stems can be 2 inches in diameter! It can be mistaken for plants like wild carrot with catastrophic results.

This plant has no relation to the conifer tree, western hemlock (*Tsuga heterophylla*). Avoid harvesting near poison hemlock, as it is a common victim of chemical herbicides.

Poison hemlock is a central-nervous-system blocker that causes paralysis that begins at the feet and moves upward until it reaches the lungs and causes asphyxiation.

Flower

Seeds

Lacy leaves resemble wild carrot and parsley

Stem

Water Hemlock ☠

Cicuta spp.
Apiaceae (carrot family)

Water hemlock is considered even more poisonous than poison hemlock. Thankfully, it is must less common, for the most part. As the name suggests, this plant prefers to grow in ponds, ditches, and streams, so this is an important plant to keep an eye out for when harvesting aquatic species such as watercress and cattail.

The leaf shape is different from poison hemlock, with less lacy leaves that are closer to the angelicas. The root often has chambers inside it (visible when the root is cut vertically).

The toxins in water hemlock are similar to those in poison hemlock. They can cause seizures and convulsions (among other nervous system symptoms), which eventually lead to asphyxiation.

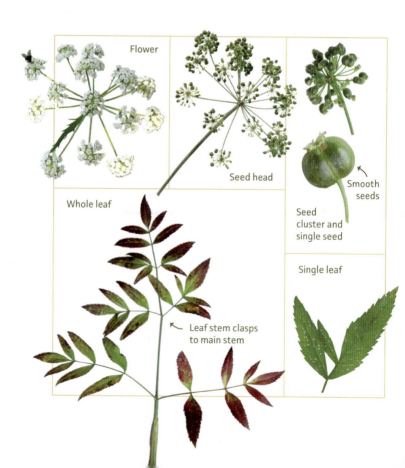

Baneberry ☠

Actaea rubra
Ranunculaceae (buttercup family)

Baneberries are especially toxic, affecting the heart when ingested. They have a characteristic cluster shape and uniquely shaped leaves. There is usually only one berry cluster per plant, and the plants can be found solo or in clusters of two to ten. These plants are not super abundant, found scattered among the understory of moist forests throughout our region. They share a habitat with plants like sword fern, foam flower, twin flower, and star-flowered false Solomon's seal.

Leaf

Berry cluster

Bittersweet Nightshade ☠

Solanum dulcamara
Solanaceae (nightshade family)

Bittersweet nightshade berries are toxic, having harmful effects on the heart, if eaten. They look like tiny bright-red tomatoes and have a characteristic star-shaped stem attachment at the top of the berry. The leaves have a unique irregularly lobed shape—a good way to identify this somewhat elusive vine. This plant can sometimes climb up into other berry bushes, such as cramp bark (*Viburnum opulus*), and fool the picker, so keep an eye out.

Flowers

Berry cluster

Leaves

Cascara Sagrada ☠

Frangula purshiana
Rhamnaceae (buckthorn family)

These dark-purple berries look a lot like cherry fruits but are toxic and should not be mistaken. The year-aged bark of cascara sagrada is used medicinally as a laxative, though it is advisable not to touch the fresh bark, as even exposing your hands to the fresh bark can cause serious intestinal distress. The berries also have a laxative effect, which is why humans should not eat them.

The leaves of the tree can also resemble cherry-tree leaves, so take extra care when identifying. Cascara leaves are much thicker and waxier than cherry leaves, and the fruits contain several seeds rather than a single pit like cherry. Chokecherry, in particular, also has a very different cluster shape, which in botany is called a spike.

Berry cluster and single berry

Leaf

English Ivy ☠

Hedera helix
Araliaceae (ginseng family)

English ivy is highly invasive throughout the region, strangling whole trees in city parks. Many people do not realize that the plant has berries, which ripen in late winter and are toxic to humans. Thankfully, ivy is fairly easy to identify with its characteristic leaf shape, waxy coating, and vining habit. The berry clusters have the characteristic shape of the aralia family, which is like an exploding firework or a pom-pom.

Interestingly, birds consume English ivy berries, though they appear to limit the amount they eat, perhaps due to the toxicity.

Berries and leaves

Berry cluster

Leaf front and back

Manroot ☠

Marah oregana
Cucurbitaceae (cucumber family)

This unique vining plant is a relative of cucumber and has a spiky fruit that seems like it should be edible but is quite toxic to eat. Apparently, they were once used by Native peoples in small doses as a purgative and laxative, which gives you an idea of what will happen if you try to eat one of these. Manroot grows in western Washington, western Oregon, and in a tiny coastal portion of Northern California. The name manroot comes from its enormous and strangely shaped roots.

Fruit

Flower

Leaf

Flower cluster

Root tendril

Snowberry ☠

Symphoricarpos albus
Caprifoliaceae (honeysuckle family)

Snowberries are toxic to humans but fairly easy to identify and avoid. Basically, don't eat white berries. The leaves of snowberry can be another giveaway. They have characteristic irregularly lobed leaves, some of which look like mittens. Snowberry is often used in native plantings in parks and restoration projects. Their white berries persist on the vine into late fall and can make a nice addition to fall and winter flower arrangements; just don't eat any part of it!

Flowers   Berry cluster   Leaves are irregularly lobed

Twinberry ☠

Lonicera involucrata
Caprifoliaceae (honeysuckle family)

Though not considered poisonous, twinberries are toxic and can induce nausea and vomiting when consumed. Thankfully, these very dark berries are distinct, growing in pairs. Twinberry is in the same genus as honeysuckle, as the tubular yellow flowers suggest. This plant is found in wetlands, ponds, streams, and other wet areas growing alongside other shrubs, such as willow (*Salix* spp.), red osier dogwood (*Cornus stolonifera*), and hardhack (*Spirea douglasii*).

Twin berries

Berry clusters

Leaves

Pacific Yew ☠

Taxus brevifolia
Taxaceae (yew family)

Yew has the leaves of western hemlock and the berries of red huckleberry. Thankfully, the leaves are so different from red huckleberry that once you know it, you are unlikely to make the mistake of eating it. All parts of the plant are highly toxic, potentially causing damage to the heart and nervous system. Yew tips could also be mistaken for some other species of edible conifer tips, so take care when harvesting the spring tips of spruce, hemlock, fir, or Douglas-fir. I look for the characteristic green stem of yew. Note that some foragers actually do eat the technically edible flesh of the mucilaginous berries, carefully avoiding the toxic seed inside. Personally, I am not that bold.

Acknowledgments

I want to start by thanking all my teachers, and their teachers.

I have so many to thank at Mountaineers Books, who has been a fantastic publisher for me to work with on both of my books so far. Thank you to my editor Erin Cusick, who did an impeccable job of making things consistent and clear. To my project manager, Beth Jusino, who not only spent time on the phone answering all my big-picture and small-picture questions but also supported all my efforts to outline crucial sustainability issues in foraging. Finally, to Kate Rogers, for seeing my potential as an author, bringing me in to write a second book with Mountaineers, and being a delight to work with.

I also want to thank my husband, who was my number one ally during this process. He charged camera batteries, offered technical photography tips, came along and helped on countless field excursions over a two-year period, harvested a lot of berries with me, gave me constant encouragement, and sampled almost all the recipes I tested.

Thanks to my parents, Megan and Firelight, who helped support me with this project in their own ways. Thank you to the many friends who tagged along, helped harvest, and waited for me on the trail when I took pictures.

A special thank-you to Jason Knight from Alderleaf Wilderness College and Megan Gurule of Wild Women Herbs for taking me out on special outings.

I also want to thank everyone who generously let me use their recipes in this book.

Resources

Learning about wild plants is a lifelong journey, so I have created a resources section to give you more tools to aid you on your journey. A big mission of this book is to encourage folks to plant native wild edibles in their yards, so I have included a fairly exhaustive list of native plant nurseries and seed sources. I have also included plant ID resources and some of my favorite books on wild foods.

Online Sources of Native Plants Starts and Seeds

Inside Passage Seeds & Native Plant Services
www.insidepassageseeds.com/

Northwest Meadowscapes
https://northwestmeadowscapes.com/

Rose Creek Seed
https://www.rosecreekseed.com/

Native Plant Nurseries

BRITISH COLUMBIA

Coast Salish Plant Nursery
North Vancouver, British Columbia
https://wildbirdtrust.org/coast-salish-plant-nursery/

Streamside Native Plants
Bowser, British Columbia
https://www.streamsidenative-plants.com/

OREGON

Bosky Dell Natives
West Linn, Oregon
https://www.boskydellnatives.com/

Doak Creek Native Plant Nursery
Eugene, Oregon
https://doakcreeknursery.com/

Echo Valley Natives
Sandy, Oregon
https://www.echovalleynatives.com/

Humble Roots Nursery
Mosier, Oregon
https://www.humblerootsnursery.com/

Native Foods Nursery
Dexter, Oregon
https://nativefoodsnursery.com/

Sauvie Island Natives
Portland, Oregon
https://sauvienatives.com/

WASHINGTON

Calendula Farm and Earthworks
Tacoma, Washington
https://calendulafarm.com/

Derby Canyon Natives
Peshastin, Washington
https://derbycanyonnatives.com/

Desert Jewels Nursery
Spokane, Washington
https://www.desertjewelsnursery.com/

Oxbow Farm & Conservation Center
Duvall, Washington
https://www.oxbow.org/

Plantas Nativa
Bellingham, Washington
https://www.plantasnativa.com/

Salish Trees Nursery
Kingston, Washington
https://www.salishtreesnursery.com/

Tadpole Haven Native Plants
Woodinville, Washington
https://tadpolehaven.com/

Tapteal Native Plants
West Richland, Washington
https://www.taptealnativeplants.com/

Woodbrook Native Plant Nursery
Gig Harbor, Washington
https://woodbrooknativeplantnursery.com/

Plant Identification and Information

Burke Herbarium Image Collection (website)
https://burkeherbarium.org/imagecollection/
An online database for images of plant specimens and information about naturalized plant species in Washington State.

Calflora
https://www.calflora.org/
Lists all the naturalized plants of California.

iNaturalist
https://www.inaturalist.org/
A global database of nature observations contributed to by users all over the world. A great resource for plant ID and to find out what's in your area.

OregonFlora
https://oregonflora.org
Lists naturalized plants of Oregon.

Plants of the Pacific Northwest Coast by Jim Pojar and Andrew MacKinnon. Lone Pine, 1994

Plants of Southern Interior British Columbia and the Inland Northwest by Roberta Parish, Ray Coupé, and Dennis Lloyd. Lone Pine, 2018

The Biota of North America Program
http://bonap.org
A project seeking to catalog the flora of North America. They have distribution maps of almost all plants that grow in the mainland United States, and other map-based resources.

Wild Foods

Edible Wild Plants: Wild Foods from Dirt to Plate by John Kallas. Gibbs Smith, 2010

Edible Wild Plants: Wild Foods from Foraging to Feasting by John Kallas. Gibbs Smith, 2023

Foraged & Grown: Healing, Magical Recipes for Every Season by Tara Lanich-LaBrie. Countryman Press, 2024

The Forager Chef's Book of Flora by Alan Bergo. Chelsea Green Publishing, 2021

Recipe Index

Pantry Staples and Condiments

Bittercress and Chickweed Italian Salsa Verde, 63
Blackberry Syrup, 68
Classic Rowanberry Jelly, 188
Chokecherry Jam, 96
Oregon Grape Oxymel, 202
Oven-Dried Salal Berries, 224
Rose-Petal Jam, 216

Savory Snacks

Dock-Seed Crackers, 108
Hawthorn Fruit Leather, 131
Pickled Maple Blossoms, 59
Roasted Hazelnuts, 137
Serviceberry Fruit Leather, 232
Thimbleberry Muffins, 253

Salads

Chickweed Spring Salad, 84
Greek Salad with Purslane, 210
Waldorf Salad with Sheep Sorrel, 236

Soups

Watercress Soup, 266
Wild-Green Soup, 182

Main Dishes

Italian Sausage with Wild-Harvested Fennel Seeds, 113
Nettle Frittata, 194
Wild Lambsquarters Ricotta Tart, 172

Side Dishes

Boiled Dandelion Leaf with Creamy Sesame-Ginger Sauce, 103
Boiled Sow Thistle Leaves, 243
Easy Slow-Cooker Applesauce, 53
Fiddleheads with Butter and Garlic, 167
Kinpira Gobo, 78
Sautéed Mallow Greens with Garlic, 177
Wild Greens with Olive Oil and Garlic, 126

Dessert

Blueberry and Japanese Knotweed Pie, 161
Huckleberry Sorbet, 145
Pavlova With Salmonberries, 227
Rose And Strawberry Kanten, 248
Sweet Violet Infused Pot De Crème, 260
Wood Sorrel and Douglas-Fir Sorbet, 271

Drinks

Dried Pineappleweed Tea, 206
Fermented-Fireweed Tea, 120
Iced Fermented-Fireweed Tea, 121
Indian Plum Shrub, 155
Roasted Chicory Coffee, 90

Index

A

acorns, 42–43
aggregate fruits, 251
Alaska huckleberry, 146
alder, 230–1
alpine lady-fern, 164
alpine spring-beauty, 179
animals, staying safe from wild, 21
apple, 34–35, 49–54
applesauce, easy slow-cooker, 53

B

bald-hip rose, 213–9
baneberry, 285
beach strawberry, 245–9
beaked hazelnut, 31, 134–9
Bergo, Alan, 188
berries
    See also specific plant
    toxic, 277
    trail, 73
bigleaf maple, 34–35, 55–60
bitter cherry, 95
bitter nightshade, 286
bittercress, 34–35, 61–64
bittercress and chickweed Italian salsa verde, 63
black hawthorn, 31, 127–33
blackberry, 34–35, 39, 43, 65–70
blackberry syrup, 68
blackcap raspberry, 228
blackcaps, 34–35, 69
bleeding heart, 258
bluebells, 27
blueberry and Japanese knotweed pie, 161
bohemian knotweed, 20, 157–63
boiled dandelion leaf with creamy sesame-ginger sauce, 103
boiled sow thistle leaves, 243
books about wild foods, 296
bracken fern, 40, 166
bristly stem checker-mallow, 177
broadleaf dock, 104–9, 163
buckthorn, 95
buckwheat, 109
bull thistle, 24
Burbank, Luther, 67
burdock, 34–35, 75–80
buzz pollination, 251

C

calendar, seasonal harvest, 34–37
camas, 27, 28
Canadian thistle, 242
Cascade blueberry, 141, 146
cascara sagrada, 287
cattail, 34–35
cedar-apple rust, 231
checker-mallows, 174, 177, 178
cherry laurel, 223
chickweed, 32, 34–35, 38, 43, 63, 81–85, 183
chicory, 34–35, 86–91, 101
chocolate lily, 27
chokecherry, 17, 34–35, 92–97
chokecherry jam, 96
classic rowanberry jelly, 188
cleaning harvests, 38
clover, 269
coffee, roasted chicory, 90
Columbian monkshood, 277, 278
common burdock, 75–80
common mallow, 174–8
common sow thistle, 239–44
contaminated sites, avoiding, 22–25
cooking wild edible plants, 41
cooking with (plant listing), 48
Cooley's hedge nettle, 195
crab apples, 31, 51

crackers, dock-seed, 108
creeping buttercup, 265–6
creeping Oregon grape, 198–203
creosote, 23
crystoliths, 196
cultivated cranberry, 146
cyanogenic glycosides, 189

D

dandelion, 32, 34–35, 88, 89, 98–103
dead-nettle, 195
death camas, 277, 279
Department of Natural Resources (DNR), Washington State, 18
devil's club, 258, 276
devil's tongue, 41
dock, 26, 34–35, 42, 104–9
dock-seed crackers, 108
dog rose, 212–19
dried pineapple weed tea, 206
drying evergreen huckleberries without dehydrator, 149
dwarf mallow, 174–8
dwarf nettle, 193

E

early blue violet, 255–62
ecosystems, harvesting for health of, 25–31
English ivy, 288
Environmental Protection Agency (EPA) Superfund sites, 23
equipment for harvesting plants, 20–21
Essiac formula, 234
European hazelnut, 134–9
European mountain-ash, 185–90
evergreen huckleberry, 141, 146, 147–51, 222
evergreen violet, 255–62

F

false azalea, 144
false hellebore, 276, 277, 280
false lily of the valley, 259
false Solomon's seal, 119
families, plant, 14–15
fecal contamination, 24
fennel, 34–35, 110–5
fennel seeds with Italian sausage, 113

fermented-fireweed tea, 120
fermenting wild edible plants, 43
fiddlehead, 164–8
fiddleheads with butter and garlic, 167
field sow thistle, 239–44
filberts, 134–9
fireweed, 34–35, 116–22
flowers, harvesting, 33
Forager Chef's Book of Flora (Bergo), 188
foraging
  finding good spots, 16–17
  on private land, 19–20
foxglove, 277, 281
freezing harvests, 39
fruits, harvesting, 33

G

Geller, Cascade Anderson, 197
genus, plant, 14–15
giant hogweed, 276
giant knotweed, 157–63
glyphosate (herbicide), 160–1
goldenrod, 119
great lettuce, 242
groundsel, 242–3
grouseberry, 141, 143
Grow Your Own Drugs (BBC), 131
grow your own (plant listing), 47–48
guide, how to use this, 9

H

hairy cat's ear, 34–35, 101, 123–6
harvesting
  for health of ecosystems, 25–31
  limits, 18
  plants. *See specific listing*
  preparing for, 16–25
  on private land, 19–20
  on public land, 17–19
    regulations, 18–19
  sensitive wild edibles to avoid, 27
  shoots, leaves, flowers, fruit, seeds, roots, rhizomes, 32–33
  tools, 20–21
  wild foods, 12–13
harvests
  processing and storing, 33, 38–39
  scaling, 27–28
  seasonal harvest calendar, 34–37

INDEX

299

timing your, 30–31
hawksbeard, 99
hawthorn, 127–33
hawthorn fruit leather, 131
hazelnut, 36–37, 134–9
hedge nettle, 195
herbicides, 24–25
high-bush blueberry, 146
Himalayan blackberry, 25, 26, 65–70, 72–73
holly, 201
hollyhock, 174
how to harvest (plant listing), 46
huckleberry, 36–37, 140–6
huckleberry, evergreen, 141, 146, 147–51
huckleberry sorbet, 145

I

iced fermented-fireweed tea, 121
identifying plants, 13–15
Indian plum, 31, 36–37, 152–6
Indian plum shrub, 155
inulin, 79, 103
invasive species controlled by herbicides, 25
Italian sausage with wild-harvested fennel seeds, 113
Ivan chai, 120, 122

J

jam, chokecherry, 96
Japanese knotweed, 25, 29, 32, 36–37, 43, 157–63
jars, sterilizing, 96

K

Kallas, John, 223
kinpira gobo, 78
konjac root, konnyaku, 41

L

laceleaf blackberry, 65–70
lady fern, 31, 36–37, 164–8, 257
lambsquarters, 36–37, 43, 169–73
larkspur, 277, 282
leaves, harvesting, 32–33
Linnaeus, Carl, 14
look-alikes (plant listing), 46–47
low Oregon grape, 198–203

M

mallow, 36–37, 174–8
manroot, 289
maple, bigleaf, 55–60
maple, pickled blossoms, 59
mapleleaf goosefoot, 173
maps, 22
mariposa lily, 27
marsh violet, 256–62
marshmallow, 174, 178
Medicinal Plants of the Pacific Northwest, 110, 203
milk spurge, 84
miner's lettuce, 36–37, 179–84
mines and soil pollutants, 23
mock strawberry, 248–9
mountain ash, 36–37, 185–90
mountain huckleberry, 146
mountain strawberry, 245–9

N

narrow-leaf plantain, 237
native plant nurseries, 294–5
native wild edibles, power of growing, 30–31
nettle, 32–33, 36–37, 191–7
nettle frittata, 194
Nootka rose, 11, 212–9
northern blue violet, 260
nurseries, native plant, 294–5
Nuttall's violet, 261

O

Olympic violet, 260
one-seed hawthorn, 28–29, 34–37, 127–33
online sources of native plants starts and seeds, 294
Oregon boxleaf, 151
Oregon grape, 31, 36–37, 38, 198–203, 222–3
Oregon grape oxymel, 202
Oregon wood sorrel, 268–72
oval-leaf blueberry, 143
oven-dried salal berries, 224
oxalates, 15, 40, 42–43, 109, 122, 162, 172, 173, 184, 237, 259, 272

P

Pacific crab apple, 31, 51
Pacific yew, 292

patch tending, 29
pavlova with salmonberries, 227
peeling wild edible plants, 43
Pennington, Amy, 59
pesticides, 24–25
Phos-Chek flame retardants, 23
pickled maple blossoms, 59
pigweed, 171
pineapple weed, 204–7
plant ID, 13
plant taxonomy and scientific names, 14–15
plants
    See also specific plant
    cooking with (plant listing), 48
    grow your own (plant listing), 47–48
    how to harvest (plant listing), 46
    identification and information (resources), 295–6
    listings generally, 46
    look-alikes (plant listing), 46–47
    native, nurseries, 294–5
    poisonous and toxic, 274–92
    sustainability (plant listing), 47
    where to find it (plant listing), 46
poison hemlock, 25, 275, 277, 283
poisonous and toxic plants
    generally, 274–6
    most poisonous, 276–7
poppy greens, 40
prickly lettuce, 89, 242
prickly sow thistle, 239–44
private land, harvesting on, 19–20
processing and storing harvests, 38–39
prostrate knotweed, 210
public land, harvesting on, 17–19
purslane, 36–37, 208–11

R

radicchio, 86
red elderberry, 154, 185, 187, 225
red huckleberry, 141–6
red miner's lettuce, 179–84
redwood sorrel, 268–72
refrigerating harvests, 39
resources, 294–6
rhizomes, harvesting, 33
ridge-seed spurge, 209–10
ripassata, 262
roasted chicory coffee, 90
roasted hazelnut, 137
roots, harvesting, 33

rose, 36–37, 212–9
rose and strawberry kanten, 248
rose hips, 212, 219
rose-petal jam (rose confit), 216, 217
roses, 28
rugosa rose, 212–9

S

safety, making wild foods safe for consumption, 40–43
salads
    boiled sow thistle leaves, 243
    chickweed spring, 84
    Greek salad with purslane, 210
    sautéed mallow greens with garlic, 177
    Waldorf salad with sheep sorrel, 236
    wild greens with olive oil and garlic, 126
salal, 31, 36–37, 220–4
salicylates, 259
salmonberry, 31, 36–37, 69, 72–73, 225–8, 252
salsa verde, 63
salsify, 101–2
saponins, 259
sautéed mallow greens with garlic, 177
scarlet pimpernel, 84–85
Schemmel, Tonia, 216
scientific names, plant, 14–15
Scouler's corydalis, 258
seasonal harvest calendar, 34–37
seeds
    harvesting, 33
    online sources of native, 294
serviceberry, 31, 36–37, 229–33
serviceberry fruit leather, 232
sheep sorrel, 36–37, 42, 234–8, 271
shooting star, 27
shoots, harvesting, 32
Siberian miner's lettuce, 179–84, 257–8
Sitka mountain-ash, 185–90
smartweed, 171
smooth hawksbeard, 101
Snoqualmie Tribe Ancestral Lands Movement, 28
snowberry, 290
soaking wild edible plants, 41
soil pollutants, 22–24
sorting harvests, 38
sow thistle, 239–44

species, plant, 14–15
Speckhardt, Bernice, 227
spring-beauty, 183
starts, online sources of native plant, 294
sterilizing jars, 96
stinging nettle, 191, 276
storing harvests, 38–39
strawberry, 36–37, 245–9
stream violet, 255–62
Superfund sites, 23
sustainability (plant listing), 47
sweet violet, 257–62
sweet violet infused pot de crème (dairy free), 260, 261
syrup, blackberry, 68

T

tall bluebells, 27
tall huckleberry, 143–4, 146
tall Oregon grape, 198–203
taxonomy and scientific names, plant, 14–15
thimbleberry, 36–37, 250–4
thimbleberry muffins, 253
thistle, 242
tools for harvesting plants, 20–21
topographical maps, 22
toxic berries, 277
toxic plants. *See* poisonous and toxic plants
trail berries, 73
trailing blackberry, 65–70, 72–73, 228
twinberry, 277, 291

V

violet, 36–37, 255–62

W

Waldorf salad with sheep sorrel, 236
wapato, 27
washing harvests, 38–39
water hemlock, 266, 277, 284
watercress, 36–37, 263–7
western mountain-ash, 185–90
western teaberry, 221
where to find it (plant listing), 46
wild edible plants
    See also specific plant
    books about, 296
    foraging and preparing, 10–43
    the power of growing native, 30–31
wild ginger, 259
wild greens with olive oil and garlic, 126
wild lambsquarters ricotta tart, 172
wild lettuce, 242
wild-green soup, 182, 183
willow dock, 107
winged dock, 107
wintergreen, 220
Wong, James, 131
wood sorrel, 31, 36–37, 268–72
wood sorrel and Douglas-fir sorbet, 271
woodland strawberry, 245–9

Y

yellow dock, 104–9

About the Author

I have been teaching about wild plants since 2016, when I founded the Adiantum School of Plant Medicine, based in the Seattle area. I have taught thousands of people on topics such as herbal medicine, foraging, wild edibles, and basket weaving. In 2024, I published my best-selling book *Medicinal Plants of the Pacific Northwest: A Visual Guide to Harvesting and Healing with 35 Common Species*.

One of my biggest goals in my work is that my readers and students become respectful participants in nature and advocates for it. I am proud to say that many of my students do the hard work of slowing down, harvesting with respect, and teaching others to do the same.

I live in Roslyn, Washington, with my husband, where we enjoy a lot of time outdoors and close to nature. I offer online programs and classes in Roslyn and Seattle. Learn more on my website, adiantumschool.com, or on social media.

Photo: Wren Morrow

About Skipstone

Skipstone is an imprint of independent, nonprofit publisher Mountaineers Books. It features thematically related titles that promote a deeper connection to our natural world through sustainable practice and backyard activism. Our readers live smart, play well, and typically engage with the community around them. Skipstone guides explore healthy lifestyles and how an outdoor life relates to the well-being of our planet, as well as of our own neighborhoods. Sustainable foods and gardens; healthful living; realistic and doable conservation at home; modern aspirations for community—Skipstone tries to address such topics in ways that emphasize active living, local and grassroots practices, and a small footprint.

Our hope is that Skipstone books will inspire you to effect change without losing your sense of humor, to celebrate the freedom and generosity of a life outdoors, and to move forward with gentle leaps or breathtaking bounds.

All of our publications, as part of our 501(c)(3) nonprofit program, are made possible through the generosity of donors and through sales of 700 titles on outdoor recreation, sustainable lifestyle, and conservation. To donate, purchase books, or learn more, visit us online:

www.skipstonebooks.org | www.mountaineersbooks.org

SKIPSTONE

LIVE LIFE

MAKE RIPPLES

YOU MAY ALSO LIKE

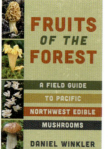
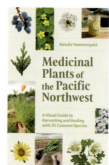